INTEGRATING DISABILITY CONTENT IN SOCIAL WORK EDUCATION

A Curriculum Resource

Senior Editor

Stephen French Gilson

Contributing Editors

Elizabeth DePoy
Heather MacDuffie
Katherine Meyershon

In conjunction with the Council on Social Work Education

Commission on Disability and Persons with Disabilities

From the series

**Teaching Social Work:
Resources for Educators**

D1065925

Council on Social Work Education
Alexandria, Virginia

OTHER TITLES IN THE SERIES

TEACHING SOCIAL WORK: RESOURCES FOR EDUCATORS

CURRICULUM RESOURCES

Teaching Social Work Values and Ethics: A Curriculum Resource

CASE STUDIES

Case Scenarios for Teaching and Learning Social Work Practice

ANNOTATED BIBLIOGRAPHIES

Lesbian, Gay, Bisexual, and Transgender Issues in Social Work
Social Work with the First Nations
Spiritual Diversity and Social Work

COLLECTIONS OF MODEL COURSE OUTLINES

FORTHCOMING

Teaching Gerontological Social Work, Volume 2
Teaching Social Policy in Social Work Education
Integrating Domestic Violence Content into Social Work Education

IN STOCK

Teaching Racial, Ethnic, and Cultural Diversity in Social Work
Teaching School Social Work
Teaching Forensic Social Work
Integrating Gender in the Social Work Core Curriculum
Approaches to Teaching Health Care in Social Work
Educating for Child Welfare Practice
Teaching Qualitative Research
It Could Be Otherwise: Course Outlines on Social Work Epistemology

Council on Social Work Education
1725 Duke Street, Suite 500
Alexandria, VA 22314-3457

Printed in the United States of America

Integrating Disability Content in Social Work Education: A Curriculum Resource

ISBN 0-87293-089-0

Contents

Foreword

On behalf of the Council on Social Work Education, I am pleased to present this collection of resource materials on the topic of disability in social work. The collection provides curriculum content on disability that is current with progressive views of persons with disabilities and that reflects the profession's commitment to respect for human diversity and social justice for all populations. The work of the CSWE Commission on Disability and Persons with Disabilities, as well as the task force that was the commission's predecessor in the 1990s, has been instrumental in efforts within the Council to advocate for integration of contemporary disability content throughout the curriculum.

The materials included in this compendium respond to a need expressed by educators for model syllabi, assignments, and references on social work and disability. To this end we hope it serves the profession well.

Frank R. Baskind, President, Council on Social Work Education

Series Introduction

In the interest of improving the availability and quality of instructional materials in social work, the Council on Social Work Education's Publications and Media Commission has developed a series entitled *Teaching Social Work: Resources for Educators*. This collection of essays, course outlines, and annotated bibliographical references, compiled by Stephen French Gilson, Elizabeth DePoy, Heather MacDuffie, and Katherine Myerson, in conjunction with the Commission on Disability and Persons with Disabilities, represents a component of this effort.

Although the resources in this collection are not intended to serve as official, CSWE-approved models for curriculum development, they are examples of high-quality, peer-reviewed resources that may be of use to social work faculty at a variety of institutions.

Ruth G. McRoy, Chair, Publications and Media Commission

Preface

This project was an outgrowth of a meeting held in 1999 with the Board of Directors of the Council on Social Work Education (CSWE). By invitation from the Board, Commissioner Barbara White and I represented and discussed the seminal issues and concerns about the current state of disability content in social work education identified by the Commission on Disability and Persons with Disabilities (CDPD). At that meeting the need to reform and develop new curricula to assure that disability could be examined in light of contemporary theory and research was asserted. However, Board members identified a major impediment to this aim as the general lack of familiarity on the part of social work educators with the scholarly resources and models of how to address disability content in the classroom.

Following the presentation, Dr. Michael Monti, director of publications and media for CSWE, and I began discussions, during which he not only suggested but guided the development of a proposal to the Publications and Media Commission for a resource guide to disability education in social work. Without Dr. Monti's unwavering support and direction this project would not have been initiated or completed.

In the spring of 2000 a call for submission of curriculum materials and entries for inclusion in a disability and social work bibliography was published and circulated. The submissions were reviewed by myself, Elaine Jurkowski, Southern Illinois University, and Romel Mackelprang, Eastern Washington University, using the instrument published here as an appendix. Suggested references were also collected and evaluated according to the criteria described at the beginning of each section of the bibliography.

There are numerous individuals who were instrumental in this project. Among them are the authors, students, and individuals who have created the body of literature on disability. However, I wish specifically to acknowledge the extensive contributions of a few individuals.

First, I wish to thank the contributing editors, Dr. Elizabeth DePoy, Ms. Heather MacDuffie, and Ms. Katherine Meyershon, who devoted countless hours to searching the literature and identifying bibliographic entries. I would also like to acknowledge the reviewers named above and various contributors, including those who submitted syllabi and those who called attention to important bibliographic resources.

This project could not have been done without the support and participation of both the past and present members of the CDPD. The discussions and work of the CDPD provide an ongoing forum for analysis and clarification of the needed directions for disability content in social work education.

Finally, I want to thank all of the social work educators who use this resource to advance the principles of social justice on behalf of individuals with disabilities.

Stephen French Gilson, Senior Editor

Disability and Social Work Education: A Multitheoretical Approach

STEPHEN FRENCH GILSON | ELIZABETH DEPOY | HEATHER MACDUFFIE

Over the past several decades, theoretical perspectives on disability have undergone a major paradigm shift from a view of disability as deficit to that of disability as element of human diversity. Recent academic trends suggest that definitions of disability have been reconsidered, stretched, revised, and politicized to locate disability within multicultural and diversity discourses. Despite the focus on diversity and social justice that is foundational to the social work curriculum, discussion and analysis of disability in social work courses typically occurs through a deficit-treatment lens. In this chapter, disability is defined as the interplay of diverse human conditions and environmental barriers to full community inclusion. This contemporary view of disability, although consistent with the mission and values of social work, receives limited attention in social work curricula (DePoy & Miller, 1996; Liese, Clevenger, & Hanley, 1999).

DISABILITY PERSPECTIVES

Historical accounts of disability reveal nonlinear and multidirectional movement of the meaning of disability spanning a continuum from the diagnostic-medical approach to an interactive complex person-in-environment perspective (Stiker, 1999). On the one hand, the diagnostic-medical explanation of disability places the locus of disability within the individual who has experienced illness, insult, or anomaly. This internal focus results in an interpretation of the disabled individual as "defective." The person-in-environment lens, on the other hand, considers factors external to an individual that interact with and influence the creation of a disabling condition. Between these two views, numerous other perspectives of disability exist, including spiritual demonization or glorification of individuals with disabilities (Gilson & DePoy, 2000).

Influenced by pluralism, contemporary theorists have positioned disability within the complex and diverse universe of human experience, resulting in the notion of disability as a multilevel social justice concern embedded within cultural, sociopolitical, economic, and relational environments (Linton, 1996; Scotch, 1984). From this perspective in the United States, legislation and protective regulations have emerged prohibiting segregation and externally imposed control over the lives of people with disabilities (e.g., Americans with Disabilities Act of 1990). But even these laws and regulations advance diverse definitions and determinations of disability. For example, the Social Security Act defines disability as the inability to engage in remunerative employment as a result of a disabling condition (Kiernan & Stark, 1986), whereas the ADA defines disability more broadly as limitation in life activities due to impairment. Even with such legal protections, people with disabilities continue to face significant under-representation and limitations in their ability to exercise their civil rights and fully participate in community life, employment, and education (National Organization of Disability, 1994; N.O.D./Harris, 2000).

DISABILITY AS DIAGNOSTIC CONDITION

The diagnostic approach to disability is based on medical explanations of human conditions. As such, disability is defined as either long-term to permanent impairments that position individuals with disabilities as "less able" than those who can recover from illness or who are nondisabled

(Mackelprang & Salsgiver, 1999). A form of biological determinism, this definition focuses on physical, behavioral, psychological, cognitive, and sensory inadequacy. As a result, the problem to be addressed by disability services is situated within the disabled individual (Shakespeare, 1996). Interventions are designed to be curative, and services are aimed at remediating the disability (Mackelprang & Salsgiver, 1999). Not unexpectedly, the diagnostic approach to disability does not bode well for those with conditions that cannot be cured, modified, or changed by professional intervention (Quinn, 1998). In this view, the individual who cannot be "fixed" remains deficient (Longmore, 1997).

DISABILITY AS A CONSTRUCTION

The "constructed" category of disability may be defined as the forces that socially, economically, culturally, and physically construct disabling conditions in the environment (Shakespeare & Watson, 1997). In this category, while the medical condition is acknowledged, it is not necessarily undesirable, in need of remediation (Quinn, 1998), or even relevant to understanding the circumstance of disabled people. Moreover, the notion that individuals have diverse conditions is central to this approach. A fundamental question raised by this framework is why some conditions are constructed as disabilities (e.g., mobility impairments in which individuals cannot walk) and others are not (mild nearsightedness), despite both being generally correctable with adaptive equipment.

The incapacity to function is in large part attributed to a disabling environment in which barriers to inclusion and civil rights are constructed and maintained (Hahn, 1993). Negative attitudes, limited or nonexistent physical and communication access, and the denial of rights and privileges are examples of just some of the barriers that interfere with the disabled individuals' potential to actualize their desired roles (Barnes, Mercer, & Shakespeare, 1999). Thus, disability has been traditionally presented in health-related curricula as inequity in how the environment responds to and interprets diversity of the human condition rather than as an undesirable diagnostic condition to be cured, remediated, or fixed.

Within constructionist conceptualizations of disability, there are many different emphases, each of which have been posited as models of disability in and of themselves. For example, looking at the political construction of disability, the barrier creating the disabling condition is disempowerment due to unequal earning opportunity for individuals with conditions that are socially constructed as disabilities. Discrimination and exclusion from the workplace limit the capacity of the disabled individual to exchange earned resources for privileges, goods, and services.

Another important focus within the constructed approach to disability is the view of disability as culture. This focus suggests that all individuals who define themselves as disabled choose to belong to a unique group, which shares circumstance, experiences, tacit rules, language, and discourse. In this view, the notion of disability is one of group belongingness and distinction from other groups who do not share the disability identity (Mackelprang & Salsgiver, 1999). Those individuals who perceive their conditions to be unfairly treated and constructed as undesirable by dominant social institutions can therefore be members of the culture of disability in that they share disadvantage and curtailment of civil rights (Linton, 1998). Within this framework, issues involving race, class, gender, sexual orientation, and disability identification are important determinants of the shared experiences that bind people together in single, identifiable communities of concern (Charlton, 1998).

DISABILITY CONTENT IN SOCIAL WORK CURRICULA

For the most part, the academy has focused on disability as a diagnostic condition. As suggested above, disability is viewed as a medical phenomenon to be understood by professionals and treated through the provision of services and supports that counterbalance personal deficits. Unfortunately, despite the change in disability theory from an individual deficit model to a view of disability as constructed, disability rarely is integral to the diversity discourse on college campuses.

Assessing the nature of disability content in social work education can be done on multiple levels. For the purpose of the present discussion, our national consideration will involve evaluation of the Council on Social Work Education's Educational Policy and Accreditation Standards, approved in 2001, and its 1992 *Curriculum Policy Statement* (CPS) and 1994 *Handbook of Accreditation Standards and Procedures*. Even a cursory reading of the documents reveals an ambiguous approach to disability definition and content requirements. Prior to the 1994 document, social work curricula were guided to organize their programs around either populations or problem areas. In this taxonomy, disability was included under problem areas, while other vulnerable groups were named in populations. Thus disability was seen as an undesirable rather than a group characteristic.

The 1992 CPS reflected some attempt to address more thoughtfully or progressively the issue of disability. However, in addition to the term "disability," the use of phrases such as "populations at risk" (B6.6), which deny positive experiences of disability and position it within a medical and pathological perspective continued to be used without further positioning disability in the category of diverse populations along with other devalued "at risk groups."

With the 2001 Educational Policy and Accreditation Standards (EPAS), the topic of disability is placed within a somewhat problematic context. In contrast to the 1992 CPS and 1994 *Handbook*, where there was at least the struggle to discuss and present disability, EPAS omits that discussion except under Accreditation Standard 6: Nondiscrimination and Human Diversity, which reads in part,

> The program makes specific and continuous efforts to provide a learning context in which respect for all persons and understanding of diversity (including age, class, color, disability, ethnicity, family structure, gender, marital status, national origin, race, religion, sex, and sexual orientation) are practiced. (p. 16)

Accreditation Standard 6 is intended to provide a general framework for the evaluation and assessment of a social work program. The ability to apply multiple interpretations and determinations of the degree to which any program meets the standards of Nondiscrimination and Human Diversity is highlighted by the following,

> The program describes how its learning context and educational program (including faculty, staff, and student composition; selection of agencies and their clientele as field educational settings; composition of program advisory or field committees; resources allocation; program leadership; speakers series, seminars, and special programs; research and other initiatives) and its curriculum model understanding of and respect for diversity. (p. 16)

We would advance two possible positions given the more generalized statement of disability in the 2001 document. First, the placement of disability on a "laundry list" of human diversity does little to assure that enlightened education about disability will occur. Because disability as medical diagnosis is foundational to much of social work education, limited attention to disability as diversity may serve to perpetuate a narrow view of the social, economic, and political issues faced by disabled people.

Second, while Accreditation Standard 6 does require that programs describe how they "model understanding of and respect for diversity" (p. 16), it does not insure that populations who are considered to be consumers of clinical practice also be understood in light of systemic macro issues. Thus, the changes in the EPAS, while intended to eliminate identity politics, may have the unintended potential to restrict the discussion of disability to diagnosis and treatment of individuals.

It is of great concern that disability in social work curricula is primarily presented and examined through a diagnostic lens, not only because of the current academic trends towards pluralism, but because of the fundamental commitment of social work to eradicating oppression and disenfranchisement, promoting equal opportunity, and advancing self-determination. While we do not suggest that pathology be totally removed from an examination of disability, we posit a framework below that critically examines each perspective of disability and applies it thoughtfully to the curriculum areas of human behavior in the social environment, practice, research, and policy.

MODEL DISABILITY CURRICULA

As presented in Table 1, the two views of disability correspond to different theoretical, methodological, and action approaches in the primary social work curriculum areas. The social work curricular content areas on which we focus are human behavior and the social environment (HBSE), social work practice, social welfare policy and services, and research. We have not included a section on the field practicum, nor is it included in the syllabi in this volume, due in part to the great number of practicum settings in which students are placed and because this educational component tends to have an experiential rather than didactic focus. Our discussion considers baccalaureate and master's content. In the syllabi selected for this volume, the predominant number of master's-level syllabi that have been included are foundation year courses; however, some advanced-year courses are included based on a belief that all or part of the material could readily be adapted into foundation-year curriculum content. Given that many graduate schools of social work offer two or more courses on specific policy topics, a concentration disability policy course syllabus has been included in this text as an example of an advanced-year policy course. All of the syllabi included in this text reflect "state of the art" thinking and development in the area of disability, to the extent that we have also included an "online" foundation year research course.

Human Behavior and the Social Environment

As we mentioned above, the, *diagnostic* approach to disability defines disability as a long-term or permanent, physical, behavioral, psychological, cognitive, or sensory impediment to be treated by working with individual recovery, adaptation, or both (Longmore, 1997). Given this definition, disability can be examined in the HBSE curriculum area through developmental, psychodynamic, biological, behavioral, and psychopathological theories. That is to say, these theories provide the "normal backdrop" from which disability can be distinguished. Medical model theories that are studied within the HBSE curriculum provide a foundation for assessing functional adequacy and providing intervention for individual improvement. As such, interpretations and impressions made at this level provide a normative/deviance theoretical framework for viewing humans in direct practice, policy practice, and research practice.

TABLE 1. Diagnostic and Constructionist Approaches to Disability Content across Four Major Curriculum Areas

	HBSE	Practice	Policy	Research
Diagnostic	Developmental	Clinical intervention	Rational models	Clinical, outcomes oriented
	Psychodynamic	Case management		
	Psychopathology			
	Behavioral			
	Biological			
Constructionist	Systems	Problem Solving	Rational and nonrational models	Integrated
	Sociohistorical/ economic context	Community/group organization		Critical theory approach
	Social construction		Participatory	
	Humanistic	Psychoeducational		Ethnography
	Multiculturalism	Legislative intervention		
		Direct action (e.g., lobbying, civil disobedience)		

As discussed above, in the *constructed* view, while diagnostic condition may be acknowledged, it is not necessarily undesirable, in need of remediation (Quinn, 1998), or even relevant to disability. Consistent with the constructed view of disability, the HBSE curriculum would be informed by several perspectives. Interactions with broader systems would be most useful in examining the constructed phenomenon of disability. These interactions would provide a large part of the theoretical discussion of disability. Negative attitudes, discrimination, oppression, limitations in civil rights, devalued cultural groups, and limited access to resources, privilege, and community life compared to that accessed by counterparts without specific medical conditions would be targets of change. Social learning theory, social constructivism, pluralistic approaches to view of humans, identification of the factors that interact to construct some diagnostic conditions as undesirable, and multiculturalism would serve as lenses through which to examine disability and the marginal social/cultural positioning assigned to individuals and subgroups whose diagnostic conditions are constructed as "disabilities." A specific focus on social, economic, political, cultural, and environmental barriers that prevent individuals from full community participation might be a point from which to define and examine disability (Hutchison, 1999). Further examination of disability as minority culture would not only analyze members of disabled groups as marginalized, but would also examine the intersection of disability, race, gender, and class as interactive factors that serve as barriers to civil rights and social justice. Disability would therefore be located within the larger discussion of domination, power, and oppression experienced by marginalized cultural groups.

Social Work Practice

Guided by the *diagnostic* category, the direct practice aim, and thus direct practice education, would center on clinical strategies to "normalize" or "fix" individuals with disabilities to the degree possible. Environmental modification may be appropriate here, as well, to assure that individuals can navigate their surroundings and occupy desired normative roles that have been hampered by the diagnostic condition. These strategies may be collaboratively developed with clients, but also may be determined as best practice by the social worker or professional team.

Working from the *constructionist* approach, the social worker in collaboration with the client/consumer would determine the nature and extent of social worker involvement. Whether in a central or peripheral role, the practice approach would be based on theory in which disability is seen as a social construction within oppressive systems (Chetkow-Yanoov, 1992). Practice education would therefore take on problem-solving, emancipatory approaches (Gambrill, 1997) in which multiple systems would be challenged and culturally competent methods to eliminate barriers to community inclusion and social justice for disabled individuals would be posited (Longres, 1995).

Social Welfare Policy and Services

In the social welfare policy sequence, rational models of policy, practice policy, or policy implementation analysis and development are often taught. Consistent with the philosophical cause-and-effect underpinnings and economic context of medical *diagnosis*, rational models are based on linear reasoning (Jansson, 1994; Netting, Kettner, & McMurtry, 1998), and a market economy model of society. These models of policy and administrative and management analysis, development, and implementation are grounded on assumptions that (a) the individual's well-being is determined by trading choices and (b) individual self-interest is a given. This perspective is therefore concentrated on individual worth and productivity. Within disability practice, the social worker would therefore advance policies through an approach to agency management that promotes the maximum functioning of a disabled individual for the least social/economic cost, while maintaining clinical models of professional intervention.

Policy and services work framed within a *constructionist* view of disability would focus on a continuum of rational to nonrational approaches at multiple system levels (Stone, 1997), including the local agency level as well as at larger community, state, and federal systems levels. As described above, the rational model of policy analysis suggests a planned and linear approach to the development of policy. In contrast, the nonrational model provides a perspective that views policy creation as resulting from multiple and often competing value-based interests. Stone's model is based upon a framework that assumes that the analysis of policy development, modification, and overturn occur within a paradoxical political environment in which value and stake-holding supercede evidence-based, reasoned policy change. The nonrational model focuses on social values, political decision making, community interests, and the *polis.*

Consistent with Schneider and Netting's (1999) call for social workers to "embrace ambiguity and to connect the often-invisible struggles of individuals with the more public actions of decision makers in powerful positions" (p. 349), a combined, rational/nonrational approach would help the worker begin to appreciate the multiple and competing meanings of social welfare policy and services as they affect individuals and communities.

Research

In concert with the *diagnostic* category, research methods to examine disability from a researcher-driven perspective are emphasized in the research sequence. In particular, clinical outcome research relying on predetermined standardized testing is indicated. Social work students are taught strategies such as single case study designs, experimental, quasi-experimental, and nonexperimental approaches to examining client and family outcome (Yegidis, Weinbach, & Morrison-Rodriguez, 1999). Research methods to maintain accountability and measure the outcomes of interventions are emphasized, along with cost-benefit investigation strategies. Consistent with the *constructionist* approach, both experimental and interpretive research methods (DePoy & Gitlin, 1998) would be taught so that students could examine disability from pluralistic and multilevel viewpoints. Experimental-type models of research yielding quantitative findings might be most useful in concert with interpretive approaches. Quantitatively supported service needs and outcomes could be examined within a context of socially constructed attitudes, barriers, and advantages that could be mobilized to advance equal opportunity and access to community, economic, and political resources. Ethnographic methods hold the members of a culture as experts in their own lives and experiences, and thus the investigator would look to cultural members to answer questions about language, rules, traditions, rituals, and so forth that would inform social work knowledge and practice in disability. Along with ethnographic approaches, participatory action research would be indicated to identify areas and methods for cultural and social change. Research from a critical theory perspective (that which is conducted for the purpose of political change, DePoy & Gitlin, 1998) would guide inquiry towards the production of knowledge for the purpose for social, political, and economic change. Studies based on this epistemological position would enhance both understanding of power relationships as well as action strategies designed to provoke change. Mixed methods would provide the complex integration of experimental and interpretive understandings of constructed and experienced social functioning as a basis for targeting change actions.

CONCLUSION

The diagnostic perspective of disability in social work education remains prevalent. However, by itself this approach is seriously outdated and does not illuminate or educate social workers to engage in practice, thinking, inquiry, and policy change which is aimed at the eradication of social injustice resulting from discrimination towards arbitrarily targeted human conditions. As indicated in the literature, disability coexists with poverty, limitations in civil rights, prejudice, and devaluation. In concert with the mission and values of social work to advance social justice and eliminate oppression, the current conceptualizations of disability which fall broadly within the constructed approach are critical to an informed, contemporary understanding of and work with disadvantage resulting from disabling environmental factors.

The knowledge, theory, and skills that would emerge from a complex, multifaceted, and contemporary treatment of disability would position disability not only within the professional commitment to social justice but within the larger discourse of diversity. While we do not deny that diagnostic content is still necessary to an understanding of diverse medical conditions experienced by humans, we assert that decreasing the emphasis on diagnosis and increasing content and analysis of disability as constructed are not only warranted but essential if social work is to actualize its mission and values. Moreover, critically approaching disability in a manner similar to the approach that has been taken with other vulnerable groups such as ethnic and sexual minorities enriches the universality of diversity dialogue.

REFERENCES

Americans with Disabilities Act of 1990, Pub. L. No. 101-336, 104 Stat. 327. (1990).

Barnes, C., Mercer, T., & Shakespeare, T. (1999). *Exploring disability: A sociological introduction.* Cambridge: Polity.

Charlton, J. I. (1998). *Nothing about us without us: Disability oppression and empowerment.* Berkeley, CA: University of California Press.

Chetkow-Yanoov, B. (1992). *Social work practice: A systems approach.* Binghamton, NY: Haworth.

Council on Social Work Education. (1992). *Curriculum policy statement for baccalaureate and master's degree programs in social work education.* Alexandria, VA: Author.

Council on Social Work Education. (1994). *Handbook of accreditation standards and procedures* (4th ed.). Alexandria, VA: Author.

Council on Social Work Education. (2001). *Educational policy and accreditation standards* [Online]. Retrieved January 7, 2002, from http://www.cswe.org/accreditation/EPAS/epas.pdf.

DePoy, E. & Gitlin, L. (1998). *Introduction to research: Understanding and applying multiple strategies* (2nd ed.). Chicago: Mosby Yearbook.

DePoy, E. & Miller, M. (1996). Preparation of social workers for serving individuals with developmental disabilities: A brief report. *Mental Retardation, 34*(1), 54-57.

Gambrill, E. D. (1997). *Social work practice: A critical thinker's guide.* New York: Oxford University Press.

Gilson, S. F. & DePoy, E. (2000). Multiculturalism and disability: A critical perspective. *Disability & Society, 15*(2), 207-218.

Hahn, H. (1993). The politics of physical differences: Disability and discrimination. In M. Nagler (Ed.), *Perspectives on disability* (2nd ed, pp. 37-42). Palo Alto, CA: Health Markets Research.

Hutchison, E. D. (1999). *Dimensions of human behavior: Person and environment.* Thousand Oaks, CA: Pine Forge.

Jansson, B. S. (1994). *Social policy: From theory to policy practice* (2nd ed.). Belmont, CA: Wadsworth.

Kiernan, W. E. & Stark, J.A. (1986). *Pathways to employment for adults with developmental disabilities.* Baltimore, MD: Paul H. Brookes.

Liese, H., Clevenger, R., & Hanley, B. (1999). Joining University Affiliated Programs and schools of social work: A collaborative model for disabilities curriculum development and training. *Journal of Social Work Education, 35*, 63-69.

Linton, S. (1998). *Claiming disability: Knowledge and identity*. New York: New York University Press.

Longmore, P. K. (1997). Conspicuous contribution and American cultural dilemmas: Telethon rituals of cleansing and renewal. In D. T. Mitchell & S. L. Snyder (Eds.), *The body and physical difference: Discourses of disability* (pp. 134-160). Ann Arbor, MI: University of Michigan Press.

Longres, J. F. (1995). *Human behavior in the social environment*. Itasca, IL: F. E. Peacock.

Mackelprang, R. W. & Salsgiver, R. O. (1999). *Disability: A diversity model approach in human service practice*. Pacific Grove, CA: Brooks/Cole.

National Organization of Disability. (1994). *N.O.D./Harris survey of Americans with disabilities*. New York: Louis Harris and Associates.

Netting, F. E., Kettner, P. M., & McMurtry, S. L. (1998). *Social work macro practice* (2nd ed.). New York: Longman.

N.O.D./Harris. (2000). *The 2000 N.O.D./Harris Survey of Americans With Disabilities: Survey program on participation and attitudes*. [Online]. Available: http://www.nod.org.

Quinn, P. (1998). *Understanding disability: A lifespan approach*. Thousand Oaks, CA: Sage.

Schneider, R. L. & Netting, F. E. (1999). Influencing social policy in time of devolution: Upholding social work's great tradition. *Social Work, 44*, 349-357.

Scotch, R. K. (1984). *From good will to civil rights: Transforming federal disability policy*. Philadelphia: Temple University Press.

Shakespeare, T. (1996). Disability, identity and difference. In G. Barnes & G. Mercer (Eds.), *Exploring the divide: Illness and disability* (pp. 94-113). Leeds, United Kingdom: Disability Press.

Stiker, H. J. (1999). *A history of disability*. Ann Arbor, MI: University of Michigan Press.

Stone, D. A. (1997). *Policy paradox: The art of political decision making*. New York: W. W. Norton.

Yegidis, B. L., Weinbach, R. W., & Morrison-Rodriguez, B. M. (1999). *Research methods for social workers*. Boston: Allyn and Bacon.

Social Work Practice with Persons of Disability

ROMEL W. MACKELPRANG

Social work practice is continually evolving. Historically, the profession has employed varying approaches that are still apparent in practice today. In Mary Richmond's friendly visitor approach, social workers visited individuals and families to help them with their problems. Her approach approximates today's clinical and direct social work practice. Jane Addams, on the other hand, worked to help people in the context of their communities, much as community development workers do today. One theme that has transcended Richmond's, Addams's, and subsequent approaches has been the profession's commitment to devalued and oppressed people and groups. Awareness of and attention to social contexts and societal policies have guided, and continue to guide, the profession today (Hepworth, Rooney, & Larson, 2002).

SOCIAL WORK PRACTICE WITH DIVERSE POPULATIONS

Social workers acknowledge that social problems of disadvantaged groups such as people of color, women, and gay, lesbian, bisexual, and transgendered (GLBT) individuals are embedded in a history of racism, sexism, heterosexism, and homophobia. Social work practice at all levels, from individual and family intervention to community development to policymaking, factors in discrimination and oppressive social policies in effective interventions. For example, individual job training cannot negate the effects of racism in hiring or sexism in determining pay for work. The commitment to social justice is reflected nationally in the fact that the National Association of Social Workers (2001) "supports three national committees on equity issues: the National Committee on Women's Issues, the National Committee on Racial and Ethnic Diversity and the National Committee on Gay, Lesbian and Bisexual Issues" (p. 1). Social work practice with devalued groups such as women, people of color, and GLBTs is guided by common beliefs. These include:

1. Problems faced by members of devalued groups are primarily a result of discrimination and oppression rather than individual pathology.

2. Social workers identify these groups not only for their vulnerability but, more importantly, for the contributions they make to the diverse tapestry of our society.

3. The removal of community and societal barriers faced by devalued groups will ameliorate the majority of problems they face.

4. Given equal opportunity, members of devalued groups will achieve the same success as members of advantaged groups.

SOCIAL WORK PRACTICE WITH PERSONS WITH DISABILITIES

Given the profession's rich tradition in advocating for human rights of devalued groups, where is our profession in advocating for effective social work practice with persons with disabilities? From the profession's outset, social workers have worked with persons with disabilities. Traditionally, social work jobs have been in agencies and institutions that employ a medical model, that is, a professional orientation in which social workers and other professionals provide treatments to cure, treat, or ameliorate the limitations imposed by disability. Psychiatric hospitals and mental retardation "training schools" have warehoused people with mental health and intellectual disabilities. In social service agencies, professionals intervene on behalf of, or "manage" cases/clients. Social work practice has primarily focused on treating or curing individual problems. While social work practitioners have worked on behalf of clients and patients, these practice contexts expect social workers to work on individual problems with little or no attention to societal discrimination and devaluation (Mackelprang & Salsgiver, 1996; Morris, 1991; Shapiro, 1994).

However, in the 1970s alternate views of disability emerged, views based on social construction rather than the supposed objective reality of disability as a problem condition (Linton, Mello, & O'Neill, 1995). An early proponent was Ed Roberts. Roberts, who had quadriplegia from polio, was denied access to California Vocational Rehabilitation services and was denied admission to the University of California at Berkeley because he was too disabled. Eventually, however, Roberts graduated from Berkeley and was appointed director of the California Division of Rehabilitation. He was instrumental in creating the Independent Living movement that puts disabled people in charge of their lives with social workers and other professionals as consultants (Priestly, 1998; Shapiro, 1994).

The birth of the independent living movement in Berkeley has resulted in federally funded Centers for Independent Living (CIL) throughout the country. By law, persons with disabilities must comprise a majority of CIL boards and administrative staff. Self-advocacy organizations, deinstitionalization, and civil rights laws such as the Americans with Disabilities Act are opening possibilities to participate in society. As John Woodward (1996), an MSW at a CIL in Florida states,

> We proclaim that we are born free and equal human beings.... We proclaim that we have the same value as people who are not disabled.... We reject the idea that institutions must be created to "care" for us.... We reject the notion that we need "experts" to tell us how to live, especially experts from the able-bodied world.... We assert our rights of self-determination. (p. 1)

In the social model of disability, barriers to functioning reside in a society with negative attitudes, discrimination, and lack of accessibility, rather than in the disabled individual. The social model acknowledges internal conditions resulting in disability, but does not necessarily view these conditions as being in need of fixing or remediation (Gilson & DePoy, 2000). Mackelprang and Salsgiver (1999) articulate six principles in working with people with disabilities from a social perspective.

1. *People with disabilities are capable and have potential.* Forty years ago, people with Down's syndrome and other intellectual disabilities (ID) were routinely consigned to lives of institutionalization. Society's low expectations led to institutionalization and living conditions that ensured people with intellectual disabilities would meet those low expectations. Today, with adequate social supports, people with Down's syndrome and other IDs attend regular schools, obtain jobs, and live in the community. Social workers have a responsibility to identify people's strengths and potential strengths, then collaborate with disabled individuals to develop and maximize strengths. For example, as we help them develop skills to care for themselves and manage their own lives, people with Down's syndrome are becoming active contributors to society and their quality of life has greatly improved. Given the opportunity, they are developing their potentials into capabilities.

2. *Devaluation and the lack of resources, not individual pathology, are the primary obstacles facing persons with disabilities.* The following case illustrates this principle. Bob T. was a 19-year-old-male with C-4 quadriplegia (paralyzed from the shoulders down) as a result of being hit by a car. His parents were deceased and he had little family support. At the time of his accident, he was working at a minimum wage labor job. After Bob's hospitalization, he was transferred to a nursing home where he was the only resident under the age of 65. His wheelchair had no power controls. He had to rely on an overtaxed nursing home staff for his social and all physical needs. When Bob became suicidal, his emotional condition was attributed to his quadriplegia. However, after more than a year of working with a social worker, Bob was able to procure a power wheelchair that gave him mobility, and he was able to move into the community, hire an attendant, and live

near others with disabilities. Bob's quality of life and emotional status improved greatly once resources were made available; however, for nearly two years he was consigned to a fate he considered worse than death. Once resources were available to enhance his life, Bob no longer wished to die.

3. *Disability, like race and gender, is a social construct, and the primary intervention emphasis with people with disabilities must be social and political in nature.* As a cost-cutting measure, a local public transit authority decided to cut funding for paratransit services for disabled persons while maintaining mainline transportation services for nondisabled riders. As an employee at the local center of independent living, the social worker, herself a wheelchair rider, helped mobility-disabled people to find alternate transportation options. However, she also mobilized disabled and elderly people to pressure the transit authority to restore services. Public testimony to the transit board, protest demonstrations, a media campaign, and the threat of a lawsuit led to the restoration of paratransit services. In this case, individual services helped individuals; however, sociopolitical action was needed to right a social injustice.

4. *There is a disability culture and history of which professionals should be aware to facilitate the empowerment of persons with disabilities.* There is a thriving Deaf American Culture (DAC) that is distinct from mainstream American culture. A relatively small but thriving group, DAC members differentiate being deaf, a physical condition, with being Deaf, a socio-cultural construct (Wilcox, 1989). Deb was a 25-year-old deaf single mother living in an isolated rural community. She was in danger of losing custody of her infant daughter due to "poor parenting skills," yet was resistant to public health nurse and social work interventions to improve parenting skills. The social worker consulted a past college professor to explore options. She was then referred to the Deaf Center in a community 30 miles away. Subsequently, a Deaf mother and a culturally competent hearing social worker, the daughter of Deaf parents who was fluent in ASL, were contacted. They provided Deb support services and parenting education, consulted with the local social worker and the public health nurse, and helped develop trust between Deb and the professionals involved in her case. Deb developed social supports and parenting skills that accounted for her disability, and she kept her child.

5. *There is joy and vitality to be found in disability.* Tim was a 30-year-old man with a leg amputation from an industrial accident. An avid recreational runner and basketball player before his accident, he dropped all sports activities after his accident. A year later, he contacted his rehabilitation social worker to help him deal with depression. He continued to work in his accounting job but had no social, recreational life. The social worker, who was also a coach for the local wheelchair basketball team, contracted with Tim to attend a practice. Within weeks, Tim was a team leader on and off the court. He developed close friendships with teammates and was soon heard using disability slang like "TAB" (temporarily able-bodied) and "Walkies" (non-wheelchair users). Tim later told the social worker that it was not his disability but his reaction to his disability and his social isolation that led to his depression.

6. *Persons with disabilities have the right to self-determination and the right to guide professionals' involvement in their lives.* The story of Bob T., the man with quadriplegia described above, is illustrative. While Bob resided in the nursing home, professionals decided when he would get in and out of bed, eat, use the bathroom, and every other activity of daily living. When Bob was able to move to the community, he hired his attendant, who became Bob's employee. Bob directed his attendant care. The social worker from the local center for independent living was a consultant and helped Bob obtain services. He was *not* Bob's "case manager"; Bob was his own case manager. There were times when the social worker did not agree with Bob's decisions, yet the social worker honored Bob's self-determination and his right to direct his own care.

In another case, Magda, a 42-year-old woman who had lived with AIDS for 10 years, decided to terminate all aggressive treatment, such as highly aggressive antiretroviral treatment, and "let nature take its course." She informed the social worker that she was becoming increasingly frustrated and depressed with the side-effects of her mediations and with the disease itself. She rebuffed the efforts of her physician, who stated that her decision would "substantially shorten" her life, to change her mind. Her health care providers discussed the possibility of action to have her declared incompetent. However, though depressed, Magda had made a reasoned decision. Though the social worker disagreed with Magda's decision, she honored her self-determination, supporting her decision, and working with Magda until her death.

Sociopolitical models of disability move disability into the domain of power and resources in which privileges afforded to nondisabled people are withheld from disabled individuals. They also articulate a "cultural definition" of disability that focuses not on individuals with disabilities but on the collective experiences of disabled people that create disability identity and culture. These approaches redefine work with persons with disabilities as well. Traditional approaches focus on providing society's resources to help the less fortunate or the less able. In sociopolitical approaches, societal resources are used to invest in people with disabilities who can, in turn, provide a return on investment (Gilson & DePoy 2000; Mackelprang & Salsgiver, 1999; Sleeter, 1996).

So what does all this mean for social workers' practice with persons with disabilities? How do social workers practice effectively in settings that define disabled people according to their limitations (e.g., hospitals, mental health centers) and in a society that requires pathological diagnoses for service eligibility? What approach do we take in work with people who are newly disabled and perceive their disability as pathology rather than identity? What changes are needed for persons with disabilities to enjoy the same rights as nondisabled people? What is society's responsibility to individuals with disabilities as well as disabled people as a class?

SOCIAL WORK PRACTICE IN CONTEXT

For the profession to operationalize cardinal social work values, such as respecting the inherent worth of all persons and the right to self-determination, social workers must strive to bring about social justice and eliminate discrimination and to work with persons with disabilities (rather than on their behalf). This means allying ourselves with disability advocates as well as including persons with disabilities as equals and embracing them as members of the profession. As we do this, the profession will be strengthened, just as it has been strengthened by embracing other diverse groups.

There are five practice issues each social worker should assess in practice with persons with disabilities. First, we need to evaluate our own attitudes and values relative to disability. Second, we must assess the professional contexts in which we practice. Third, we need to respect and honor the views of those with whom we work. Fourth, the right to self-determination must be respected. Finally, our interventions must extend beyond individual treatment and encompass changing social policies and societal practices that limit the rights of people with disabilities.

First, effective practice begins with an evaluation of one's personal and professional beliefs and values. Social workers who practice with persons with disabilities must evaluate the beliefs they have adopted about disability. To assess our personal attitudes and beliefs, we might ask ourselves questions such as the following. (1) What is my first reaction when I see someone in a wheelchair? (2) If I were pregnant and found my child had spina bifida, how would I react? (3) If, in hiring a social worker, I found an applicant had a history of depression, how would it affect my hiring decision? (4) When I think of someone using a wheelchair, do I think of them as being "confined" to a wheelchair or as someone who uses a wheelchair for mobility? (5) Would my reactions be positive, negative, or neutral if I learned a group home for intellectually or psychiatrically disabled residents was opening in my neighborhood?

Just as society can perpetuate sexism, racism, and heterosexism, it can also perpetuate ableism, the belief that life with disabilities or people with disabilities are inferior. Some social workers have been raised with ableist ideas and attitudes including pity, shame, and fear. Some have been taught that disability is a result of sin or imbalance in nature. To work effectively, social workers must identify ableist attitudes, eschew disability stereotypes, and adopt a stance that disabled people have the same value and rights to function in society that persons without disabilities enjoy.

Second, the settings and contexts in which social workers practice influence disability-related practice. We have an ethical obligation to work in the interests of our employing organizations. In most professional settings, disabled service recipients are defined by their personal problems, and agencies employ social workers to reduce, ameliorate, or solve those problems. For example, hospitals, mental health centers, special education programs, and social service agencies treat individuals' medical, mental health, educational, emotional, and resource needs. In these settings our primary, or even exclusive, responsibility may be to serve the individual patient, client, or student. However, social workers also have an ethical responsibility to clients and to combat social injustice.

Ethical social work practice, therefore, may also require social workers to balance agency mandates for individual intervention while acting on the recognition that many problems persons with disability face are societally imposed. For example, the job description for social workers for persons with acute physical disabilities may direct them to assist with emotional and family adjustment, and help apply for financial resources. In addition, ethically social workers should also work to change conditions that lead to unemployment, poverty, and social isolation for persons with disabilities, even when these activities are not part of one's job description.

Third, social workers must honor the views of those with whom we work. An old social work adage continues to be, "Start where the client is." In disability practice especially, the adage might better be stated as, "Find out where the client is." People with disabilities perceive their disabilities from a wide range of perspectives. Some people, particularly newly disabled persons and those who acquire disability late in life, hold mainstream societal views of disability as an unfortunate or even tragic condition. At the other end of the spectrum are persons who maintain a disability identity with pride (Mackelprang & Salsgiver, 1999). For example, an adult born deaf and who is part of Deaf culture finds joy in being deaf. However, an adult who becomes deaf from illness or accident may have difficulty finding anything positive about being deaf.

Social workers in disability practice need to balance two core social work values. Social workers respect the right to self-determination, including the right to believe as one might. However, while it is inadvisable to impose disability affirming values on others, the profession's respect for the dignity and worth of all people can prompt social workers to suggest alternate ideas and views when people's attitudes are based on ableist societal attitudes or are self-destructive. Thus, an adult deafened individual can be connected to peer role models and can be taught to use supplemental communication strategies to enhance quality of life and, consequently, change perceptions of the meaning of being deaf.

Fourth, self-determination is of paramount importance. We must work to keep the locus of control with the individual. Persons with disabilities are not cases to be managed; they are people who have rights and in whom society should make investments. In those instances in which our employing or sanctioning agencies use ableist or discriminatory policies and practices, we have a responsibility to change those conditions.

Finally, social workers and the social work profession need to recognize people with disabilities are not only a population at risk, which has experienced discrimination, devaluation, and oppression, but also a diverse population that offers unique contributions to society. Social work practice must encompass all levels. At the micro level we can utilize roles such as counselors, educators, mediators, and advocates to help individuals and families with personal needs and to integrate into the community. At the meso level we can engage in community building activities, work to enhance accessibility within neighborhoods, and collaborate with other disability advocates to make transportation and housing available. On the macro level, social work can strive to change discriminatory social policies and practices that limit opportunity and access. For example, recent changes in Social Security policies have helped people with disabilities to work while maintaining medical benefits. Social work should be actively involved in further changes that encourage employment among persons with disabilities.

CONCLUSION

Historically, social work has joined forces with devalued and oppressed groups. We have been at the forefront of advocating for groups such as immigrants, people of color, women, and gays and lesbians. This curriculum project is intended, in part, to help social workers engage in effective practice with persons with disabilities. To do this, we must view disability within a human rights context in which people have the right to self-determination. Further, persons with disabilities have as much value in our society as nondisabled persons. It is essential that we work not only to help with individual problems, but to change oppressive social attitudes and conditions. Finally, the profession has a responsibility to embrace persons with disabilities as full members of our profession with unique and important contributions.

REFERENCES

Gilson, S. F. & DePoy, E. (2000). Multiculturalism and disability: a critical perspective. *Disability and Society*, *15*(2). 207-218.

Hepworth, D. H., Rooney, R. H., & Larson, J. (2002). *Direct social work practice: Theory and skills.* (5th ed.). Pacific Grove, CA: Brooks/Cole.

Linton, S., Mello, S., & O'Neill, J. (1995). Disability studies: Expanding the parameters of diversity. *Radical Teacher*, *47*, 4-10.

Mackelprang, R. W. & Salsgiver, R. O. (1996). Persons with disabilities and social work: Historical and contemporary issues. *Social Work*, *41*, 7-14.

Mackelprang, R. W. & Salsgiver, R. O. (1999). *Disability: A diversity model approach in human service practice.* Pacific Grove, CA: Brooks/ Cole.

Morris, J. (1991). *Pride against prejudice.* London: Women's Press.

National Association of Social Workers. (2001). *Diversity and equity issues* [Online]. Retrieved January 7, 2002, from http://www.naswdc.org/diversty.htm.

Priestly, M. (1998). Constructions and creations: Idealism, materialism and disability theory. *Disability and Society*, *13*(1), 75-94.

Shapiro, J.P. (1994). *No pity: People with disabilities forging a new civil rights movement.* New York: Times Books.

Sleeter, C. (1996). Radical structuralist perspectives on the creation and use of learning disabilities. In T. M. Skrtic (Ed.), *Disability and democracy: Reconstructing (special) education for postmodernity* (pp. 153-165). New York: Teachers College Press.

Wilcox, S. (Ed.). (1989). *American Deaf Culture: An anthology.* Burtonsville, MD. Linstock.

Woodward, J. R. (1996). *A disabled manifesto.* Retrieved January 7, 2002, from http:// freenet.buffalo.edu/ ~ wnydf/library/rights.text.

SAN FRANCISCO STATE UNIVERSITY
SCHOOL OF SOCIAL WORK | SAN FRANCISCO, CA
REIKO HAYASHI* | TERESA FAVUZZI

Disability Rights and Social Work Practice

SW655 (Spring 1999)

INTRODUCTION

People with disabilities are one of the oppressed groups that have suffered from discrimination and economic deprivation in this ableist society, and they have been fighting for their civil rights. Social work education should provide students information about oppressed groups, including people with disabilities, that has been generated through their struggles against discrimination.

The disability rights movement was born alongside other social movements of the 1950s and 1960s, including the civil rights, feminist, and gay and lesbian rights movements. The focus of the disability rights movement was, and still is, challenging institutionalized oppression, segregation, and the lack of basic rights (physical accessibility, equal employment, health care, housing, and transportation among others). It was also the leading force in the enactment of the Americans with Disabilities Act (ADA) of 1990 and current disability advocates are fighting for the implementation and preservation of the ADA.

This course is an elective for the Bachelor of Social Work degree but it is also open to other students who are interested in disability issues. It will examine ableism (discrimination against people with disabilities) in U.S. society and its historical development, and the philosophy of disability as expressed in various social institutions including social welfare agencies and schools of social work. The course will also explore organized efforts by various disability groups to address and ameliorate the oppression they suffer. The *minority group model* and the *socio-political model* of disability, as opposed to the *medical model*, will be emphasized. Students will explore how our own personal and professional values, beliefs, and behaviors can empower or disempower our work with people with disabilities.

DESCRIPTION

The course integrates community service, distance education using a computer interactive program and websites, and on-campus lectures. The class meets on campus every three weeks. The class time is used for lectures, films, exercises, and discussions. During the weeks when the class does not meet, students interact with each other and with the instructors through the computer interactive program. The computer program is used for discussions and reflection, support, class evaluations, and to obtain reading materials through its links.

As a community service learning course, students are required to commit 40 hours per semester in a supervised service experience with a community organization espousing the perspective of the those in the disability movement. Community service enhances the opportunity to achieve student learning objectives by connecting classroom learning with real-life activism, both with and for people with disabilities.

*Reiko Hayashi is now an assistant professor at the Graduate School of Social Work, University of Utah.

OBJECTIVES

By the end of this course students will be able to

1. Understand the concepts of ableism

2. Develop self-awareness regarding the impact of institutional ableism on their personal beliefs, behaviors, and professional practice

3. Analyze the historical development of oppression towards people with disabilities in the United States and how that history continues to shape current circumstances

4. Understand the nature and pervasiveness of individual, cultural, and institutional ableism and its influence on social welfare policies and social work practices in the United States

5. Analyze how oppression shapes the lives of people with disabilities as well as those who do not have disabilities

6. Develop an appreciation for the disability culture

7. Identify existing gaps and contradictions between the social work value system and the delivery of social services to clients with disabilities

8. Develop appropriate frameworks for social policies, social work programs, and social work practices that will overcome the problems of oppression to better serve clients with disabilities

9. Recognize the capacity of people with disabilities to cope with discrimination in their daily lives and to develop support systems

10. Plan and participate in advocacy activities with and for people with disabilities

11. Utilize computer interactive programs to enhance their education

COURSE UNITS

Unit I: Introduction to Course Format and Expectations. This unit orients students to a distance learning environment by providing detailed instruction on the use of the Internet based computer-mediated learning program. This unit provides students with an overview of their Community Service Learning placement options.

1. Course overview

2. Creating distance learning Internet accounts

3. Instruction in the use of the interactive computer-mediated learning program

4. Community Service Learning agencies present the philosophy, goals, and activities of their organizations.

5. Community Service Learning Agency representatives meet with students

Unit II: Disability and Society. This unit begins a dialogue regarding disability and society. Professional stereotypes, including various models of disability, are examined and the concept of disability culture is introduced. Disability history and the disability rights movement is explored and life stage development in relation to disability is also discussed.

1. Society and professional stereotypes

2. Disability culture

3. Disability history in the United States

4. Life stage development

Unit III: Disability Diversity I. This unit begins an exploration of the diversity and commonality of life experiences for people living with disabilities. Critiquing the medical model of disability, which classifies, categorizes, and isolates people by diagnosis, this review of disability diversity is based on the tenets of the Independent Living movement which assert that people living with various disabilities share a common experience and culture. Disability Diversity I provides an overview of the major mobility, hearing, and visual disabilities, as well as the unique life and cultural experiences of individuals living with these disabilities.

1. Persons with mobility disabilities
2. Deaf and hard-of-hearing people
3. Persons with visual disabilities and blindness

Unit IV: Disability Diversity II. This unit continues the exploration of disability diversity. Students will be able to compare and contrast the medical, social, and political definitions of disabilities and understand how these models affect individuals with disabilities. Included is an examination of the social construct of disability and how social stigma, stereotyping, and prejudice affect all people with disabilities. The major developmental, psychiatric, and cognitive disabilities and the experiences of persons with these disabilities are outlined in this unit.

1. Persons with developmental disabilities
2. Persons with psychiatric disabilities
3. Persons with cognitive disabilities

Unit V: Human Service Practice Framework. This unit explores the limitations and implications of the medical model of assessment and proposes alternate practice models. Professional assessment guides and micro, meso, and macro levels of practice are discussed. In conclusion, this unit teaches students to develop intervention skills based on empowerment, self-determination, and independent living.

1. Assessment in human service practice
2. Models of professional practice
3. Guidelines for practice with persons with disabilities

RECOMMENDED TEXTS

Fries, K. (Ed.). (1997). *Staring back: The disability experience from the inside out.* New York: A Plume Book.

Linton, S. (1998). *Claiming disability: Knowledge and identity.* New York: New York University Press.

Mackelprang, R. & Salsgiver, R. (1998). *Disability: A diversity model approach in human service practice.* Pacific Grove, CA: Brooks/Cole.

Shapiro, J. P. (1994). *No pity: People with disabilities forging a new civil rights movement.* New York: Random House.

RECOMMENDED FILMS

- *Crip culture talks back*
- *Disabled women's alliance*
- *If I can't do it*
- *When Billy hit his head*

ASSIGNMENTS

Unit I

- Create a home Internet account for the computer distance learning site.
- Introduce yourself and your experiences with disability via computer distance learning site.
- Set appointments to visit Community Service Learning sites, choose a site, and negotiate a schedule and tasks.

Unit II

- Visit the following websites. Post your opinions about the websites, other reading materials, class discussions, your experiences with disability, and your classmates' postings at our computer distance learning site.

  - **Disability Cool** http://www.geocities.com/HotSprings/7319/
  - **Disability Social History Project** http://www.disabilityhistory.org/dshp.html
  - **Mouth Magazine** http://www.mouthmag.com/
  - **Ragged Edge Magazine** http://www.ragged-edge-mag.com/
  - **Sexual Health Network/Sexuality Following Disability** http://www.sexualhealth.com/

Unit III

- Visit the following websites. Post your opinions about the websites, other reading materials, class discussions, your experiences with disability, and your classmates' postings at our computer distance learning site.

  - **American Disabled for Attendant Programs Today** http://www.adapt.org/
  - **Blindness Related Resources and Beyond** http://www.hicom.net/ ~ oedipus/blind.html
  - **National Association of the Deaf** http://nad.org
  - **Not Dead Yet** http://acils.com/NotDeadYet/

Unit IV

- Visit the following websites. Post your opinions about the websites, other reading materials, class discussions, your experiences with disability, and your classmates' postings at our computer distance learning site.

  - **National Association for Rights, Protection, and Advocacy** http://www.connix.com/ ~ narpa/webdoc4.htm
  - **National Empowerment Center West Coast** http://www.ilrcsf.org/necwest/index.htm
  - **On The Same Page** http://amug.org/ ~ a203/
  - **Support Coalition International Human Rights** http://www.MindFreedom.org/
  - **The Invisible Disabilities Page** http://users.primushost.com/ ~ dmoisan/ invisible_disability.html
  - **Traumatic Brain Injury Resource Directory** http://www.tbi-sci.org/tbird/

Unit V

- Visit the following websites. Post your opinions about the websites, other reading materials, class discussions, your experiences with disability, and your classmates' postings at our computer distance learning site.

  - **Center for Independent Living, Oakland/Berkeley** http://www.cilberkeley.org
  - **Independent Living Resource Center San Francisco** http://www.ilrcsf.org
  - **World Institute on Disability** http://www.wid.org

UNIT READINGS

Unit II: Disability and society

Abberley, P. (1987). The concept of oppression and the development of a social theory of disability. *Disability, Handicap & Society, 12*(1), 5-19.

DeJong, G., Batavia, A. L., & McKnew, L. B. (1992). The independent living model of personal assistance in long-term-care policy. *Generations, 16,* 89-95.

Eichinger, J., Rizzo, T. L., & Sirotnik, B. W. (1992). Attributes related to attitudes toward people with disabilities. *International Journal of Rehabilitation Research, 15,* 53-56.

Fine, M. & Asch, A. (1981). Disabled women: Sexism without the pedestal. *Journal of Sociology and Social Welfare, 8,* 233-248.

Fleischer, D. Z. & Zames, F. (1998). Disability rights. *Social Policy, 28*(3), 52-56.

Kaplan, D. (1989). Disability rights perspective on reproductive technologies and public policy. In S. Cohen & N. Taub (Eds.), *Reproductive laws for 1990's* (pp. 241-247). Totowa, NJ: Humana Press.

Keer, D. W. & Placek, P. J. (1995). The international classification of impairments, disabilities and handicaps: Progress report. *International Rehabilitation Review, 46*(1/2), 17.

Longmore, P. K. (1987). Uncovering the hidden history of people with disabilities. *Reviews in American History, 15,* 355-364.

Longmore, P. K. (1995). The second phase: From disability rights to disability culture. *The Disability Rag and Resources, 16*(5), 4-11.

Unit III: Disability Diversity I

Gregory, S. & Hartley, G. M. (1991). Defining the deaf community. In S. Gregory & G. M. Hartley (Eds.), *Constructing deafness* (pp. 21-22). London: Pinter.

Groce, N. E. (1985). *Everyone here spoke sign language.* Cambridge, MA: Harvard University Press.

Hahn, H. (1988). Can disability be beautiful? *Social Policy, 18,* 26-32.

Hahn, H. (1988). The politics of physical differences: Disability and discrimination. *Journal of Social Issues, 44,* 39-47.

Johnson, M. (1997). Those ol' Kevorkian blues: Give me dignity or give me death. *Ragged Edge,* Mar/April. Available at http://www.raggededgemagazine.com/archive/p9story.htm.

Lane, H. (1995). Constructions of deafness. *Disability & Society, 10*(2), 171-189.

Longmore, P. K. (1985). Screening stereo types: Images of disabled people. *Social Policy, 16,* 31-37.

Unit IV: Disability Diversity II

Bogdan, R., Biklen, D., Shapiro, A., & Spelkoman, D. (1982). The disabled: Media's monsters. *Social Policy, 13,* 32-35.

Freddolino, P., Moxley, D., & Fleishman, J. (1989). An advocacy model for people with long-term psychiatric disabilities. *Hospital and Community Psychiatry, 40,* 1169-1174.

Hyler, S. E. (1988). DSM-III at the cinema: Madness in the movies. *Comprehensive Psychiatry, 29,* 195-206.

Hyler, S. E., Gabbard, G. O., & Schneider, I. (1991). Homicidal maniacs and narcissistic parasites: Stigmatization of mentally ill persons in the movies. *Hospital & Community Psychiatry, 42,* 1044-1048.

Segal, S. P., Silverman, C., & Temkin, T. (1993). Empowerment and self-help agency practice for people with mental disabilities. *Social Work, 38*(6), 705-813.

Unit V: Human Service Practice Framework

Americans with Disabilities Act of 1990, P.L. 101-336, 104 Stat 327.

Barnes, C. (1995). Disability is not measles. *Disability & Society, 10*(3), 378-381.

Burgdorf, R. L. Jr. (1991). The Americans with Disabilities Act: Analysis and implications of a second-generation civil rights statute. *Harvard Civil Rights/Civil Liberties Law Review, 26,* 413-522.

Cole, B. S., Christ, C. C., & Light, T. R. (1995). Social work education and students with disabilities: Implications of section 504 and the ADA. *Journal of Social Work Education, 31*(2), 261-269.

Morris, J. (1993). Feminism and disability. *Feminist Review, 43,* 59-70.

Moxlely, D. (1992). Disability policy and social work practice. *Health & Social Work, 17*(2), 99-104.

Pfeiffer, D. (1994). Eugenics and disability discrimination. *Disability and Society, 9*(4), 481-499.

Quinn, P. (1994). America's disability policy: Another double standard. *Affilia, 9*(1), 45-60.

Reeser, L. C. (1992). Students with disabilities in practicum: What is reasonable accommodation? *Journal of Social Work Education, 28*(1), 98-110.

DISABILITY RIGHTS WEBSITES

- **American Association of People with Disabilities** http://www.aapd-dc.org/

  An organization and site devoted to promoting "productivity, independence, full citizenship, and total integration of people with disabilities into all aspects of society and the natural environment."

- **American Disabled for Attendant Programs Today** http://www.adapt.org/

  A grassroots organization fighting so that people with disabilities are able to live in their communities with any necessary supports, as opposed to institutionalization.

- **Blindness Related Resources and Beyond** http://www.hicom.net/ ~ oedipus/blind.html

  An extensive collection of links, this site is a starting point for the exploration of topics related to blindness, low vision, or vision loss.

- **Center for Independent Living, Oakland/Berkeley** http://www.cilberkeley.org

  A national leader in assisting people with disabilities to live independently and become productive, fully participating members of society. The staff and board, most of whom have disabilities, are strongly committed to supporting others in their efforts towards self-sufficiency.

- **Consortium for Citizens with Disabilities** http://www.c-c-d.org

  A national coalition of 100 disability organizations ensuring public policy reflects "self determination, independence, empowerment, integration and inclusion of children and adults with disabilities in all aspects of society."

- **disABILITY Information and Resources** http://www.makoa.org/

  The site is a meant to serve as an information resource starting point. It is simply presented and provides an extensive collection of disability related links.

- **Disability Cool** http://www.geocities.com/HotSprings/7319/

  This website challenges preconceived ideas about living with a disability. It reframes societal stereotypes that include low expectations of people with a disability and creates a new belief: disabilities are cool.

- **The National Center on Disability and Journalism** http://www.dmedia.org/

  An organization dedicated to working with the media to significantly impact, challenge, and change stereotypes and attitudes commonly portrayed and perpetuated by the media about people with disabilities. They provide resources and training for media professionals and create media that accurately represents people with disabilities.

- **Disability News Service** http://www.disabilitynews.com

  An information and disability-related news service which regularly feeds the national media. Media subscribers can purchase monthly packets of articles to republish in their publications and on internet websites.

- **The Disability Rights Activist** http://www.disrights.org/

  An excellent beginning point for people interested in exploring issues related to disability rights. It includes action alerts, a newsletter, and links to publications and organizations that will engage people in the fight for disability rights.

- **Disability Rights Education and Defense Fund** http://www.dredf.org/

  The leading disability civil rights law and policy center in the nation. This alliance of adults with disabilities and parents of children with disabilities works to advance and secure the civil rights of people with disabilities.

- **Disability Social History Project** http://www.disabilityhistory.org/dshp.html

  This community history project is reclaiming the rich, exciting, and often overlooked history of people with disabilities. It is giving shape to the way disabled people define themselves and their struggles.

- **Independent Living Resource Center** http://www.ilrcsf.org

    A San Francisco based disability rights advocacy organization. Committed to the principles of independent living and the removal of social barriers that impede equal participation for all people with disabilities.

- **Institute on Disability** http://userwww.sfsu.edu/ ~ longmore/

    An institute that focuses on a multidisciplinary approach to developing disability research, teaching, and community service opportunities. It identifies "institutionalized discrimination rather than medical pathology as the primary obstacle to the social integration of disabled persons."

- **The Invisible Disabilities Page** http://users.primushost.com/ ~ dmoisan/invisible_disability.html

    Resources and information that breaks the isolation of people living with hidden disabilities. Aimed toward people with disabilities that are not visible and therefore are misunderstood or met with hostility by society at large.

- **National Association for Rights, Protection, and Advocacy** http://www.connix.com/ ~ narpa/ webdoc4.htm

    This association is committed to empowering people who have been labeled mentally disabled, to abolishing all forced treatment laws, and to promoting the rights of recipients of mental health services as equal citizens.

- **National Association of the Deaf** http://www.nad.org

    An organization dedicated to safeguarding the civil rights and accessibility of 28 million deaf and hard-of-hearing Americans. Its areas of focus and advocacy include employment, education, social services, health care, and telecommunications.

- **National Organization on Disability** http://www.nod.org

    The only national disability organization committed to all disability issues regardless of age group or disability. This network promotes the equal and full participation in all aspects of life for America's 54 million men, women, and children with disabilities.

- **Not Dead Yet** http://acils.com/NotDeadYet/

    A grassroots disability activist organization opposed to the legalization of assisted suicide. "Americans with disabilities don't want your pity or your lethal mercy. We want freedom. We want LIFE."

- **People to People Committee on Disability** http://www.ppcd.org/

    A collection of resources and links highlighting information regarding international disability issues. Links include pathways to the United Nations and the International Labor Organization on disability employment.

- **Ragged Edge Magazine** http://www.ragged-edge-mag.com/

    Small and not-for-profit, the Advocado Press leads in the publishing of books and periodicals devoted to the disability experience and disability rights. *Ragged Edge Magazine* is among its finest publications and this is a must see website.

- **Sexual Health Network: Sexuality Following Disability or Illness** http://www.sexualhealth.com

  Provides easy access to sexuality information, education, and resources for people with disability, illness, or other health related issues. A resource for people with disabilities, health professionals, and educational groups.

- **Support Coalition International Human Rights** http://www.MindFreedom.org/

  A coalition of over 70 grassroots organizations in 11 countries, this federation is devoted to breaking the silence of psychiatry's human rights violations and promotes "humane, empowering alternatives."

- **The Action Starts Here (TASH)** http://www.tash.org/

  An international association whose mission is to "eliminate physical and social obstacles that prevent equity, diversity, and quality of life" for people with disabilities. This organization actively fights against abuse, neglect, separatism, and stigmatization.

- **World Institute on Disability** http://www.wid.org/

  This international public policy center is dedicated to overcoming obstacles to independent living and conducting cutting-edge research on disability-related issues.

- **Whirlwind Wheelchair International** http://whirlwind.sfsu.edu/

  This organization relies on wheelchair riders themselves to play a central role in its effort to develop a "worldwide network of wheelchair inventors/designers, users, and manufacturers to address the need for wheelchairs in developing nations."

Human Behavior and the Social Environment I

SWRK 300 (Spring 2002)

INTRODUCTION

The approach utilized in teaching this course places strong emphasis on challenging students to critically analyze and evaluate underlying assumptions pertaining to oppression and discrimination that permeate American society, including social or human service delivery systems. Students are expected to engage in conscious examination of the use of the self as a mechanism for actively challenging traditional paradigms that foster "isms," such as sexism, racism, able bodieism, heterosexism, ageism, and classism, and for promoting paradigms that reflect diversity-positive, disability-affirming, independent living, and empowerment perspectives. Content on disability is infused into this course and integrated into each section. Heavy emphasis is placed on the interrelationship between the physical (the biological and beyond), intrapsychic, spiritual, and cultural dimensions of the individual and other social systems and the role that the experience of disability may play in shaping this interrelationship. Traditional and alternative definitions of disability as well as paradigms pertaining to disability (the moral, medical, rehabilitation, least restrictive environment, independent living, and interdependency models) are examined. The interrelationship between such factors as body image, body awareness, visible or non-visible disabilities, as well as the distinctions between congenital and acquired disabilities are also explored.

DESCRIPTION

This course is the first of what is a two-course sequence in Human Behavior and the Social Environment. The purpose of this course is to present a comprehensive and well-integrated framework that may be utilized for effective practice (particularly in the areas of data collection and assessment) with persons from a diverse range of backgrounds. Traditional and alternative theories and paradigms pertaining to the individual as a human system as well as the other systems that the individual lives in and interacts with (families, groups, organizations, communities, and societies) are critically analyzed.

An integrated body of knowledge and theory is presented pertaining to the bio-psycho-social-cultural-spiritual dimensions of human systems of different sizes and how such dimensions influence and are influenced by the behavior that occurs within and between these systems. Content is provided on the ways in which diversity enriches and influences the interactions that take place within and between various systems. The interlocking and complex nature of culture and personal identity is explored, with particular emphasis placed on the role that disability, gender, race, and social class play in shaping the interrelationship between these two constructs.

The role that social, economic, and environmental conditions may play in deterring or maintaining the well-being of systems of various sizes and in creating at-risk potential for discrimination, oppression, and social and economic injustice is explored. An introduction to strategies that might be utilized to combat oppression, discrimination, and social and economic injustice and to promote distributive justice, human and civil rights, equality, and equity is provided. Principles pertaining to disability rights are interwoven.

Through course exercises, activities, and assignments as well as an additional 1-credit, 50-hour Social Work Service Experience Requirement that is completed in conjunction with this course, opportunities are provided for students to gain an understanding of how to begin to apply knowledge of human systems and behavior to working with systems of different sizes, as well as the beginning acquisition of skills that might be needed to advocate for social and economic justice or to eliminate discrimination and oppression. Students have the opportunity to select settings that focus on a broad range of populations, human rights, and social and economic justice issues.

OBJECTIVES

By the end of this course, learners will be able to

1. Demonstrate knowledge of traditional and alternative theories or paradigms and knowledge bases, including underlying values and assumptions that serve as constructive frameworks for data collection and assessment, as well as aspects that serve to impede utilization of diversity-positive, disability-affirming, independent living and empowerment approaches to social work practice.
   Outcome Measures Utilized: Assignment 1-4, eco map exercise, all case studies.

2. Demonstrate an understanding of the interrelationship between the biophysical-intra-psychic-psychosocial-cultural-spiritual aspects of development and begin to effectively assess, from a multi-dimensional perspective, how these aspects shape and influence the personal identity of the individual as a human system (underlying dynamics, behavior, and well being) as well as interactions between this system and systems of different sizes (families, groups, communities, organizations, societies).
   Outcome Measures Utilized: Assignment 1-4, eco map exercise, role expectations exercise, "Cultural Dimensions" exercise, and case studies—"Dealing with Children with Cystic Fibrosis: A Model for Group Intervention" and "Willow River Developmental Disabilities Center." (From: *Case Studies in Generalist Practice* by Robert Rivas & Grafton H. Hull, Jr.)

3. Critically analyze specific ways in which the various dimensions of human diversity (age, gender, race, ethnicity, social class, sexual orientation, socioeconomic status, religion, disability, culture, spirituality) influence the behavior and experiences of, and interactions within and between, human systems.
   Outcome Measures Utilized: Assignment 1-4, Cultural Dimensions exercise, and case study—"Between Two Worlds." (From: *Case Studies in Generalist Practice* by Robert Rivas & Grafton H. Hull, Jr.)

4. Identify and critically evaluate the role that social, economic, and environmental conditions may play in deterring or maintaining the well-being of systems (the individual, groups, communities, and organizations) and in creating at-risk potential for discrimination, oppression, and social and economic injustice.
   Outcome Measures Utilized: Assignment 1–4 and case studies—"Late At Night With Bea Rosen" and "Willow River Developmental Disabilities Center." (From: *Case Studies in Generalist Practice* by Robert Rivas & Grafton H. Hull, Jr.)

5. Demonstrate a beginning understanding of the interrelationship between the knowledge base that pertains to human behavior and environments and strategies that might be utilized by social work practitioners to effectively combat oppression, discrimination, and social and economic injustice and to promote distributive justice, human rights, equality, and equity.
   Outcome Measures Utilized: Assignment 1-4, all case studies, Social Work Service Experience Performance Evaluation, and Student Evaluation of Social Work Service Experience.

6. Critically assess and evaluate one's current value system including strengths, areas in which "paradigm shifts," "paradigm paralysis," or ethical incongruities might need to be addressed in order to actively promote social work values and theoretical frameworks pertaining to human behavior and the social environment.
   Outcome Measures Utilized: Assignment 1-4, all class exercises, all case studies.

POLICIES

College policies pertaining to all students are outlined in *Siena Life* and the *College Catalog*. Students are expected to review these policies and to abide by them. Questions regarding any of these policies should be directed to the course instructor. The following additional policies have been developed by the faculty of the Siena College Social Work Program and adopted across all sections of all social work courses (including elective courses and/or courses taught by adjunct instructors):

- Department Grading Policy
- Department Attendance Policy
- Academic Integrity Policy
- Human Rights Policy
- Accommodations Policy
- Accessibility Policy

These policies are listed in their entirety on course syllabi for all courses that are offered to students prior to their admission into the Social Work Program in the fall of their junior year. These policies are also outlined in the *Social Work Program Handbook* that is provided during the Orientation for incoming Social Work majors in the fall of their junior year. The text for the Human Rights, Accommodations and Accessibility Policies follows:

Academic Integrity Policy

The concept of academic integrity lies at the very heart of Siena College. Students are responsible for being familiar with and adhering to the College's guidelines on academic integrity. In any situation in which a student is unsure of what constitutes academic dishonesty, it is the student's responsibility to raise their concerns with her/his instructor. Students are expected to complete their own work and to sign and date each course assignment and examination to attest to their compliance to the College's guidelines on academic integrity. Alleging ignorance of what constitutes academic dishonesty or of the College's policy related to this subject will not be considered a valid explanation or excuse.

Students who engage in plagiarism, cheating, or any other forms of academic dishonesty may be subject to sanctions which include failure of the course, suspension from the College, or permanent dismissal. A statement of the reasons for such sanctions will be placed in the student's file.

Attendance Policy

The Social Work Program is a professional education program that is designed to prepare students for entry into generalist social work practice at the baccalaureate-level. In this context, the classroom is viewed as a "microcosm" of Social Work practice. Ongoing participation in class lectures, discussions, and activities are necessary to ensure that students have effectively mastered the course content. While engaged in course work, students are expected to display the same behaviors they might demonstrate when working in the field, including punctuality and regular attendance. Assessment of student readiness for upper-level course work and advancement into the field experience will take into consideration the ability of the student to demonstrate consistent behavior in these areas.

Students are allowed one absence (one two-hour and forty-five minute segment of classroom instruction) for a course offered once a week, two absences (two one-hour and twenty minute segments of classroom instruction) for a course offered twice a week, and three absences (three fifty-five minute segments of classroom instruction) for a course offered three times a week. One gradient (a three-point interval) will be deducted from an individual's final grade for each absence incurred beyond three absences (or the equivalent as outlined above) for up to and including six absences (the equivalent of three, fifty-five minute segments of classroom instruction). Students who exceed six absences will be required to withdraw from the course and may receive a failing grade for excessive absence.

In the case of inclement weather, the instructor will not count this as an absence as long as the conditions are clearly hazardous. Students must contact the course instructor (783-4283) or the Coordinator of Administrative Services (783-4123) and leave a message regarding the specific class that will be missed.

Human Rights Policy

The Social Work Department/Program is deeply committed to ensuring an effective learning environment that is free from discrimination, harassment, sexual harassment, and violence of any type. It is an expectation that faculty and students will conduct themselves in a manner which demonstrates a regard for every individual and which abides by the human rights policies established by the College, the Department, and State and Federal Law. It is recognized that there may be instances in which individuals may engage in behavior that they did not intend to be offensive to other/s. In such instances, the ability to acknowledge errors in judgment is critical as is openness to feedback. It should be noted, however, that it is the *impact* that an act/s might have on other/s rather than the *intent* that dictates if it is a violation of these policies. The College and Social Work Department/Program has extensive guidelines on student and faculty rights and responsibilities pertaining to human rights as well as established procedures for how to seek redress. These aspects apply both on and off campus and in relation to the Social Work Service and Field Education Experiences. For more information, please contact the Social Work Program Director, the Dean of Students and/or the Chair of the Human Rights Committee.

Accommodations Policy

Students who may need accommodations due to a disability and/or a condition that may become disabling are strongly encouraged to work through and with the College's Office for Students With Disabilities (Siena Hall, Rm. 111) to communicate their needs to department faculty. However, student/s are not required to disclose the nature of their disability to this Office in order to make a request for accommodation with a faculty member. A student may choose to discuss a request for accommodation/s directly with a department faculty member and/or adjunct instructor at any time. Requests for accommodations that extend into the realm of the Social Work Service Experience and/or Field Education Experience should be addressed with either the Coordinator of the Social Work Service Experience and/or the Coordinator of Field Education, respectively.

In order to address a request for accommodations in a timely manner, Department faculty should be informed of a need for accommodations, either directly by the student and/or through the Office of Students with Disabilities as soon as possible and/or prior to the beginning of the semester, if feasible. Once a faculty member has received a request, s/he will make every effort to accommodate the student's needs. Students who choose to request accommodations directly from a faculty member should note that this request will not be shared with other faculty. Therefore, requests for such accommodations need to be addressed to *each* faculty member separately. However, with the student's consent, faculty may need to work directly with the Office for Students with Disabilities to determine the feasibility of addressing specific accommodations that extend beyond the scope of what resources s/he has immediately accessible on an as-needed basis. Faculty advisors are also willing to assist any advisee in their efforts to obtain resources that may be needed (both within and outside of their Social Work classes) to address their needs pertaining to disability in order to maximize their educational experiences with the College.

Accessibility Policy

The Social Work Department is deeply committed to having courses and Program-sponsored activities and events fully accessible (both physical as well as psychological) for students, faculty, adjunct instructors, presenters, Advisory Board members, field educators and any other individuals whom participate in the Social Work Program. Faculty will make every effort to work with the College to ensure that accessibility and a full range of accommodations such as technology, assistive devices, etc. are provided on an as-needed basis.

REQUIRED TEXT AND READINGS

Schriver, J. M. (2001). *Human behavior and the social environment: Shifting paradigms in essential knowledge for social work practice.* Needham Heights, MA: Allyn & Bacon.

Rivas, R. F. & Hull, G. H. (2000). *Case studies in generalist practice.* Pacific Grove, CA: Brooks/Cole.

Mackelprang, R. & Salsgiver, R. (1999). *Disability: A diversity model approach in human service practice.* Pacific Grove, CA: Brooks/Cole.

Course packet of miscellaneous readings.

OUTLINE

The following outline highlights the key points in each module and the corresponding assigned readings. The instructor reserves the right to make alterations in the course and readings or modify the readings as dictated by the combined needs of the learners and the instructor.

I.   Establishing a Contextual Framework

- Overview of purpose, foundations, and underlying assumptions of the HBSE Sequence.

- Major distinctions between HBSE I and HBSE II courses.

- Introduction to the Human Behavior Assessment Framework.

- Overview of traditional paradigms pertaining to human behavior such as masculinity/patriarchy, the concept of the norm of "rightness," eurocentrism, ethnocentrism, privilege, the isms (heterosexism, racism, ageism, classism, sexism, able bodieism, and handicapism), and the concept of interlocking oppressions.

- Overview of alternative paradigms such as the concept of holism, diversity and multiple diversities, feminism, the person as political, populations-at-risk, empowerment, wellness, inclusion theories, person-in-environment and social systems, social and economic justice, advocacy, activism, and cultural competency.

Required Readings: Course Texts

Schriver, Chapter 1—"HBSE and Paradigms," pp. 6-12 and 17-29, Chapter 2—"Traditional and Alternative Paradigms," pp. 62-71 and 86-100 and "The Social Systems and Strengths Perspectives," pp. 138-147.

Rivas & Hull: Case Study #9—"Late Night with Bea Rosen," pp. 55-61.

Required Readings: Reading Packet

Compton, B.R. & Galway, B. (1999). *Social Work Processes (6th edition)*. Pacific Grove, CA: Brooks/Cole. Chapter 2 - "The Eco-System Perspective and the Use of Knowledge," pp. 28-65. Chapter 4 - "Theoretical Perspectives in Social Work Practice," pp. 123-132.

Kirst-Ashman, K. & Hull Jr., G. (2001). *Generalist Practice with Organizations and Communities*. Pacific Grove, CA: Brooks/Cole. "Advocacy and social action with populations-at-risk," pp. 356-364.

Van Den Bergh, N. & Cooper, L.B. (1995). Introduction to Feminist Visions for Social Work. In J. Tropman, J. Erlich, & J. Rothman (Eds.), *Tactics and Techniques of Community Intervention* (pp. 74-81). Itasca, IL: F. E. Peacock.

Onken, S. (1997). *Disability resource curriculum*. CSWE 44th Annual Program Meeting, Orlando, Florida. "Infusing Content on Service Paradigms Applied to People with Disabilities," pp. 23-35.

NASW National Committee on Racial and Ethnic Diversity. (2001, June 23). *NASW Standards for Cultural Competency in Social Work Practice*, pp. 4, 7-9. Available at http://www.socialworkers.org/pubs/standards/cultural.htm.

Individual Learning Application: Analysis of social systems: eco-map exercise.

Professional Practice Application: Case Study #9, pp. 55-61, and discussion questions, "Late Night with Bea Rosen," (see below).

II. The Individual

- Concept of holism as it applies to the development of personhood: definition and key aspects of the physical self (the body as a physical entity, the interrelationship between physical and biological systems, the concept of physicalness or physicality, the role of sexuality), the intra-psychic self (the construct of "personality" and traditional and alternative paradigms pertaining to how personality is structured, the role that internal factors such as perception, affect, cognition, and intuition, as well as external factors such as socialization, play in shaping the intra-psychic self), the spiritual self (definition of what may constitute spirituality, distinctions between organized religion, religious belief systems and spirituality, various conceptualizations of the soul, interrelationship between the soul and spirituality, exploration of the link between the personal and the professional—social work practitioner's beliefs and practices in relation to religion and spirituality), and the cultural self (the interrelationship between cultural constructs and the shaping of cultural identity based on factors such as belief systems, language, symbols, race/ethnic/gender/sexual orientation/disability identification, socioeconomic status).

- Interrelationship between the physical, intra-psychic, spiritual, and cultural dimensions of the self and body image, body awareness, and disability: the concept of embodiment, the role that perception, affect, and cognition play in influencing body image and body awareness as physical and intra-psychic constructs, physical and intra-psychic constructs pertaining to disability, cultural constructs pertaining to disability (moral, medical, rehabilitation, independent living, least restrictive environment, and interdependency), current definitions of disability, including legal or legislative perspectives (Rehabilitation Act of 1973, ADA of 1990), ways in which disabilities may be grouped or categorized and factors influencing "classification," distinctions between congenital and acquired disabilities, the role of visible and non-visible disabilities in shaping definition of the self in relation to disability, interrelationship between eating disorders as a personal as well as a social or cultural construct—the "body politic"—the use of the body to make a social or political statement, the concept of health and wellness from an integrated or holistic self perspective.

- Disabilities pertaining to the physical or intra-psychic dimensions of the self: definition and major characteristics of physical or mobility disabilities, mental or psychiatric disabilities (i.e. Mackelprang & Salsgiver), interrelationship between the spiritual and cultural dimensions of the self, societal and cultural constructs, and the experiences of persons with physical or mobility disabilities and disabilities of an intra-psychic nature.

- Role of the practitioner: link between social work assessment criteria pertaining to the individual as a social system and development of strategies for addressing oppression and discrimination, and promotion of distributive, social and economic justice.

Required Readings: Course Text

Schriver, Chapter 3—"Paradigm Thinking," pp. 121-126, 262-268, and Reading 8.1—"Persons with Disabilities - I am John," pp. 479-486.

Mackelprang & Salsgiver, Part Two: Disability Groupings, pp. 82-101 and 167-179 (mobility disabilities and psychiatric disabilities).

Required Readings: Reading Packet

Berger, R., Federico, R. & McBreen, J. (1988). *Human behavior: A perspective for the helping professions*. New York: Longman. Chapter 2 - The Dimensions of Human Behavior, pp. 23-40.

Estes, C. P. (1995). *Women who run with the wolves: Myths and stories of the wild woman archetype*. NY: Ballantine Books. Chapter 7—"Joyous Body: The Wild Flesh," pp. 197-212 and Chapter 9—"Homing: Returning To Oneself," pp. 255-296.

Fine, M. & Asch, A. (1988). *Women with disabilities: Essays in psychology, culture, and politics*. Philadelphia: Temple University Press. "On Embodiment: A Case Study of Congenital Limb Deficiency in American Culture," pp. 41-68.

Redfield Jamison, K. (1995). *An unquiet mind.* New York: Random House. "Flights of the Mind," pp. 67-68, "Missing Saturn," pp. 90-109, and "A Life in Moods," pp. 211-219.

Canda, E. (2000). *Spiritual diversity in social work practice.* New York: Haworth Press. Chapter 3— "Human Diversity, Spirituality and Social Work Practice," pp. 79-96.

Millet, M. (2000). "Soul Fragmentation," pp. 1-3, available at http://website.lineone.net/%7Edr.mgm/ index-soul.html

Louis, R. (1998). "Contemporary Soul Retrieval: An Interview with Sandra Ingerman." *Shaman's Drum*, (50), pp. 25-30.

Keen, S. (1992). *Fire in the belly: On being a man.* New York: Phantom/DoubleDay. "The Soulful Quest: Pilgrimage into Self," pp. 125-151.

NASW Committee on Racial and Ethnic Diversity. (2001). NASW Standards for Cultural Competency in Social Work Practice, pp. 4, 7-9.

Yamasaki, T. (1999, April 12). Special report: Wasting away—Eating disorders on campus. *People Magazine*, pp. 54-65.

Steiner-Adair, C. (1986). "The Body Politic: Normal Female Adolescent Development and the Development od Eating Disorders." *The Journal of American Academy of Psychoanalysis*, 14(1), 95-114.

Optional Readings (in packet)

Wyldkat. (2000). "Shamanism, Power Animals, and Animal Wisdom," pp. 1-4, available at http:// www.wicca.com/celtic/wyldkat/shmnindex.htm

Moore, T. (1992). *Care of the soul: A guide for cultivating depth and sacredness in everyday life.* New York: HarperCollins. Chapter 1—"Honoring Symptoms as a Voice of the Soul," pp. 3-21.

Voss, R., Douville, V., Little Soldier, A., and Twiss, G. (1999). Tribal and shamanic-based social work practice: A Lakota perspective. *Social Work*, 44(3), pp. 228-239.

Individual/Group Learning Application: Embodiment and Body Image: Class Discussion Questions, Cultural Dimensions: Exercise

Individual Assignment #1: Individual as a Human System—The Interrelationship between the Physical, Psychological, and Spiritual Dimensions of Human Behavior

Video: *Mr. Jones* (Richard Gere—experiences of an individual with bipolar disorder)

Professional Practice Application: Discussion Questions—Religion, Spirituality, and the Soul.

III. The Family

- Reconsidering traditional definitions of the family: the concept of familieness and the diversity of family structures.
- The family as a social system: characteristics of healthy families; properties and rules that govern family functioning (boundaries, open and closed systems, power structures, roles and rules, interrelationship between societal values and expectations, and family interactions).
- Concept of the family as a physical/intrapsychic/spiritual/cultural entity (holism): the interrelationship between the physical, psychological, and spiritual dimensions of the family and family health, impact of social class or socioeconomic status on family health, the interrelationship between the development of cultural identity—as it pertains to age, gender, race, ethnicity, culture, disability, sexual orientation, religion, and spirituality within the context of various family structures—and the nature of interactions within the family as well as between the family and other systems.

- Traditional paradigms and effective family functioning: the interrelationship between traditional paradigms such as patriarchy (i.e. good provider role), eurocentrism, ethnocentrism, norm of "rightness," privilege, isms (i.e. sexism, racism, classism, able bodieism, and heterosexism), obstacles that hinder family well-being and effective family functioning, mezzo and macro level strategies for promoting distributive justice, human rights, equality, and equity in relation to the family as a system.

- Alternative paradigms and effective family functioning: the interrelationship between alternative paradigms such as the strengths or capacities, empowerment, diversity-positive, disability-affirming, social and economic justice perspectives, and promotion of the well-being and effective functioning of the family as a unit on a mezzo and macro level.

- Role of the practitioner: link between social work assessment criteria pertaining to the family as a social system and development of strategies for addressing oppression and discrimination and promotion of distributive, social and economic justice.

Required Reading: Course Text

Schriver, Chapter 6—"Perspectives on Familieness," pp. 317-328, 333-336, and 365-373. Reading 1.1: "Toward Understanding The Association of Socioeconomic Status and Health: A New Challenge for the Bio-psycho-social Approach," pp. 32-46. Reading 6.2: "Quiet Success: Parenting Strengths among African Americans," pp. 377-389.

Rivas & Hull, Jr.: Case Study #13—"Between Two Worlds," pp. 88-94.

Required Readings: Reading Packet

Coontz, S. (2000). "The American Family: An Essay." *Life Magazine*, pp. 98-109.

Hepworth, D. & Larsen, J. (1990). *Social work practice.* Pacific Grove, CA: Brooks/Cole. Chapter 10— "Assessing Family Functioning in Diverse Family and Cultural Contexts," pp. 287-310.

Skolnick, A. & J. (1988). *Family in transition,* IL: Scott, Foresman, and Co. Chapter 3—Jessie Bernard, "The Good Provider Role: Its Rise and Fall," Chapter 6—Rosanna Hertz, "More Equal Than Others: Women and Men in Dual-Career Marriages," pp. 291-300, and "Single Mothers: A Review and Critique of Current Research," pp. 440-454.

Kirn, W. (2000, September 25). Should you stay together for the kids? *Time Magazine*, pp. 75-82.

Knox, D. & Schacht, C. (2000). *Understanding relationships.* Belmont, CA: Wadsworth/Thomas Learning Co. Chapter 15—"Remarriage," pp. 396-405.

Schriver, J. (1998). *Human behavior and the social environment: Shifting paradigms in essential knowledge for social work practice (2nd edition).* Needham Heights, MA: Allyn and Bacon, Reading 6.1—"The Black Family in America," pp. 246-260.

Ewalt, P., Freeman, M., & Poole, L. (1998). *Community building: Renewal, well-being, and shared responsibility.* Washington, DC: NASW Press, Chapter 4—"Kinship Care: The African American Response to Family Preservation," pp.182-188.

Badillo Ghali, S. (1982). Understanding Puerto Rican traditions. *Social Work, 27*(1), 98-102.

Schriver, J. (1998). *Human Behavior and the Social Environment: Shifting Paradigms in Essential Knowledge for Social Work Practice.* Needham Heights, MA: Allyn and Bacon, Reading 6.1— "Brooke Medicine Eagle," pp. 353-363.

Individual/Group Learning Application: Role Expectations Exercise.

Professional Practice Application: Case Study and Discussion Questions—Between Two Worlds
Assignment #2: Genogram and Family Analysis.

Guest Speaker: Uses and Interpretations of Family Genograms.

IV. Groups

- Introduction to groups: link between course content introduced in this course and future content presented in SWRK 400 Social Work Practice II (Mezzo and Macro Practice).

- Definition, purposes, functions, and types of groups: primary and secondary groups, formal and informal, task and treatment group typology.

- The group as a social system: boundaries, homeostasis, process and product dimensions, interfacing, and other aspects of social systems theory applied to the group.

- Concept of the group as a physical/intrapsychic/spiritual/cultural entity (holism): role of physical environment in shaping group interactions, intrapsychic dimensions of group behavior (communication and interaction patterns, group attraction and cohesion), power structure, social control, group membership, roles and role behavior, factors shaping the cultural identity of the group as an entity and in relation to individual membership composition (role of cultural values, norms, traditions, as well as age, gender, race, ethnicity, culture, sexual orientation, disability, socioeconomic status, and social class) in influencing behavior and interactions within and between groups, the concept of the spirit and the soul as it applies to the group as a social and cultural construct.

- Traditional paradigms and effective group functioning: the interrelationship between traditional paradigms such as patriarchy, eurocentrism, ethnocentrism, norm of "rightness," privilege, and isms (i.e. sexism, racism, classism, able bodieism, and heterosexism) and obstacles that hinder effective group functioning, mezzo and macro level strategies for promoting distributive justice, human rights, equality and equity in relation to the group as a social system.

- Alternative paradigms and effective group functioning: the interrelationship between alternative paradigms such as the strengths or capacities, empowerment, diversity-positive, disability-affirming, social and economic justice perspectives and promotion of the well-being and effective functioning of the group as a unit on a mezzo and macro level.

- Role of the practitioner: link between social work assessment criteria pertaining to the group as a social system and strategies for the promotion of distributive, social, and economic justice.

Required Readings: Course Text

Schriver, Chapter 7—"Perspectives On Groups," pp. 394-399, 402-409, and 414-417, and Reading 9.1 "Hip-Hop Nation: The Undeveloped Social Capital of Black Urban America," pp. 544-551.

Required Readings: Reading Packet

Toseland, R. & Rivas, R. (2001). *Introduction to group work practice, (4th ed.).* Needham Heights, MA: Allyn & Bacon. Chapter 1—"Introduction," pp. 12-46, Chapter 2—"Historical Developments," pp. 48-56, and Chapter 3—"Understanding Group Dynamics," pp. 69-94.

Brown, D., Guida, D., Krieg, K., & Belluck, F. (1995). "A model for group intervention with the chronically ill: Cystic fibrosis and the family." Published simultaneously in *Social Work in Pediatrics,* pp. 81-94, and *Social Work in Health Care, 21*(1), 81-94.

Individual/Group Learning Application: Group Dynamics Exercise.

Professional Practice Application: Case Study: Ari and Simone: Notes From the Group.
Assignment #3: Group Analysis.

V. Communities and Organizations

- Introduction to communities and organizations: link between course content introduced in this course and future content presented in SWRK-310 HBSE II, SWRK-320 Social Work Practice I (Micro Practice) and SWRK 400 Social Work Practice II (Mezzo and Macro Practice).

- Communities and organizations as biophysical/intra-psychic/cultural/ spiritual entities (holism): environment as a biophysical, social, and cultural construct, application of systems theory constructs such as boundaries, interfacing, patterns of activity, and power structures, social networking theory as it pertains to communities and organizations (vertical and horizontal linkages, directions of influence; levels of inclusiveness).

- Traditional and alternative definitions of communities: as "target/service populations," as "populations-at-risk," based on physical or geographic locations and boundaries, as racial/ethnic/cultural entities, as established neighborhoods or social networks, as "intentional" communities based on ways of relating or common interest or identification, the "virtual" community.

- Traditional and alternative definitions of organizations: social units or human grouping systems, profit/not-for-profit/public sector/private sector/non-governmental, community-based/global/world class entities united by common purpose/mission/goals (sources for public consumption of goods and services, social or human service providers, "agents" of social/political/economic distributive justice or change), categories of human service or social work organizations (direct service, social equity, social justice/advocacy/activist).

- Traditional and alternative purposes and functions of communities and social work organizations: production-distribution-consumption; socialization and social control mechanisms; direct and indirect service delivery, cultivation and preservation of fictive kinship/natural helping networks/ other types of community-based networks and neighborhoods, utilization of organized religion and spiritual support systems, promotion and maintenance of social/political/cultural/spiritual identity (i.e. Grey Panthers, Independent Living Movement, Urban League, Act-Up, other community-based movements), social development, community building and renewal, community organizing, social and political action, advocacy and social change.

- Dynamics influencing the health and well-being of communities: rural, suburban, urbanization, suburbanization, centralization, gentrification, social stratification (social class and socioeconomic status) economic resource allocation (distribution of financial/human/social capital), diversity paradigms (strengths/capacities/assets vs. pathology and dysfunction), access to environmental resources, and social, political, and environmental patterns of oppression and discrimination (environmental racism, sexism, ageism, able bodieism).

- Relationship between purpose/functions/resources of human service and social work organizations and the promotion of social and economic justice: the role that factors such as organizational mission and mandate, organizational philosophy (moral, medical, rehabilitative, independent living, empowerment), organizational structure, geographic locale, service boundaries, organizational culture (values, norms, traditions pertaining to service delivery), and access to social/political/ economic resources play in influencing the effectiveness of human service organizations and social work organizations in relation to the promotion of social and economic justice.

Required Readings: Course Text

Schriver, Chapter 9—"Perspectives on Community(ies)," pp. 501-513, 520-525, and 530-541.

Required Readings on Reserve at Library and in Reading Packet

Kirst-Ashman, K. & Hull, G. (2001). *Generalist practice with organizations and communities.* Brooks/ Cole: Pacific Grove, CA. Chapter 3—"Mezzo Skills in the Macro Environment," pp. 89-98 and Chapter 8—"Understanding Neighborhoods and Communities," pp. 268-282 and 288-291.

Rubin, H. & Rubin, I. (1988). *Community organizing and development*. New York: Macmillan Publishing, Chapter 5—"Communities and Organizations," pp. 81-88 and 93-100.

Ewalt, P., Freeman, M., & Poole, L. (1998). *Community building: Renewal, well-being, and shared responsibility*. Washington, DC: NASW Press, Chapter 10—"Strengthening Neighborhoods by Developing Community Networks," pp. 107-114.

Grossman, K. (1991). Environmental racism, *Crisis, 98*(4), 14-17 & 31-32.

NASW Delegate Assembly (2000, April). NASW Environmental policy statement. Reprinted with permission from NASW Press in *NASW/NYS Chapter Update, 24*(9), 9.

Hoff, M. & McNutt, J. (2000). *Rogge's Social Work Practice with Environmental Issues Matrix.* Available at Social Welfare, Social Justice, and Environmental Degradation Website: University og Tennessee College of Social Work (http://web.utk.edu/ ~ merogge) and Boise State University Social Work Department (http://www.idbsu.edu:80/social work/).

Love Canal Collection. (2000). *University of New York at Buffalo Archives*. Who will help them?, pp. 1-2 and Testimony Presented to House Committee on Oversight and Investigations, pp. 1-15.

Individual/Group Learning Application: Assessing Communities: Class Exercise.

Professional Practice Application: Assignment #4: Organizational and Community Analysis.

Guest Speaker: Mobilizing Communities for Community Development/Preservation.

EXERCISES

"Late Night With Bea Rosen" Case Study and Discussion Questions

Students are assigned the case study "Late Night With Bean Rosen," from *Case Studies in Generalist Practice*. This case study is utilized in the introductory unit to this course and highlights the experiences of an individual who has recently lost her partner and is experiencing grief and loss as well as managing long-term health conditions that periodically become disabling. Through this case study, students have the opportunity to apply concepts pertaining to systems theory as well as course content on the diversity and strength perspectives, with particular emphasis on disability. Students are asked to complete their individual responses to the following questions. (NOTE: Questions have been developed by the course instructor to ensure that they are tailored to course content.)

1. Provide a brief overview of the key aspects of Bea as an individual. Address this from a holistic perspective. Include an overview of her major strengths.

2. What would you identify as Bea's major needs at this point in time?

3. What are your views regarding the concerns raised by Kathleen when she did not want to question Bea any further about her fears and possible phobias because it would have been intrusive? Do you agree? Disagree? Why?

4. In what ways have Bea's support systems changed since her husband's death? What affect has does this appear to have had on Bea's current life circumstances (issues and needs)?

5. In what ways might Bea's support systems need to be strengthened or further developed to better address her current and anticipated future needs (health/social/emotional/spiritual)?

6. What other steps might need to be taken to address Bea's needs?

7. In what ways did Kathleen effectively utilize the agency supports that she had available to her as a worker in relation to this situation? What impact did this have? What other steps might she have taken? Why?

Embodiement, Body Image, and Body Awareness: Discussion Questions

This set of discussion questions is distributed to students in relation to readings assigned in the course unit pertaining to the individual as a social system. Students are asked to review the readings assigned on "Joyous Body…" by Clarissa Pinkola Estes and "Embodiement" by Gelya Frank. Students are asked to complete their individual written responses to the following:

* Identify and write down some examples of the major messages that are conveyed in each of these articles about the body and the concept of body image.

* Compare these messages to your impression of the messages given by the broader society about these areas. Write down some examples of these messages.

* Explain what you think is meant by concept of "embodiement" both from a societal as well as the author's perspective. (key words and phrases are fine!)

* Identify and write down examples of major factors that seem to have shaped Diane Devrie's concept of body image.

* Discuss what role prosthetic devices played in influencing both Diane's concept of body image as well as the messages that she received from others regarding her ability to function effectively in relation to these devices.

* Identify some similarities and differences between the experiences of Opalanga and Diane Devrie— in terms of the messages that each individual received about their bodies and the ways in which they "reframed" their experiences—challenged negative perceptions and reassigned new and different meanings.

Students are assigned these questions to coincide with the readings noted and are asked to bring their responses to the next class. Students are broken into dyads and provided with some time to process their responses. The instructor then draws from these responses as part of the class lecture and discussion.

Mental Health and Psychiatric Disabilities—Bi-Polar Disorder: Discussion Questions

Students are assigned excerpts from *An Unquiet Mind* by Kay Redfield Jamison and asked to write down their responses to this reading in relation to the following questions:

* What thoughts and feelings surfaced as you read about Kay's experiences?

* Were there any aspects of her portrayal of her experiences that you found to be disturbing? If so, which aspects? Why?

* What is your perspective on Jamison's quote "We are all, as Bryon put it, differently organized. We each move within the restraints of our temperament and live up only partially to its possibilities?"

* With regard to Bi-Polar Disorder as well as other psychiatric disabilities, how might this relate to our class discussions on the concept of a continuum of functioning as it pertains to disability?

* How might this reading challenge perspectives you may have on what constitutes "normalcy" as compared to "mental illness?"

* Do you agree or disagree with the perspective highlighted through these readings on mental health? Why? Why not?

Students are assigned these questions to coincide with the readings noted and asked to bring their responses to the next class. The instructor then draws from these responses as part of the class lecture and discussion.

"Between Two Worlds" Case Study and Discussion Questions

Each student reads the entire case study "Between Two Worlds," in the text *Case Studies in Generalist Practice*. This case study is utilized in relation to the course unit on the family as a social system. It focuses on a young woman of Hmong descent who is experiencing physical symptoms that are very much interrelated with emotional distress that she is feeling in relation to family pressures and expectations. The case study highlights the interrelationship between cultural and spiritual beliefs and family traditions and provides a cross-cultural perspective on embodiement, body awareness, and able bodieism. Drawing from this case study and a course reading from Hepsworth and Larsen, students write down their responses to the questions below.

Group 1:

1. Based on the data provided, describe what you know about Bea as an individual. In this description, include, but don't limit it to, the initial problem or need identified by Bea.

2. Identify the major characteristics of Bea's family structure based on ethnicity and cultural background—key considerations with regard to history, power structure, decision- making processes, expression of feelings, goals, needs, and roles.

Group 2:

1. Discuss the role of ethnicity and culture in relation to the conflict and stressors being experienced by Bea (think physical/intra-psychic/spiritual/cultural).

2. Describe the role of spiritual practices in assisting Bea in dealing with conflicts and stressors being experienced.

3. Discuss the possible role that constructs such as embodiement, body awareness, and able bodieism may have played in influencing the initial responses that Bea received from the health care system in relation to her situation.

Group 3:

1. Discuss the possible role that constructs such as embodiement, body image, and able bodieism may have played in influencing the initial responses that Bea received from the health care system in relation to her situation.

2. Discuss the goals targeted by the worker and identify how these goals changed over time.

3. Discuss the role that cultural differences played in shaping both Bea's and the worker's problem-solving style and approach to their counseling relationship.

Group 4:

1. Identify the interventions used by the worker.

2. Were the interventions selected by the worker appropriate based on Bea's ethnicity/culture/spirituality? If so, why? If not, why not? Anything you might have done differently? What? Why?

Students are broken into small groups and compile collective responses to each of the assigned questions. A large group discussion follows.

Cultural Dimensions: Individual Exercise

Student Directions. You are uncommitted romantically to any particular individual at this point in time. A friend has just arranged a date for you with someone you have not met before. Review the list of attributes below and then complete the following exercise. (Note: Strive to be as candid with yourself as possible.)

- Place an *A* next to any attribute that you might view as acceptable or which would not influence your decision of whether or not to date this individual in the future.

- Place an *R* next to any attribute that through your direct contact on your first date with this individual and information s/he shared during the first date might make you hesitant to become romantically involved with or to seriously date this person.

- Place an *M* next to any attribute that might lead you to rule out the possibility of ever marrying/partnering with that individual. (Note: You may have both an *R* & *M* next to the same item.)

- Develop a list of any other attributes that might apply to any of the areas above that are not in-cluded in the list below—i.e. that would fall under *A*, *R*, or *M*.

_ Puerto Rican heritage	_ Italian heritage	_ Heterosexual
_ Chinese heritage	_ Mexican heritage	_ Uses a wheelchair for mobility
_ Japanese heritage	__Islamic	_ Protestant
__Blind	__Cerebral Palsy	_ Canadian
_ HIV Positive	__Muslim	_ Baptist
_ African American heritage	__Paraplegic	_ Polish heritage
_ Schrizophrenic	__Transvestite	_ Bi-Polar Disorder
_ Iranian heritage	__Vietnamese heritage	_ Cuban Heritage
_ Deaf	__Bisexual	_ Jehovah's Witness
_ Obese	__Previously Divorced	_ Recovering addict
_ Native American heritage	__IRA Supporter	_ French Heritage
_ Jewish Heritage	__Latino/a Heritage	_ Biracial (Dad is African Am. Mom is Euro. Am.)
_ Diagnosed as having cancer in the terminal Stages	__ Atheist	
__Convicted Felon	__Transgendered	_ In the U.S. Illegally (Immigrant)
__Catholic	__German Heritage	_ Epilepsy

Part One:

Complete the attached exercise.

Part Two:

After completing the attached exercise, write down your answers to the following:

- Provide a brief summary of any items that you placed an *A* next to, as well as any items that you included on the list that you developed and were not included in the list provided. Provide a brief explanation regarding why you rated these items as an *A*.

- Provide a brief summary of those items next to which you placed an *R* or an *M* as well as any items that you included on your list that were not part of the list provided.

- Complete an analysis of the items that you placed an *R* or an *M* next to as follows:

  - Provide a brief rationale or explanation of why you assigned the ratings you did to these items.

  - Identify any items that you might have any "qualifiers" for (i.e., might be willing to reconsider) and, if so, explain what the specific circumstances are that might influence you to change any of your ratings (i.e., if someone who was currently in the United States as an immigrant illegally were here to escape political or religious persecution, etc.)

  - Identify what you learned from completing this exercise and what conclusions you might draw (i.e., thoughts or feelings that you have about completing it, about the ratings you assigned, and about your responses to any of the above areas).

Bring your responses to this exercise with you to the next class. These responses will be collected.

Part Three:

Drawing from the prior responses that you completed for the "Cultural Dimensions" exercise, complete your responses to the follow-up questions below:

1. Define the meaning of and discuss the role that the following paradigms may have had in influenc-ing some of your responses: strengths, feminism, empowerment, independent living. (Note: Select the two perspectives that you feel are the most relevant to your responses.) Give examples of some specific items and your ratings to illustrate your points.

2. Review the rationales that you provided for why you assigned the ratings that you did. Identify and provide a list of those items for which ratings might be based on qualities or behaviors you associate with THE LARGER GROUP that the attribute you were asked to consider is most commonly viewed as representative of—rather than any actual experiences you have had with a particular individual. Select two of these items and discuss underlying assumptions that you have about the larger group and how these assumptions might have shaped your responses in these areas.

3. Define the meaning of and discuss the role that the following paradigms may have had in influencing some of your responses: eurocentrism, ethnocentrism, privilege, isms (such as racism, sexism, heterosexism, able bodieism). (Note: Select the two perspectives that you feel are the most relevant.) Give examples of some specific items and your rating to illustrate your points.

4. Identify two or three conclusions that you might draw regarding how your responses to this exercise—i.e., factors that influence how you might approach the development of personal relationships with others based on cultural attributes—may relate to your current personal values and beliefs about culture. Drawing from the NASW Standards on Cultural Competency, identify specific ways that you might further develop your cultural competency (knowledge and skills) as a future social work practitioner.

ASSIGNMENTS

Students are given extensive instructions for the four assignments in the course. The full-text of the assignments are available in printable format online at http://www.cswe.org/disabilityresource. The assignments are abstracted here.

Assignment 1: Individual as a Human System—The Interrelationship between the Physical, Psychological and Spiritual Dimensions of Human Behavior

Paper length: Minimum of 10 pages, typewritten and double-spaced
Grade weight: 100 points

Clarissa Pinkola Estes maintains that "our body is considered a sensor—an informational network, a messenger with myriad communication systems—cardiovascular, respiratory, skeletal, autonomic, as well as emotive and intuitive." The concept of body and body image is shaped by the various dimensions—physical, psychological, religious or spiritual, and cultural—that comprise the essence of one's personhood. The purpose of this assignment is to provide an opportunity for you to examine the relationship that exists between the concept of one's body, body image, and one's religion or spirituality. The interrelationship between beliefs about disability, one's body image or self-concept and one's concept of spirituality will also be explored. The ability to understand the interrelationship between these various aspects is essential for effective social work practice.

In this assignment students are told to draw heavily from course readings but also to draw a clear distinction between educational and academic sources and their own personal perspectives. The analysis is to be broken down into four parts:

Part One (20 points)

Body awareness and body image are often influenced by one's level of awareness of what our body means to us at a particular point in time. Drawing from the assigned reading from Clarissa Pinkola Estes, "Joyous Body: The Wild Flesh," Gelya Frank, "Embodiement...," Steiner-Adair, "Body Politic," and the student's own life experience, the students are asked to discuss their current values and beliefs, including, among other things, factors that shape their own body image and level of body awareness and ways that concepts of embodiement and able bodieism inform this image.

Part Two (25 points)

Clarissa Pinkola Estes notes, "Some say the soul informs the body. But what if we were to imagine for a moment that the body informs the soul…" Drawing from the readings by Canda, Millet, Louis, Estes, and Keen from Unit II, students reflect on their religious or spiritual beliefs.

Part Three (30 points)

Disability is a major dimension of our human experience. The reality is that most if not all of us either have or will acquire a disability or develop a disabling condition during the course of our lifetimes. This part requires students to research and provide an overview of a condition (physical and/or psychological) of interest. The overview should draw from a minimum of four and a maximum of eight sources, two of which must be professional journal articles and only two of which can be websites.

Part Four (25 points)

Next, students envision that they have been identified as having the condition or disability discussed in Part Three. They discuss how this condition might influence their current body image from an intrapsychic (emotions, affect, cognition), cultural, religious or spiritual perspective. Students are given 10 areas in which to focus for this section.

Assignment 2: Family Systems Analysis

Paper length: Minimum of 10 double-spaced pages, excluding genogram
Grade weight: 100 points
This assignment provides an opportunity for students to examine the role that family history and intergenerational themes play in influencing the family as social system. They use a genogram to analyze these dynamics. Students construct a genogram and complete an analysis of their family as a reference point for application of course concepts. They are asked to review readings from Unit II, The Family. The assignment is broken down into three parts.

Part One: Family History - Genogram (25 points)

Students construct a genogram and display it on poster board or a large piece of paper. They include family structures, educational and professional or occupational information, ethnic or cultural heritage, and several other factors in the genogram, as directed by the instructor.

Part Two: Analysis of Intergenerational Themes (55 points)

A. **Overview of Background History (10 points).** Students provide a succinct, written summary (minimum of 3, maximum of 5 pages) that presents an overview of your family background from an intergenerational perspective.

B. **Assessment of Intergenerational Patterns (45 points).** Students review the entire genogram and identify and analyze the major themes and patterns that cut across or are woven through it. This includes looking within each generation, across generations, and within their own immediate family unit.

Part Three: Closing Summary (20 points)

Students tie in their previous analysis with alternative and traditional paradigms influencing their family patterns, strengths, and obstacles to family development, and other factors that affect family interactions. They are also asked to discuss how these components inform their knowledge and understanding about practicing as a social worker.

Assignment 3: Group Analysis

Length: Minimum of 8 pages, double-spaced

Grade weight: 100 points

The purpose of this assignment is to enhance students' understanding of groups as social systems. In preparation, students observe the inner workings of a group, either through viewing a video that highlights group dynamics or through observing at least two live group sessions or meeting (e.g., in an agency setting). The final group analysis paper draws from the observation or group experience, course readings, and class discussion. The paper is divided into three parts.

Part One: Introduction (5 points)

Students give a brief introduction that identifies the movie or group observed for the completion of this assignment.

Part Two: Group Analysis (85 points)

Students discuss (a) group attraction and cohesion, (b) communication and interaction patterns, (c) group culture (including, for example, values demonstrated, language and rituals used to help group spirit develop), and (d) social controls that define group dynamics.

Part Three: Summary (10 points)

Students draw from Rivas and Toseland to select a group stage development model that most fits this particular group's process. They are also asked to evaluate the group in terms of its defined purposes or tasks or other components that served as strengths and obstacles to its activities.

Examples of Possible Videos and Group Experiences

(Video/group observation must be approved in advance by the course instructor)

Videos

1.	The Breakfast Club	7.	Toy Story
2.	Stand By Me	8.	The Homecoming
3.	Stand And Deliver	9.	Saving Private Ryan
4.	Alive	10.	Girl Interrupted
5.	Lord of the Flies	11.	K-Pax
6.	Dead Poets Society	12.	28 Days

Group Experiences That Might Be Utilized for Group Observations

1. Clubs you are involved with on campus.

2. Task groups that the agency that you are volunteering with might be running (Socialization skills, educationally based groups—must be a group that meets at least 4-6 times versus a one-time group experience).

3. Community-based groups such as "self-help" or peer support groups (same ground rules apply as for #2).

4. Community-based groups such as coalitions or task forces that are working on a specific issue (same ground rules apply as per noted above).

Assignment 4: Communities and Organizations

Length: 8-10 pages, double-spaced
Grade weight: 100 points

The purpose of this assignment is to enhance students' understanding of communities and organizations with regard to the role that organizations may play in working to effectively promote social, economic, and political justice and to eradicate such injustices in conjunction with the target populations and communities they seek to serve.

Students must conduct in-person interviews with an individual from a community-based human service organization that focuses on the promotion of social or economic justice. Students are able to use their field agency, if appropriate.

Students are told that the interviewee should be an individual within the organization who has the knowledge and ability to discuss the organization and the points outlined in the assignment and is willing to set aside at least 90 minutes for meetings. Students are encouraged to give their interviewees their assignment in advance. Students must also gather an organizational chart and resource materials or literature on the organization. The paper is divided into four parts.

- Organizational Profile (35 points).

- Interrelationship between Organization, Target Population, & Community (40 points).

- Assessment of Organization's Effectiveness (10 pts).

- Closing Summary (15 points). Students evaluate the strengths and obstacles of the organization, discuss ways the organization might better serve its target population or community, and provide other insights about the workings of the organization.

Human Behavior and the Social Environment II

SWRK-310 (Spring 2002)

INTRODUCTION

The approach utilized in teaching this course continues (from HBSE I) to place strong emphasis on challenging students to critically evaluate underlying assumptions pertaining to traditional and alternative paradigms. Students are expected to draw from their knowledge of these paradigms as well as prior content pertaining to the physical, intra-psychic, spiritual, and cultural self and to begin to effectively integrate these constructs into the broader, comprehensive data collection and assessment frameworks for generalist practice presented in this course. Content on disability as well as other dimensions of one's personhood continue to be infused into this course and integrated into each section. Utilizing developmental life span, life course, life stage and identity formation perspectives as vantage points from which to explore the commonality as well as uniqueness of each individual, heavy emphasis is placed on the strengths, diversity-positive, "diversity-within-diversity" and disability-affirming perspectives. Through the collection of assessment data via first-person narratives and other primary as well as secondary data sources, students apply course content to practical, real-life experiences and examine the various factors and social systems that serve to promote or deter persons in their efforts to maintain or achieve well being.

DESCRIPTION

This course is the second course is the HBSE Sequence. Building upon on course content presented in SWRK-300 HBSE I, this course provides a comprehensive understanding of the interactions between the dimensions of the self as an individual and systems of various sizes as well as how this interrelationship may serve to influence human behavior throughout one's life course. Strong emphasis is placed on concepts such as developmental assets, resiliency, protective factors, and risk assessment. Within the context of each stage, students examine the interrelationship between each of these concepts and life events/occurrences that serve to shape growth and development. Resources that might be utilized to develop/build upon individual strengths are also emphasized.

OBJECTIVES

By the end of this course, learners will be able to:

1. Demonstrate an understanding of the traditional and alternative theories pertaining to human development and critically evaluate the underlying values and ethics related to these theories as well as how to begin to apply them to understanding client/consumer situations.

   Outcome Measures Utilized: Assignment 1-3, Case studies, quizzes and final examination

2. Demonstrate an understanding of the interactions between the bio-psycho-social-spiritual dimensions of the individual as a system and systems of other sizes and begin to assess how such interactions may serve to influence human behavior throughout the life course and within the context of the social environment.

   Outcome Measures Utilized: Assignment 1-3, Class activities: Force Field Analysis, Fetal Drug and Alcohol Syndrome; Case study on older adulthood, quizzes and final examination.

3. Assess the role that various dimensions of one's personhood such as age, gender, socioeconomic status, social class, sexual orientation, religion and/or spirituality, disability, race, ethnicity, and culture play in influencing client life experiences throughout the life course.

   Outcome Measures: Assignment 1-3; Class activities: Children and Spirituality, Adolescent Sexuality, Sexual Orientation; Midterm and final examination

4. Assess the interrelationship between aspects of client's life situations such as developmental assets, strengths/ capacities, protective factors, risk factors, resiliency, and coping behaviors.

   Outcome Measures Utilized: Assignments 1-3; Narratives and case studies; speaker presentations on inclusion and foster care; final examination

GRADING

- Assignment 1:   Pregnancy, Childbirth, and Infancy/Toddlerhood: Developmental Assessment
  15 pts.
- Assignment 2:   Middle Childhood/Adolescence: Data Collection and Assessment Criteria
  20 pts.
- Assignment 3:   Middle/Older Adulthood: Life Event Assessment
  25 pts.
- Quiz 1   15 pts.
- Quiz 2   10 pts.
- Final Exam   15 pts.
  TOTAL   **100 pts.**

Criteria

Course objectives are achieved through a combination of lecture, class discussion, class assignments, assigned readings, guest speakers, films, papers, and exams. Written assignments will be graded on the basis of the student's ability to integrate course content into the structure of the prescribed assignment, conceptual clarity, organization and flow, and grammatical accuracy. Written assignments are due on the date specified. Extensions will be granted only under extenuating circumstances and only by direct permission of the instructor. Under no circumstances will extensions be granted on the day an assignment is due. No extensions will be granted via electronic mail. Assignments handed in late, without prior permission of the instructor, will automatically be graded down one gradient (a three-point interval) for each day.

PROGRAM POLICIES AND REQUIREMENTS

The following academic policies pertaining to Social Work students have been discussed and were outlined on the SWRK 300 Human Behavior and the Social Environment I course syllabus and are also outlined in the Social Work Program Student Handbook:

- Attendance Policy
- Accommodations Policy
- Accessibility Policy
- Human Rights Policy
- Academic Integrity Policy

Additional policies pertaining to students are outlined in *Siena Life* and the *College Catalog*. Students are expected to review these policies and to abide by them. Questions regarding any of these policies should be directed to the course instructor.

REQUIRED TEXT AND READINGS

Zastrow, C., and Kirst-Ashman, K. (2001). *Understanding human behavior and the social environment.* Nelson-Hall Publishers, Inc.

Schriver, J. M. (2001). *Human Behavior and the Social Environment: Shifting Paradigms In Essential Knowledge For Social Work Practice.* Allyn and Bacon, 2nd Edition.

Mackelprang, R., & Salsgiver, R. (1999). *Disability: A Diversity Model Approach in Human Service Practice.* Brooks/Cole Publishers.

Reserved readings are also interwoven into each section of the course syllabus. A copy of these readings has been provided as part of the course reading packet and is also on reserve in the Siena library.

OUTLINE

This is an overview of the course content and a schedule of the assigned readings to help you plan for this course. The Instructor reserves alter the course and/or readings as dictated by the combined needs of the learners and the instructor.

I. ESTABLISHING A CONTEXTUAL FRAMEWORK

*   Link between the HBSE Sequence, the Human Behavior Assessment Framework and the Generalist Problem Solving Methodology utilized in Generalist Social Work Practice.

*   Overview of theories (traditional/alternative) pertaining to human growth and development (life span, life stage, life course, identity formation—individual and family perspectives).

Required Readings: Course Texts

Zastrow, C. & Kirst-Ashman, K. (2001) *Human Behavior and the Social Environment.* Brooks/ Cole. Chapter 5—"Interaction in Family Systems: Choosing a Personal Lifestyle," pp. 321-323.

Schriver, J. M. (1997) *Human Behavior and the Social Environment: Shifting Paradigms In Essential Knowledge For Social Work Practice,* Boston: Allyn & Bacon. Chapter 4 – Traditional/Dominant Perspectives on Individuals, pp. 128, 132-133, "Guidelines for Strengths-Based Assessment," p. 140-top of p. 147, "Critiques of Traditional, Stage-Based Theories," p. 169-middle of p. 173, "Developmental Risk Assessment," middle of pp. 175-176, "Erikson's Model," pp. 197-199, "Levinson: Adult Development," p. 204-middle of p. 207, "Developmental Perspectives and People of Color, pp. 249-255, "Life Span and Adult Developmental Models and People of Color," bottom of pp. 256-261 & pp. 266-268.

Required Readings: Reading Packet

Berger, McBreen, & Rifkin. (1996). *Human Behavior: A Perspective for the Helping Professions,* N.Y.: Longman, New York. Chapter 4—"Human Behavior Throughout the Life Course," pp. 129-141.

Rhodes, S.. (1987). Social Casework. "A Developmental Approach To The Life Cycle of the Family," pp. 301-310.

Kirby, L. A., & Fraser, M. W. (2000). Chapter 2—Risk and Resilience in Childhood," pp. 10-19. In *Risk and Resilience in Childhood,* NASW Press, Washington, D.C.: Mark W. Fraser, ed.

Benard, B. (1991). Western Regional Center for Drug-Free Schools & Communities/Far West Laboratory for Educational Research & Development. "Fostering Resiliency in Kids: Protective Factors in the

Family, School, and Community," pp. 2.1-2.13.

II. The Interrelationship Between Individual Growth and Development, Social Systems, and Human Behavior Throughout the Life Course

A. Infancy, Toddlerhood, and The Preschool Years (Early Childhood)

- Overview of conception, pregnancy, and childbirth as life course events.
- Death and loss as part of the life course—miscarriage, neonatal, and perinatal loss.
- Evaluation of major theories (including strengths, drawbacks, underlying values and ethics) pertaining to human growth and development of the infant/toddler/preschooler.
- Individual and family developmental milestones in relation to the infancy/toddler/preschool years.
- Role of attachment, bonding, separation and individuation in shaping infant/toddler/preschool psychosocial development (primary and alternative caregivers).
- Role of diversity in relation to infant/toddler/preschool growth and development.
- Promoting healthy development of young children with disabilities.
- Role of social systems during the infancy/toddlerhood/preschool years – kinship and extended family networks, open vs. closed adoption processes, the foster care system.
- Variations in life experience & at-risk potential: fetal drug and alcohol syndrome, unresolved grief pertaining to the adoption process.

Required Readings: Course Text

Zastrow, C., & Kirst-Ashman, K.: Chapter 2—"Dynamics of Human Reproduction," pp. 52-73 and pp. 86-97; Chapter 3 – "Cognitive Development: Piaget, " pp. 114-118 & "Emotional Development," pp. 121-middle of 124 and Chapter 4—Membership in Sibling Sub-Systems, " bottom of pp. 177- middle of pp. 179 & "Social Aspects of Play with Peers," middle of pp. 182-middle of pp. 184.

Schriver, J. M.: Chapter 1—"Toward Understanding the Association Between Socioeconomic Status and Health," 32-43, Chapter 4—"Traditional Developmental Assessment Tools," pp. 176-184, Chapter 5—"Variables Associated with Positive Child Development," p. 238-middle of 241 and "Multiracial Identities," pp. 262-265.

Required Readings: Reading Packet

Lopez, M. (March 20, 1994). *Times Union.* "Birth Without the Breathing (Bradley & Lamaze Methods Compared)," pp. 1-3.

Walsh, M. (1997, January-February). *Times Union.* "Postpartum Depression is Serious and Common," pp. 1-7.

Rando, T. (1988) *Grief, Dying, and Death: Clinical Interventions For Caregivers*, Ill: Research Press. Chapter 6 – "Miscarriage, Stillbirth, Neonatal Death, and Sudden Infant Death Syndrome," pp. 131-144.

Glenn Dowling, C. (2000). *Life Magazine.* "Rituals: A Time to Grieve," pp. 83-87.

Nash, M. (February 3, 1997). *Time Magazine.* "Fertile Minds," pp. 49-56.

Pillar, V. (1988). *Human Behavior in the Social Environment*, Ca.: Brooks/Cole. Chapter 3—"Infancy," pp. 69-94.

Kirby, L. A., & Fraser, M. W. (2000). Risk and Resilience in Childhood, Chapter 2—pp. 20-27. Zipper, I.

N., & Simeonsson, R. J., Promoting the Development of Young Children with Disabilities, Chapter 12—pp. 244-259. In *Risk and Resilience in Childhood*. NASW Press, Washington, DC: Mark W. Fraser, ed.

White, J. (May 5, 1997). *Time Magazine*. "Race is no longer as simple as black and white," pp. 32-38.

Curtis, P. A. (October, 1986). *Child Welfare*. "The Dialectics of Open Versus Closed Adoption of Infants," pp. 437-445. (Volume LXV, #5)

Federal Department of Education. (1998). *Subchapter VIII of Federal Education Law on Handicapped Infants and Toddlers* (20 U.S.C. 1401-1485), pp. 37-40.

New York State Education Department (1998). *Updated Regulations of the Commissioner of Education—Subchapter F/Part 200 (Pursuant to Sections 207, 4403 and 4410 of Education Law)*, pp. 4-7.

New York State Board of Regents. (1998). *Statement on Least Restrictive Environment*, pp. 1-8.

Hopkins, E. (October 18,1990). *Rolling Stone Magazine*. "Childhood's End: Babies Born to Crack-Addicted Mothers", pp. 68-72, pp. 108 & 110. DHHS Publication. (1991). "Cocaine/Crack: The Big Lie." Publication # (ADM) 91-1427.

Cloud, J. (October 9, 2000). *Time Magazine*. "Protecting the Unborn," pp. 51-52.

Roche, T. (November 13, 2000) *Time Magazine*. "The Crisis of Foster Care," pp. 74-82.

Video: "A Cry For Help: Fetal Drug and Alcohol Syndrome."

Guest Speaker: "The Foster Care System: Key Considerations." (County Department of Children &Family Services)

B. Middle Childhood

- Evaluation of major theories (including strengths, drawbacks, underlying values and ethics) pertaining to human growth and development during middle childhood.

- Overview of key developmental tasks/milestones and the role of bio-psycho-social-cultural and spiritual dimensions in shaping individual and family development during middle childhood.

- The role of diversity in relation to human growth and development in middle childhood – gender, race/ethnicity, culture, socioeconomic status, religion/spirituality, disability.

- Role of broader social systems during early and middle childhood – the peer group, the educational system, organized religion, the health and/or social welfare systems.

- Variations in life experience & at-risk potential: poverty, developmental and learning disabilities, and child abuse, neglect and maltreatment.

Required Readings: Course Text

Zastrow, C, & Kirst-Ashman, K.: Chapter 3 -"Piaget," pp. 119; "Self Concept and Self-Esteem," pp. 124-127; "Intelligence Testing," pp. 127-132; and "Persons With Cognitive and Learning Disabilities," pp. 132-141; Chapter 4—"Behavior Management: Parenting Techniques, " pp. 164-172 & pp. 174-176; "Membership in Family Systems," pp. 176-177; "Child Abuse and Neglect, " pp. 189-197. Chapter 7- "Kohlberg's Stages of Moral Development," pp. 285-287.

Mackelprang, R., & Salsgiver, R. Chapter 8—"Persons with Developmental Disabilities—Mental Retardation, Down's Syndrome, Autism, & Epilepsy," pp. 147-160 and Chapter 10—"Persons with Cognitive Disabilities—Learning Disabilities," pp. 191-195 & 201-204.

Required Readings: Reading Packet

Coles, R. (1990). *The Spiritual Lives of Children*, Boston: Houghton Mifflin. Chapter 7 – "Young Spirituality: Visionary Moments," pp. 148-166.

Brislin, R. (1993). *Understanding Culture's Influence In Shaping Human Behavior.* Texas: Harcourt Brace. Chapter 6 – "Formal Educational Experiences," pp. 141-168.

Wang, M. C., Reynolds, M. C., & Walberg, H. J. (January, 1995). *Educational Leadership.* "Serving Students at the Margins," pp. 12-17.

Heubert, J. (July/August, 1994). *Harvard Education Letter.* "Point/Counterpoint: Assumptions Underlie Arguments about Inclusion," p. 4 and "New Research Supports Inclusion for Physically Disabled—Vocational Ed Prevents Dropping Out."

Shevin-Sapon, M. (January, 1995). Educational Leadership. "Why Gifted Children Belong in Inclusive Schools," pp. 64-66 & 69.

Shaywitz, S. E. (November, 1996). *Scientific American.* "Dyslexia," pp. 99-104.

DSM-IV. (1998) "Disruptive Behavior Disorders: Attention-deficit Hyperactivity Disorder (ADHD)," pp. 78-85.

Hancock, L. (March 18, 1996). *Newsweek.* "Mother's Little Helper," pp. 51-56.

Gibbs, N. (November 30, 1998). *Time Magazine.* "The Age of Ritalin," pp. 88-96.

Shute, N. Locy, T., & Paternak, D. (March 6, 2000). *U.S. News & World Report.* "Are These Drugs Safe for Your Kids?: The Perils of Pills," pp. 45-50.

Video: "The Moral Development of Children." (Robert Coles)

Guest Speaker: "The Role of the Educational System in Addressing the Needs of School Age Children with Disabilities."

C.   Adolescence and Young Adulthood

- Evaluation of major theories (strengths, drawbacks, underlying values and ethics) pertaining to human growth and development during adolescence and young adulthood.
- Overview of individual and family developmental tasks/milestones and role of bio-psycho-social-cultural-spiritual dimensions in shaping development during adolescence and young adulthood.
- The role of diversity in relation to human growth and development during adolescence and young adulthood—gender and separation and individuation behavior of adolescents, exploration of sexuality and sexual identity, the "outing" process related to sexual orientation and non-visible disabilities.
- The role of mezzo and macro systems during adolescence and young adulthood – the peer group, the work group, organizations as workplaces, the interrelationship between leisure time and organized social/community systems, involvement with health maintenance organizations and other aspects of health care systems.
- Variations in life course & at-risk potential: sexual abuse, cutting/self-mutilation, addiction/chemical dependency, HIV/AIDS, suicide. (NOTE: Eating Disorders content presented in SWRK 300/HBSE I)

Required Readings: Course Text

Zastrow, C & Kirst-Ashman, K: Chapter 4—"Sexual Abuse, " pp. 197-202; Chapter 6-"Adolescence," pp. 243-248, "Sexual Activity in Adolescence," pp. 255-275, & "Young Adulthood," pp. 248-255;

Chapter 7- "Identity Formation," pp. 280-282 & "Suicide," pp. 292-301. Chapter 11—"Effects of HIV," pp. 414-416 & 422-425 and "Specific Drugs: What They Are and What They Do," pp. 451-452 & 455 and Chapter 13—"Sexual Orientation," pp. 529-531.

Mackelprang, R., & Salsgiver, R. Chapter 10—"Persons with Cognitive Disabilities—Traumatic Brain Injury (TBI)," pp. 197-201.

Required Readings: Reading Packet

Lemonick, M. (October 30, 2000). *Time Magazine*. "Teens Before Their Time," pp. 67-74.

Collier Cool, L. (March 21, 2000) *Ladies Home Journal*. "The Secret Sex Lives of Kids," pp. 157-159.

Adler, J., & Wright, L. (December 9, 1991). *Newsweek Magazine*. "Safer Sex," pp. 52, 54-56.

Van Biema, D. (April 4, 1994). *Time Magazine*. "AIDS: In the Deaf Community, Silence Equals Death," pp. 76-78.

Gorman, C. (June 23, 1997). *Time Magazine*. "If the condom breaks—a morning-after treatment may protect you from "AIDS, but don't count on it," p. 48.

Rounds, K. (2000). Chapter 2—"Preventing Sexually Transmitted Infections Among Adolescents," pp. 175-188 in *Risk and Resilience in Childhood*. NASW Press, Washington, D.C.: Mark W. Fraser, ed.

Morrow. (November, 1993). *Social Work*. "Social Work With Gay and Lesbian Adolescents," pp. 655-659. (Volume 38, #6)

Firestone, R. *Journal of Psychotherapy*. (Fall, 1986). "The 'Inner Voice' and Suicide," pp. 439-447. (Volume 23, #3)

Summit, R. C. (1990). *Child Abuse & Neglect*. "The Child Sexual Abuse Accommodation Syndrome," pp. 177-193. (Volume 7)

Plessner, Lyons, N. (1988) Chapter 2—"Two Perspectives: On Self, Relationships, and Morality," pp. 32-43. In *Mapping out the Moral Domain*. Harvard University Press, MA: Carol Gilligan, ed.

Trotter, J. *Life Magazine*. (1999). "My Life Turned Upside Down," pp. 59-65.

Berkow, I. *New York Times*. (October 1, 1995) "An Athlete is Dead at 17 & No One Can Say Why," pp. 1-4.

Nash, M. *Time Magazine*. (May 5, 1997). "How We Get Addicted," pp. 1-5.

Jampolsky, L. (1995). *Healing The Addictive Mind*. Chapter 2—"The Structure of the Addictive Thought System," pp. 23-37 and Chapter 3—"The Core Beliefs of the Addictive Thought System," pp. 39-51. CA: Celestial Arts.

Guest Speakers: "HIV/AIDS Awareness" and/or "Cutting/Self-Mutilation."

Video: "Delayed Discovery of Sexual Abuse." (20/20 Segment)

D. Middle and Later Adulthood

- Evaluation of major theories (including strengths, drawbacks, underlying values and ethics) pertaining to human growth and development during middle and older adulthood.
- Overview of key individual and family developmental tasks/milestones and the role of bio-psycho-social-cultural and spiritual dimensions during middle and older adulthood.
- The role of diversity in relation to human growth and development during middle and older adult-

hood – interrelationship between gender, race/ethnicity, culture, and views on aging; feminization of poverty as it applies to middle and older adulthood; impact of gender, race/ethnicity and socio-economic status and at-risk potential for certain health conditions; role of extended kinship and family networks

- Managing transitions: redefining career and/or work, life review process; coping with grief and loss; the living will and health care proxy.

- Role of mezzo and macro systems during middle and/or older adulthood—adapting to changes in support networks; confronting societal biases/discrimination; negotiating health and social service systems; adapting to changes in one's living environment; the use of support groups and recreational networks for social/emotional support.

- Variations in the life course & at-risk potential: the "second" middle adulthood; aging and wellness; widowhood; onset of disability in middle and/or later adulthood; managing life-threatening and/or disabling conditions; the "sandwich" generation, depression, pseudo-dementia, and dementia; abuse of older adults; the concept of an appropriate vs. inappropriate death.

Required Readings: Course Text

Zastrow, C. & Kirst-Ashman, K: Middle Adulthood: Chapter 10—"The Age Span of Middle Adulthood," pp. 398-410. Chapter 11—"Psychological Systems & Their Impact on Middle Adulthood," pp. 428-429, "As Lesbians and Gay Men Age," pp. 548, & "Alcohol Addiction and Recovery," pp. 467.

Zastrow, C. & Kirst-Ashman, K: Older Adulthood: Chapter 14—"Biological Systems and Their Impacts On Later Adulthood," pp. 554-572; Chapter 15 – "Developmental Tasks of Later Adulthood," pp. 580-592 and "The Impact of Life Events On The Elderly," pp. 592-597; Chapter 15—"The Elderly: A Population-at-Risk," pp. 607-613 & 615-621.

Required Readings: Reading Packet

Bronte, L. (1993). *The Longevity Factor*. Chapter 2 – "The Longevity Factor," pp. 20-28, 34-37 and Chapter 4—"Patterns of Aging," pp. 60-72. NY: Harper-Collins.

In *Time Magazine*:

Drummond, T. (September 13, 1999) "Elixirs For Your Memory," pp. 60-61.

Gorman, C. (January 28, 1998). "An Attack on Aging," p. 60.

Handy, B. (May 4, 1998). "The Viagra Craze," pp. 50-57.

Wallis, C. (June, 26, 1990). "The Estrogen Dilemma," pp. 46-53.

Lacato, R. (April 24, 2000). "The Testosterone Effect," pp. 57-65.

Nash, M. (Fall, 1996). "The Enemy Within: Cancer," pp. 18-23.

Nash, M. (July 17, 2000). "The New Science of Alzheimer's Disease," pp. 51-57.

Booth, C. (1999). "Taking Care of Our Aging Parents," pp. 48, 50-56 and "Elder Care: Making the Right Choice," pp. 52-56.

Life Magazine. (1994) "The Way We Live: Breast Cancer," pp. 78-88.

Parade Magazine. (March 5, 1996) "What Is the Best Way to Treat Prostate Cancer?," pp. 6-7 and attachments.

Link Newsletter for NYS Association for Independent Living Centers. (1990). "Activists Target Attendant Care for National Attention," pp. 2-4.

Wehrwein, P. (March, 1991). *Times Union*. "Lack of Skilled Workers Hampers Home Care."

Stern, C. (December 23,1990). *Parade Magazine*. "Is Your Medicine Hurting You?" pp. 8-9.

Butler, Robert N. (February, 1963). *Journal for the Study of Interpersonal Process*. "The Life Review: An Interpretation of Reminiscence In the Aged," pp. 486-496. Volume 26, #1.

Umberson, D. & Chen, D. (February, 1994). *American Sociological Review*. "Effects of a Parent's Death on Adult Children: Relationship Salience and Reaction to Loss," pp. 152-155 & 158-167. (Volume 59)

Kamerman, J. (1988). *Death in the Midst of Life*. "Grief and Bereavement in their Social and Cultural Context," pp. 65-73. N.J.: Prentice Hall.

Videos: "The Other Epidemic: Breast Cancer." (ABC News Special Presentation with Linda Ellerbee)

EXERCISES

The Instructor has several exercises and activities that are utilized in conjunction with this course. A sampling of these materials follows.

Fetal Drug and/or Alcohol Syndrome: Class Exercise

Write down your responses to the following questions and bring them to the next class.

1. Do you think all pregnant women should be automatically tested for drug usage? If not, why not? If so, should this be done only with or without her consent? What might the impact be of doing such testing without her consent?

2. Some states have attempted to introduce legislation that will allow law enforcement officials to automatically incarcerate women while pregnant as well as take custody of any other children they may have. What are the pros and cons of these perspectives?

3. Some states also have legislation that permits law enforcement officials to force women who are pregnant and addicted into mandated treatment programs. Do you agree or disagree? Why?

4. Should a woman be allowed to have her child/ren with her while in mandated treatment? Why or why not?

5. What are your thoughts about the partner in this situation? For example, if an individual is using drugs and their female partner becomes pregnant and/or an individual is engaging in drug usage with their partner while she is pregnant, should this individual face any consequences? If so, why? If not, why not?

Inclusion: Discussion Questions

After reading the compilation of articles on inclusion from Middle Childhood section (B), please write down your responses to the following questions. Bring your responses to the next class.

1. Do you agree or disagree with the concept of inclusion? Why or why not?

2. Are there certain conditions that you would place on inclusion - i.e. are you in favor of inclusion of children and/or adolescents with severe disabilities such as traumatic brain injury or severe mental retardation? Why or why not?

3. Do you believe that separate programs should be established in "inclusive" schools to ensure that the needs of gifted" children are also being met? Is so, why, If not, why not?

Adolescent Sexuality: Discussion Questions

Please review the article on "Safer Sex" and come prepared to discuss the following questions in class.

1. As the Newsweek article on "Safer Sex" points out, while adolescents definitely know enough to be worried about AIDS, it just doesn't make them any likelier to use condoms. While condoms are certainly not fool-proof, the reality is that they offer some reassurance of protection against sexually-transmitted diseases and the transmission of the HIV virus. Yet as the article notes, studies have found adolescent condom use to be inconsistent at best. What are some of the factors that might be influencing this discrepancy - i.e. why are adolescents "talking the talk" but not "walking the walk?"

2. What role might gender role expectations play in a couple's decision to even discuss wearing a condom? For example, in the article on "Safer Sex," adolescent girls seemed to be most concerned about how their partner would perceive being asked to wear a condom vs. adolescent males seemed to be most concerned about the impact of condom use on pleasure and stigma among male peers if it is known among them that they use a condom. Do you agree or disagree with these perspectives? Why? Why not?

3. Jean Baker Miller (Re: Read Schriver, pg. 292-middle of pg. 296) maintains that adolescent males are more likely to be intimate to obtain sex while adolescent females are more likely to become involved in sex as an effort to achieve intimacy. Do you agree or disagree with this perspective? Why? Why not? What role might this play in influencing either party's use of condoms and/or any other methods of contraception such as vaginal dams, etc.?

4. What kind of support is there among your group of friends for: 1)abstinence 2) condom use 3) use of any other birth control method.

5. Can you envision yourself asking your partner and/or someone that you might consider engaging in sexual activity with the questions outlined on page 56 of the "Safer Sex" article? Why? Why not? Would you be comfortable being asked these questions by someone else in a similar situation? Why? Why not?

ASSIGNMENTS

Assignment 1: Pregnancy, Childbirth, And Early Childhood: Developmental Assessment

Length: Minimum of 7 typewritten pages, double-spaced
Grade weight: 55% of total grade

Part One: Personal Interview

As part of the assessment process, students complete an in-person interview of an individual parent or a couple who have experienced the life events of pregnancy, childbirth, and the child rearing of at least one child who is, preferably, no younger than two years and no older than five years of age. While the individual or couple may have other children, one specific child should serve as the major focal point of this assessment.

Students are encouraged to ask the interviewee to allow interview to be audiotaped. The person should be given the option of having the audiotape given to them once the assignment is completed. Reassurance should be provided that this tape and the written assignment are being used solely for your educational purposes and will only be shared with your instructor for this purpose.

Part Two: Assessment

Students are given a structured format for the assessment, which is presented in narrative form and divided into clearly titled sections.

A. Introduction (5 pts.). Information on the parent or couple and their family.

B. Life Prior to the Pregnancy (10 pts.). Details of the family's life stages before the pregnancy and the social relationships and activities of the child's parents.

C. The Pregnancy Experience (10 pts.). Experiences of the family and the mother alike during the pregnancy.

D. The Childbirth Experience (10 pts.).

E. Period from Birth up to the Child's Current Age (50 pts.). Students draw from the individual or couple's recollections, course texts, readings, and class notes to construct an overview of this child's growth and development from birth through her/his current age. Students also draw from the individual or couple's recollections, course texts, readings, and class notes to construct an overview of the individual or couple's experiences with child rearing and family life since the birth of the child.

F. Summary (15 pts.).

Assignment 2: Middle Childhood/Adolescence: Research and Development of Assessment Criteria
Length: Minimum of 10 typewritten pages, double-spaced
Grade weight: 20% of total grade

As practitioners, we often are expected to assess the experience of clients and consumers as they relate to various life events and conditions. In some instances, we may have little or no prior knowledge about some of these areas. The purpose of this assignment is to provide students with an opportunity to develop and strengthen their knowledge base and assessment skills in relation to a life event or condition that is specific to a particular life stage. The assignment is organized into two parts for students: data collection and organization of research (15 points) and assessment (95 points).

First, students select the life stage that will be the focus of their work (middle childhood or adolescence) and a nonnormative life event or condition (physical/psychological/cognitive/mental) that pertains to the life stage chosen. The event or condition selected is a topic that is not covered through course content or an area that is covered but about which the student would like to gain more in-depth knowledge. Students are discouraged from using existing course materials for the completion of this assignment, with the exception of life stage/span/course materials. The topic and life stage must be pre-approved by the course instructor.

Once selected, the student conducts a library and Internet search as well as a review of other pertinent data sources. Students are encouraged to cross-reference the data search and use sources within the past five years. The results of the data collection and research efforts are attached to the end of the paper. Grading is based on the student's ability to demonstrate strong efforts to integrate both course materials and the data obtained through your research efforts into your final assessment.

The final paper, for part two of the assignment, is organized into five sections:

1. Definition of life event or condition (10 pts.)

2. Overview of possible factors contributing to onset (10 pts.)

3. Impact of life event or condition: possible assessment criteria (45 pts.)

4. Summary (15 pts.)

5. Reference list and summary of data collection and research efforts (15 pts.)

Assignment 3: Middle/Older Adulthood: Life Event/Condition Assessment

Length: Minimum of 8-10 typewritten pages, double-spaced, plus attachments
Grade weight: 25% of total grade

The purpose of this two-part assignment is to enhance students' understanding of the role that life events and interactions between systems can play in shaping growth and development during middle and older adulthood. Grading will be based on the students' ability to demonstrate a sound grasp of the course material through presenting the data gathered in a conceptually clear, succinct, well-organized, and grammatically accurate manner.

In part one (worth 25 points), students conduct a personal interview with an individual who is in either middle or older adulthood and who has experienced a significant normative or nonnormative life event or condition (one that has been accompanied by a transitional crises) within the past 1-3 years. The event or condition must have occurred during the same life stage that is the focus of this assignment. As with Assignment 1, students are encouraged to ask the interviewee to allow interview to be audiotaped. The person should be given the option of having the audiotape given to them once completed the assignment. Reassurance should be provided that this tape and the written assignment are being used solely for your educational purposes and will only be shared with your instructor for this purpose.

Students develop a list of assessment questions for the interview. They are told the questions should clearly follow the flow of the interview format, should address both the range and depth of information, and should vary in format (i.e. open, closed, probing, etc.). After the interview, students hand in the questions asked during the interview for a grade (15 points).

Students also gather resource materials for the assessment. They are asked to develop a bibliography of at least six new sources of information for the life event discussed in the interview (four of these must be professional journal articles). They also prepare an annotated bibliography of three more sources, two of which must be professional journal articles, and hand in copies of the journal articles.

In part two (worth 75 points), students prepare a written assessment with supporting materials. This write up is divided into clearly titled sections:

A. General background (20 pts.).

B. Interviewee's experience with life event or condition (35 pts.).

C. Summary analysis (20 pts.).

D. Interview questions (15 pts.).

E. Resource materials (10 pts.).

CALIFORNIA STATE UNIVERSITY, SAN BERNARDINO
DEPARTMENT OF SOCIAL WORK | SAN BERNARDINO, CA
NANCY L. MARY

Social Work with People with Disabilities
SW 690 (Spring 2002)

INTRODUCTION

Social workers encounter people with all kinds of disabilities. Over 50% of the 27,000 NASW members surveyed in the 1992 Social Work Labor Force Study reported their primary practice to be in the field of mental health (32.7%), medical clinics (12.5%), substance abuse (4.6%), gerontology (2.7%), or other areas of disability (.5%).

There is evidence, however, that social workers may not be adequately prepared to deal with the increasing numbers of people with disabling conditions. Several issues have forced us to examine the extent to which we prepare social workers for practice with people with disabilities. Among these issues are the burgeoning of the renewed disability rights movement of the nineties, the attention of CSWE evidenced in the Commission on Disability and Persons with Disabilities (CDPD), the impact of the most recent Americans with Disabilities Act on public institutions and the public marketplace, and the combined effects of vocational rehabilitation, mental health, and other agencies on meeting the needs of "welfare-to-work" clients.

How we define a condition such as *disability* drives our response to it at an individual, agency, and societal level. For example, if it is defined as a problem solely from a medical model, there is the danger of internalizing the condition to a person or group of people and ignoring institutional reactions and societal attitudes that can turn a *condition* into a *handicap*. Therefore, it is important to examine disability from the view of professionals, consumers, and the broader society. We then can look at responses to the needs of people with disabilities in terms of service models, from the earlier moral and medical frameworks to the more recent independent living, strengths perspective, case management, and consumer-centered approaches. This perspective should result in a heightened awareness of how the treatment of people with various disabling conditions depends heavily upon the worldview of professionals, service agencies, consumers themselves, and the larger society in which we live.

This course is intended to expose students to some common, as well as unique, problems faced by individuals with disabilities. It is not strictly a direct practice course. Rather, it first provides a context for practice in examining the sociological construct of *disability*, then frames practice from a bio-psycho-social perspective of the social worker, and explores some consumer perspectives on their own disabling conditions. In moving to the macro arena, the course analyzes the service delivery models that exist in disability service systems. And finally, it integrates both micro and macro content through an examination of a case management model, via Jack Rothman's work with practice with vulnerable populations.

The goal of this course is to increase student knowledge, skills, and positive attitudes in working with people with disabilities. The course frames *disability* in three primary areas: physical disabilities, developmental and cognitive disabilities, and psychiatric disabilities. Any framing of these conditions is limiting, and the course recognizes that chronic health conditions such as arthritis, diabetes, heart disease, AIDS, and other disabling conditions are important areas for student learning. Given the constraints of a 10-week course, it is important to focus. However, students are given an option, in the final paper, to explore a specific chronic disabling condition and apply the framework used throughout the course to that condition. The oral presentation also benefits other class members through the sharing of knowledge of these specific disabling conditions.

OBJECTIVES

At the end of this course students should be able to

1. Describe several perspectives on disability.

2. Describe common and distinct needs and issues of people with various disabilities and their families.

3. Identify major service providers and models of service delivery for several disability populations and discuss the roles of social work within these models.

4. Demonstrate an increased awareness of and sensitivity to the unique strengths and challenges of persons with disabling conditions via a written review and critique of a motion picture focussed on the topic.

REQUIRED TEXTS

*   Mackelprang, R. & Salsgiver, R. (1999). *Disability: A diversity model approach in human service practice.* Pacific Grove, CA: Brooks/Cole.

*   Rothman, J. & Sager, J. S. (1998). *Case management: Integrating individual and community practice.* Boston: Allyn & Bacon.

*   A packet of readings available in the bookstore (or on reserve in the library).

CONTENT OUTLINE

Unit I. Overview and Definitions (Week 1)

   A. Course framework

   B. Definitions of *disability*

   C. History of disabilities and service models

Unit II. Perspectives on Disability (Weeks 2-3)

   A. The sociology of disability, stigma, and disability culture

   B. The perspective of social work: the bio-psycho-social model

   C. Perspectives of disabled people (their own voices)

Unit III. Working with People with Physical Disabilities (Weeks 4-5)

   A. Definitions, specific populations—e.g., deaf and hard of hearing, persons with mobility disabilities, persons with visual disabilities and blindness

   B. Practice issues and use of case studies (social work roles)

   C. Service models (e.g., medical vs. vocational) and case management—evolution of independent living movement

Unit IV. Working with People with Developmental and Cognitive Disabilities (Weeks 6-7)

   A. Definitions, specific populations—e.g., developmental disabilities (autism, epilepsy, mental retardation), learning disabilities, attention deficit disorder

   B. Practice issues and use of case studies

   C. Service models (e.g., evolution of regional center system in CA), and application of case management

Unit V. Working with People with Psychiatric Disabilities (Weeks 8-9)

   A. Definitions: Use of *DSM IV*, chronic mentally ill, mental health of special population groups (e.g., women, homeless people, ethnic minorities, children)

B. Practice issues and use of case studies

C. Service models—e.g., evolution of deinstitutionalization, current "clubhouse model", consumer movement

Week 10. Student share what they've learned through presentations

READINGS

Unit I. Overview and Definitions

- Class handouts—e.g., World Health definitions of *impairment*, *disability*, and *handicap*.
- Asch, A. & Mudrich, N. (1995). Disability. In L. Beebe & N. Winchester (Eds.), *Encyclopedia of Social Work* (19th ed., pp. 752-761). Washington DC: NASW.
- Cole, B. & Cain, M. (1996). Social work students with disabilities: A proactive approach to accommodation. *Journal of Social Work Education, 32,* 339-349.
- Mackelprang, R. & Salsgiver, R. (1999). Disability. Pacific Grove, CA: Brooks/Cole. Chapter 1, Context for practice, and Chapter 3, Disability history.
- Rothman, J. & Sager, J. (1998). Case management. Needham Heights, MA: Allyn & Bacon. Chapter 1.

Unit II. Perspective on Disability

- Allison, C. (1999). Disability as diversity: A socio-linguistic construct for the new millennium. *Reflections: Narratives of Professional Helping, 5*(4), 47-51.
- Blair, R. (1999). Integrating my disability: My journey. *Reflections: Narratives of Professional Helping, 5*(4), 7-15.
- Blaska, J. (1993). The power of language. In M. Nagler (Ed.), *Perspectives on disability* (pp. 25-32). Palo Alto, CA: Health Markets Research.
- Bogdan, R. & Biklen, D. (1993). Handicapism. In M. Nagler (Ed.), *Perspectives on disability* (pp. 69-76). Palo Alto, CA: Health Markets Research.
- Devliger, P. & Albrecht, G. (2000). Your experience is not my experience. *Journal of Disability Policy Studies, 11*(1), 51-60.
- Longres, J. (1995). *Human Behavior and the Social Environment.* Itasca, IL: Peacock. Chapter 2, A systems approach to human behavior.
- Mackelprang, R. & Salsgiver, R. (1999). *Disability.* Pacific Grove, CA: Brooks/Cole. Chapter 2, Disability culture.

Unit III. Working with People with Physical Disabilities

- Ann Curry, M. (2001). Abuse of women with disabilities. *Violence Against Women, 7*(1), 60-80.
- Bader, J. (1999). Bridging personal and professional perspectives: A continuous process. *Reflections: Narratives of Professional Helping, 5*(4), 27-32.
- Hales, G. (1996). *Beyond Disability.* Thousand Oaks, CA: Sage. Chapters 3-5, Mobility impairment, Visual impairment.
- Hernandez, B. (2000) Employer attitudes toward workers with disabilities and their ADA employment rights: A literature review. *Journal of Rehabilitation, 66*(4), 4-16.
- Keller, S. & Buchanan, D. (1993). Sexuality and disability: An overview. In M. Nagler (Ed.), *Perspectives on disability* (pp. 227-234). Palo Alto, CA: Health Markets Research.
- Mackelprang, R. & Salsgiver, R. (1999). *Disability.* Pacific Grove, CA: Brookes/Cole. Chapters 5-7, Persons with mobility disabilities, Deaf and hard-of-hearing people, Persons with visual disabilities and blindness.

- Mackelprang, R. & Salsgiver, R. (1999). *Disability.* Pacific Grove, CA: Brookes/Cole. Chapter 12, Models of professional practice.

- Piastro, D. (1999). Coping with the transitions in our lives: From afflicted identity to personal empowerment and pride. *Reflections: Narratives of Professional Helping, 5*(4), 42-46.

- Rothman, J. & Sager, J. (1998). *Case Management.* Needham Heights, MA: Allyn & Bacon. Chapters 2-4.

- Schmid, W. (1997). Family-centered care: Life span issues in a spina bifidia specialty care program. In T. Kerson & Associates, (Eds.), *Social Work in Health Settings* (2nd ed.). New York: Haworth Press.

Unit IV. Working with People with Developmental and Cognitive Disabilities

- Clare, L. & Gamier, H. (2000). Parents' goals for adolescents diagnosed with developmental delays in early childhood. *Journal of Early Adolescence, 20*(4), 442-467.

- DeWeaver, K. (1995). Developmental disabilities: Definitions and policies. In L. Beebe & N. Winchester (Eds.), *Encyclopedia of Social Work* (19th ed., pp. 712-720). Washington DC: NASW.

- Ford, S. (1996). Learning difficulties. In C. Hales (Ed.), *Beyond Disability* (pp. 57-79). Thousand Oaks, CA: Sage.

- Freedman, R. (1995). Developmental disabilities: Direct practice. In L. Beebe & N. Winchester (Ed.), *Encyclopedia of Social Work* (19th ed., pp). Washington DC: NASW.

- Janecki, M. & Ansello, E. (2000). *Community supports for aging adults with lifelong disabilities.* Baltimore, MD: Paul Brookes.

- Mackelprang, R. & Salsgiver, R. (1999). *Disability.* Pacific Grove, CA: Brookes/Cole. Chapters 8, Persons with developmental disabilities, and Chapter 10, Persons with cognitive disabilities.

- Mary, N. (1998). Social work and the support model of services for people with developmental disabilities. *Journal of Social Work Education, 34*, 247-260.

- Mayberry, G. (2000). Michael the story of an autistic photographer. *PSA Journal, 68*(12), 30-33.

- Ogletree, B. (2001). Team-based service delivery for students with disabilities. *Intervention in School and Clinic, 26*(3), 138-145.

- Rothman, J. & Sager, J. (1998). *Case Management.* Needham Heights, MA: Allyn & Bacon. Chapters 5-9.

Unit V. Working with People with Psychiatric Disabilities

- Anthony, W. (2000). Musing on using metaphor. *Psychiatric Rehabilitation Journal, 24*(2), 93-94.

- Donahue, A. (2000). Riding the mental health pendulum: Mixed messages in the era of neurobiology and self-help movements. *Social Work, 45*(5), 427-438.

- Dudley, J. (2000). Confronting stigma within the services system. *Social Work, 45*(5), 449-455.

- Fellin, P. (1996). *Mental Health and Mental Illness.* Itasca, IL: Peacock.

- Gerhart, U. (1990). *Caring for the Chronic Mentally Ill.* Itasca, IL: Peacock. Chapter 1, Caring for persons who have a chronic mental illness: a historical overview, Chapter 2, Mental illness and chronic mentally ill persons, Chapter 15, Working with families.

- Herman, S., Frank, K., Mowbray, C., Ribisl, K., Davidson, W., II, Bootsmiller, B., Jordan, L., Greenfield, A., Lovelend, D., & Luke, D. (2000). Longitudinal effects of integrated treatment of alcohol use for persons with serious mental illness and substance use disorders. *Journal of Behavioral Health Services and Research, 27*(3), 286-303.

- Jackson, R., Purnell, D., Anderson, S., & Sheafor, B. (1996). The clubhouse model of community support for adults with mental illness: An emerging opportunity for social work education. *Journal of Social Work Education*, 32(2), 173-180.
- MacGregor, P. (1994) Grief: The unrecognized parental response to mental illness in a child. *Social Work*, 39(2).
- Mackelprang, R. & Salsgiver, R. (1999). *Disability*. Pacific Grove, CA: Brookes/Cole. Chapter 9, Persons with psychiatric disabilities.
- Mechanic, D. (1999). *Mental Health and Social Policy*. Needham Heights, MA: Allyn & Bacon. Chapter 1, Mental health and the mental health professions, Chapter 2, What are mental health and mental illness?
- Mu-jung P., & Lin, A. (1995). Mental health overview. In L. Beebe & N. Winchester (Eds.), *Encyclopedia of Social Work* (19th ed., pp. 1705-1711). Washington, DC: NASW.
- Potts, M. (1997). Social support and depression among older adults living alone: The importance of friends within and outside of a retirement community. *Social Work, 42*(4), 348-362.
- Rothman, J., & Sager, J. (1998). *Case Management*. Needham Heights, MA: Allyn & Bacon. Chapters 10-12.

REQUIREMENTS

1. **Midterm:** Students will view a film that involves persons with disabilities and critique it. Here are a few examples: *My Left Foot, Born on the Fourth of July, Elephant Man, Of Mice and Men, Rainman, Children of a Lesser God, Mask*. This assignment is 35% of the class grade.

2. **Final Paper:** Students will choose a specific population (e.g., children with AIDS) and write a research paper applying the course framework (see below). Sources should include library research as well as an interview with a social worker in an agency serving individuals with the disability (e.g., children with AIDS). This assignment is worth 45% of the class grade.

3. **Oral Presentation:** In the last week of class, students will share their critique (see attached guidelines) and what they found most intellectually and emotionally enlightening about the movie. This assignment is worth 20% of the class grade.

GUIDELINES FOR MIDTERM

The purpose of this assignment is for the student to gain an increased awareness and understanding of how persons with disabilities are portrayed in the media and the extent to which their unique strengths and challenges are presented. Upon completion, the final paper should be 10-15 pages in length, double-spaced, and include a bibliography.

- The **first section** should contain an introduction that guides the reader through the rest of the paper.
- **Section two** should describe the nature and scope of the challenges and conflicts being represented in the piece of media. What are the biological, psychological, social, societal problems and issues confronting the characters?
- **Section three** should include a review of a few studies that provide relevant data to the problems being depicted.
- **Section four** is an analysis of how the authors or creators present the problems and their resolutions. The following are questions to consider:

    1. How does theoretical data from your research on the issues apply to the story line and character development?

2. How are the character's strengths and conflicts portrayed?

3. How do the characters resolve the conflicts?

4. Were there any particularly effective artistic means by which the struggles of people, families, friends, or society around the issues of disability were conveyed?

5. From your own knowledge, compare and contrast the views of the creators with your view of how the topic might be handled.

- **Section five** should include a discussion about what you learned from this class experience.

COURSE FRAMEWORK

TYPES OF DISABILITIES

Physical and Cognitive   Developmental   Psychiatric

PERSPECTIVE

How does the consumer and society define and perceive the disability?

NEEDS/PRACTICE ISSUES

What are the unique needs and practice issues for individuals and their families or significant others?

SERVICES

What are the service systems and models of service for individuals and families over the life span?

DIRECT AND MACRO SOCIAL WORK ROLES

What are the client- or family-directed roles of social work within the various service models? What are the organizational or policy roles? What is the role of the consumer?

ADDITIONAL SUGGESTIONS FOR LEARNING

1. **Guest speakers** who have a disability and who are, or have been, in the roles of consumer, graduate student, or practicing social worker are very effective role models and can add a lot to this class when they are willing to share their knowledge and experience in these various roles.

2. **Case studies** are used with every unit. These can be pulled from the Disabilities Awareness Curriculum for Graduate Schools of Social Work, by Evelyn P. Tomaszewski (1993), published by the National Center for Social Policy and Practice, NASW, and modified as needed.

Disability Issues in Contemporary Society

Social Work 238 (Spring 2000)

DESCRIPTION

This course explores the important issues related to disabilities in contemporary society. The historical experience of people with disabilities will be explored with particular importance given to the implications of this history in current programs and services. Emphasis will be placed on a critical analysis of the assumptions that support contemporary thinking about disabilities and the service delivery systems based on these assumptions. Special attention will also be paid to the shift in the conceptual paradigm from a traditional rehabilitation model to *minority/empowerment* and *sociopolitical* perspectives. The range of disabilities addressed will include developmental, adventitious, hidden, and visible.

Roles and activities for social workers will be identified and discussed. The course will contribute to the student's ability and interest in taking critical perspectives in the assessment of social policy and services that affect people with disabilities.

The course will take advantage of opportunities available through the Internet to guide students to sites which are relevant to the course content via the instructor's web page. This page provides links to other credible resources, which will supplement course material and stimulate student interest in pursuing additional information. The web page will also be used to post notes, messages, assignments, and other announcements during the semester.

REQUIRED READINGS

Shapiro, J. P. (1993). *No pity: People with disabilities forging a new civil rights movement*. New York: Times Books.

Mackelprang, R. & Salsgiver, R. (1999). *Disability: A diversity model approach in human service practice*. Pacific Grove, CA: Brooks/Cole Publishing Co.

ADDITIONAL REQUIRED READINGS

Throughout the semester, articles will be distributed as additional required readings.

OBJECTIVES

The objectives of this course are as follows:

1. To offer students the opportunity to explore specific social policies from a critical perspective.
2. To introduce the student to policy options regarding disabilities.
3. To discuss the rationale and provisions of Public Law 101-336 (The Americans With Disabilities Act).
4. To explore and evaluate unintended consequences of current programs for people with disabilities.
5. To facilitate informed opinions and decision making by students regarding disability issues.
6. To challenge students to explore their personal values and beliefs regarding people with disabilities and the implications of these attitudes.

CLASS FORMAT

The class will use lecture, discussion, guest lecturers, audiovisual aids, agency visits, and experiential formats. Active student participation in class and in outside activities and information gathering is essential. Guest lecturer appearances, agency visits, and test dates will be announced in class.

GRADING

Grades will be based on the student's performance on four equally weighted standards:

1. Three non-comprehensive exams covering class content and assigned readings (100 points each).

2. An 8-10 page paper critically analyzing either the Governor's Planning Council for People with Disabilities-sponsored supported-living conference on March 14 or this year's campus disability awareness programming (100 points).

    *   The paper *must* include at least the following content areas

        a. A brief description of the activities
        b. The intended consequences of the activities
        c. The student's role in planning and implementing the activities
        d. An evaluation of the effectiveness of the activities
        e. The unintended consequences
        f. Alternatives to the activities
        g. A brief evaluation of the viability of the alternatives

    *   The paper will be predicated on the student's participation in planning and attending the conference or this year's campus disability awareness programming. Each student will be expected to participate, as appropriate, in planning, implementing, publicizing, and conducting the agreed-to activities in March 2000. Additional information and guidance regarding this assignment will be forthcoming.

The overall grade breakdown is as follows:

A	100 - 90
B+	89 - 85
B	84 - 80
C+	79 - 75
C	74 - 70
D+	69 - 65
D	64 - 60
F	59 - 00

LATE ASSIGNMENTS AND MAKE-UP EXAMS

Assignments and exams are to be completed as scheduled. Anyone who petitions for a make-up examination will be given an all-essay examination. Any late paper or assignment will have the grade reduced by five points for each day it is late. All papers and assignments submitted must be typewritten in American English and in APA format. Papers will be graded for grammar, writing style, overall quality, depth, and organization of content.

CLASS ATTENDANCE

Students who miss more than the equivalent of three weeks of classes in a semester may be dismissed from the course as specified in the attendance policy of the University of Southern Indiana Social Work Student Handbook. There is a positive correlation between attendance, student learning, and final grades. Attendance is required for scheduled exams. Make-up exams will be available only in documented cases of exceptional personal need.

DROPPING THE CLASS

The student should talk to the instructor before dropping or withdrawing from the class. After the last day for dropping the class without the instructor's permission has expired, the student must have demonstrated some interest in the class, or he or she will not receive a withdrawal.

HONOR CODE

University of Southern Indiana policies and regulations governing the conduct of students and the procedures for handling violations of these policies are found in Student Rights and Responsibilities in the University of Southern Indiana Bulletin and are on file in the Dean of Students' office. Any updates are printed once a year in the student newspaper, *The Shield*.

PLEASE NOTE

If any member of the class feels that she or he has a disability, please advise the instructor of desired accommodations by the end of the first week of class or as soon as you have written documentation. The instructor will work with you and the staff of Disability Support Services to provide reasonable accommodations that ensure you have a fair opportunity to perform and participate in class.

COURSE OVERVIEW

SESSION 1: WHO ARE THE DISABLED?

Content

- Demographic information from Bureau of the Census and elsewhere
    - 54 million persons
    - Exposure to poverty
    - Employment
    - Age
    - Geographic distribution
    - Gender
    - 85% adventitious/15% congenital or genetic
- Implications for Social Workers
    - Depiction of experience of disability (more commonplace)
    - Public policy implications
    - Implications for dreams and aspirations of persons with disabilities (videos)

Pedagogy

- Lecture
- Videos
    - *Movin' On*, produced by the Indiana Governor's Planning Council
    - *Movin' On Too*, produced by the Indiana Governor's Planning Council
- Discussion

WWW Resource
- **U.S. Census Bureau** http://www.census.gov/

SESSION 2: PERSPECTIVES

Content
- Models of disability (strengths, weaknesses, and applications)
    - Medical
    - Social
    - Empowerment
    - Civil rights

Pedagogy
- Lecture
- Discussion of assigned readings

WWW Resources
- **Ragged Edge magazine** http://www.ragged-edge-mag.com/
- **U.S. Department of Health and Human Services** http://www.DHHS.gov/

Readings
- Shapiro, 1993. Introduction & Chapter 1.

SESSION 3: PERSPECTIVES AND ACTIVISM

Content
- Views of persons with disabilities by various viewers
- Shifts in perspectives
- Implications of perspective shifts
- Nontraditional views

Pedagogy
- Lecture
- Video
    - *Vital Signs: Crip Culture Talks Back,* directed by Sharon Snyder & David Mitchell, produced by Northern Michigan University.
- Discussion of assigned readings and video

Readings
- Shapiro, 1993. Chapters 2 & 3.

SESSION 4: ORGANIZATION AND ADVOCACY

Content
- Traditional organizational services, philosophies, values, and practices
- Roles for persons with disabilities and service providers
- Relationship between traditional organizations and their communities
- Americans with Disabilities Act (ADA) as institutionalized advocacy and empowerment

Pedagogy
- Lecture
- Discussion of readings
- Sharing of personal and work experiences

WWW Resources
- *Encyclopedia of Disability and Rehabilitation* http://icdi2.hre.wvu.edu/ ~ fulmer/bob.html
- **U.S. Department of Justice, ADA Home Page** http://www.usdoj.gov/ada/adahom1.html

Readings
- Shapiro, 1993. Chapters 3, 4, & 5.

SESSION 5: ADVOCACY AND INCLUSION

Content
- "Real world" perspectives from Guest Lecturers
    - Patty Oser, Community Services Director, Southern Indiana Resource Solutions (SIRS): person-centered, community based services.
    - Barry Graves, Executive Director, Jacob's Village: a proposed segregated enclave for persons with disabilities.

Pedagogy
- Guest lecturers
- Questions & answers
- Discussion

Readings
- Shapiro, 1993. Chapters 6, 7, & 8.

SESSION 6: TEST 1

Respond to 4 of 11 essay questions (2 selected by instructor) on readings, lectures, discussion, videos, and guest presentations. Responses are to be composed and submitted online from the computer lab during class time.

SESSION 7: SHIFTING PARADIGMS

Content
- Application of various models
- The emergence of advocacy
- Implications for organizations
- Implications for persons with disabilities
- Assessment of described history

Pedagogy
- Lecture
- Discussion of readings
- Personal assessments

Readings
- Shapiro, 1993. Chapters 9 & 10, Epilogue, & Postscript.

SESSION 8: CONTEXT FOR PRACTICE

Content
- Stereotypes, social and professional
- Professional definitions of disability

- Who "owns"?
- Who "defines"?
- Why should we care?
- Disability culture
  - Does it exist?
  - How defined?
  - Advocacy and culture
- Community-based, family-centered service model

Pedagogy
- Lecture
- Discussion of readings
- Video
  - *Vietnam Veterans, Their Families, Their Legacy,* produced by Agent Orange Class Assistance Program

Readings
- Mackelprang & Salsgiver, 1999. Chapters 1 & 2.

SESSION 9: CONTEXT CONTINUED

Content
- Disability History
  - Moral model
  - Medical model
- Life stage development
  - Traditional developmental theories
  - Developmental theories and disability

Pedagogy
- Lecture
- Discussion of readings
- Personal sharing

Readings

Mackelprang & Salsgiver, 1999. Chapters 3 & 4.

SUPPORTED LIVING CONFERENCE: CONVENTION CENTRE

Content

A community forum sponsored by the Indiana Governor's Planning Council for People with Disabilities. Students were invited (for extra credit) to volunteer in this day-long program that included a presentation by Dohn Hoyle, Michigan disability advocate.

SESSION 10: DISABILITY TYPES

Content

- Persons with mobility impairments
  - Defined
  - Common issues
- Deaf and hard-of-hearing people
  - Deaf culture
  - Family
  - Language
  - Onset
- Persons with visual disabilities
  - Defined
  - Causes
  - Implications
  - Common issues

Pedagogy
- Lecture
- Discussion of readings
- Sharing of personal experiences

Readings
- Mackelprang & Salsgiver, 1999. Chapters 5, 6, & 7.

SESSION 11: TYPES CONTINUED

Content
- Developmental Disabilities
  - Defined
  - Rights
  - Institutionalization
  - Common issues
- Psychiatric Disabilities
  - Defined
  - Common characteristics
  - Family implications
  - Common issues
- Cognitive Disabilities
  - Defined
  - Learning disabilities
  - Attention Deficit Hyperactive Disorder (ADHD)
  - Traumatic Brain Injury (TBI)
  - Common issues

Pedagogy
- Lecture
- Discussion
- Site visit
  - Evansville Association for the Blind: a traditional disability service provider, including a sheltered workshop.

Readings
Mackelprang & Salsgiver, 1999. Chapters 8, 9, & 10.

SESSION 12: TEST 2

Respond to 4 of 11 essay questions (2 selected by instructor) on readings, lectures, discussion, videos, and guest presentations. Responses are to be composed and submitted online from the computer lab during class time.

SESSION 13: PRACTICE FRAMEWORK

Paper Due
Content
- Assessment in human service practice
  - Pathology and assessment
  - Models of assessment
  - Strengths and assessment

Pedagogy
- Lecture
- Discussion
- Sharing

Readings
- Mackelprang & Salsgiver, 1999. Chapter 11.

SESSION 14: FRAMEWORK CONTINUED

Content
- Models of Professional Practice
  - Strengths approach
  - Empowerment
  - Case management and service coordination
  - Independent living model
  - Individualized funding

Pedagogy
- Lecture
- Discussion
- Sharing

Readings
Mackelprang & Salsgiver, 1999. Chapter 12.

SESSION 15: FRAMEWORK CONTINUED

Content

- Guidelines for practice with persons with disabilities
- Assumptions
- Integrating a positive disability identity

Pedagogy

- Lecture
- Discussion
- Sharing

Readings

- Mackelprang & Salsgiver, 1999. Chapter 13.

SESSION 16: TEST 3

Respond to 4 of 11 essay questions (2 selected by instructor) on readings, lectures, discussion, videos, and guest presentations. Responses are to be composed and submitted online from the computer lab during class time.

Social Work and People with Disabilities

SW S827-01 (Summer 2001)

COURSE DESCRIPTION

This course is designed to provide social work students the opportunity to learn about issues and laws that affect and pertain to persons with disabilities and their families. Legislation, attitudes, and expectations are shifting from an emphasis on cure, care, and treatment to a concentration on participation, capabilities, adapting environments, and building community for people with disabilities. A cross-disability and multicultural focus will be presented throughout the course, therefore, a broad base of disability categories will be presented and discussed including physical, emotional, cognitive, and sensory disabilities. The history and current issues of the disability rights movement will be presented. Students will have an opportunity to explore their own thoughts, feelings, and perceptions about issues related to the disability community. In order for social workers to effectively interact and assist individuals with disabilities they need an awareness of everyday experiences that impact the quality of life for people with disabilities, along with an understanding of appropriate referrals to agencies and organizations.

PREREQUISITES

Completion of 18 hours of foundation coursework or permission from the instructor.

OBJECTIVES

At the conclusion of this course, each student will be able to

1. Indicate the basic legal mandates of the Americans with Disabilities Act (ADA), Section 504 of the Rehabilitation Act, and the Individuals with Disabilities Education Act (IDEA).

2. Identify and describe two agencies that provide services to people with disabilities.

3. Analyze his or her individual perceptions and attitudes toward people with disabilities.

4. Demonstrate an understanding of how the interaction between race, class, gender, and sexual orientation affects persons with disabilities.

5. Discuss the vision and goals of the disability rights movement and how she or he may be involved in achieving its success.

6. Understand parental perspectives on raising a child with a disability and recognize various family structures, cultures, and ethnic diversity.

7. Describe assistive technology devices and equipment utilized by people with disabilities.

8. Explain the roles and responsibilities of social workers in working with individuals with disabilities.

9. Recognize the professional values and ethics and the appropriate awareness and sensitivities related to working with persons with disabilities.

10. Review the history of the disability movement from a social justice viewpoint.

11. Assist the disabled community with needed legislation and social services that promote equality, self-empowerment, and independence.

TEACHING AND LEARNING METHODS

Teaching strategies incorporated into the course include cooperative learning, lecture, discussion, activities, simulation, fieldwork, videos, and reflective practice.

TEXTS

Required

Shapiro, J. P. (1992). *No pity: People with disabilities forging a new civil rights movement.* New York: New York Times Books.

Recommended

Hockenberry, J. (1999). *Moving violations.* New York: Hyperion.

METHODS OF EVALUATION

Assignments and Tasks

- **Six Reflective Journals** (10 points each)

  Students will write six journal entries. The journal entry should contain reflections about topics discussed in class, the readings assigned for the class, or topics related and pertinent but not discussed in class. 1-2 pages typed, double-spaced. **All journal entries will only be read by the instructor.**

  Point allocation and criteria

  - 1 point. The student's writing is descriptive in nature in response to a particular journal prompt.

  - 5 points. The student's writing includes description but expands to attempt some justification, rationale, or explanation for his or her views or reactions that might be accompanied by an example from class or personal experience if appropriate.

  - 10 points. The student's writing shows evidence of description, justification, and evaluation where they make judgments about the issue or actions of others. The journal entry is scrutinized and thoroughly explored with the intention of being reflective, critical and analytical in her or his reactions.

- **Book Reviews**

  Students are to select two children's books that would be useful in helping children cope with stressful or challenging life experiences related to their disability. For each book, the student will prepare a brief written summary. Books and summaries will be shared in class.

- **Two Community Resource Projects**

  1. The student will choose two resources in the community to investigate. They will find out what types of services the agencies offer to persons with disabilities and what type of referral service is used. The student will visit at least one of these resources and be prepared to share his or her observations with the class. If possible, the student will try to obtain enough written materials from the resource to share with the class.

  2. The student will visit the local offices of a state legislator, state senator, U.S. legislator, or U.S. senator. During their visit they will interview the congressman or an assigned aid regarding their stance about disability laws and their voting record in this area.

- **Final Project**

  The students will choose either to interview an adult with a disability or use a wheelchair for the day in the community and experience common attitudes and obstacles encountered daily by people with disabilities. The paper should include a description of their experiences or interview, as well as information gathered after meeting with a legislator or assigned aide. The paper should reflect the student's personal perspectives and include key disability related issues and laws that correlate with their interviews, class activities, and assigned readings. The students will write a 6-8 page (double-spaced) typed paper with appropriate documentation and an APA style bibliography. The paper will be due no later than the last day of class.

- **Final Open-Book Exam**

  The open-book exam allows the student to integrate the materials covered in class. Students will be allowed to bring notes, books, and other relevant materials distributed in class.

- **Course Requirements and Grading**

Class Attendance and Participation	100 points
Reflective Journals	60 points
Book Reviews	50 points
Final Open Book	60 points
Community Resource Projects	100 points
Final Project	130 points
TOTAL	**500 points**

- **Grading Scale**

90-100%	450-500 points	A
80- 89%	400-449 points	B
70- 79%	350-399 points	C
60- 69%	300-349 points	D
Below 60%	below 300 points	F

OTHER COURSE POLICIES

Academic Integrity and Honesty

Academic integrity is violated by any dishonesty in submitting assignments, tests, research reports, or anything thing else required to validate the student's learning. Examples of academic dishonesty would be copying from another student, copying from a book or class notes during a closed book exam, submitting materials authored by another person but represented as the student's own work, copying a passage or text directly from a published source without appropriately citing and recognizing that source, taking a test or doing an assignment or other academic work for another student, or securing or supplying an advance copy of an examination without the knowledge or consent of the instructor. Any clear violation of academic integrity will be met with sanctions. In a case of dishonesty within a course, the instructor may assign an appropriate grade and will refer the matter to the Program Director, who will determine whether additional sanctions are warranted. If the Program Director determines that additional sanctions are warranted, the Director will refer the matter to the appropriate body identified in the School of Social Service's by-laws, which will deal with the matter under the provisions of the Professional Probation and Dismissal Policy. Students are referred to the MSW Program Student Handbook for a complete presentation of the Academic Integrity and Honesty policy of the school.

Nondiscrimination Policy and Human Diversity

Saint Louis University and the School of Social Service's BSSW and MSW Programs have a strong and active commitment to promote human diversity and to ensure that all aspects of educational programs are carried forth without discrimination on the basis of age, color, disability, ethnicity, gender, national origin, race, religion, sexual orientation, or political orientation. A specific university goal is to foster "respect for diversity, other cultures, and belief systems." A related school objective is to "demonstrate skill and responsiveness to the needs of clients and client systems, especially those who are poor, oppressed, and/or members of culturally diverse groups and at-risk populations." This policy can be viewed in the university undergraduate and graduate bulletins plus the BSSW and MSW student handbooks.

Students with Special Needs

If any member of the class has a disability and needs special accommodations of any nature, please let the instructor know at some point before, during, or immediately after the first scheduled class period. The instructor will work with you and the campus Disability Coordinator to ensure that you have a fair opportunity to perform well in the class.

Writing and the APA Style

A variety of publication styles are recognized in academic and professional settings (e.g., MLA, Chicago Style). The faculty of the School of Social Service encourage graduate social work students to study, learn, and master the conventions contained in the American Psychological Association Style Manual (APA, 1994). At a minimum, students are expected to follow the rules of good grammar, syntax, punctuation, and spelling. Any student who needs assistance with her or his writing is encouraged to meet with the graduate writing assistant assigned to the school.

Instructor and Course Evaluation

The instructor and course will be evaluated at the end of the term by students through the use of a standard evaluation instrument. Each evaluation will cover the quality and relevance of course materials and the quality of instruction. The intent is to seek information which will help to improve both the quality of the course and the instructor's competence. In completing these evaluations, the student should be mindful of the extent to which the course objectives have been met.

BIBLIOGRAPHY

Supplemental readings will be assigned on a weekly basis correlating with topics being discussed. The readings will be articles selected from monthly magazines, periodicals, and journals addressing disability issues. Examples may include, but are not limited to, Mainstream, ACCENT on Living, Disability Rag, and Exceptional Parent magazines.

COURSE OUTLINE

Session 1, May 26

- Overview of course syllabus.
- History of the disability rights movement.
- Section 504 of the Rehabilitation Act.
- Video: "We Won't Go Away."
- Multicultural and equity issues and practices.
- Americans with Disabilities Act.
- Social workers' roles and responsibilities.
- Utilizing the person-centered planning and Making Action Plans (MAPS) process.
- Awareness activities, videos, and resources.
- Reading assignment: Shapiro (1992), chapters 1, 2, 3, & 4.

Session 2, June 2

- Discussion of reading assignment and journals.
- Agencies and organizations—roles and responsibilities.
- "Getting the Big Picture"—inclusive education, employment, and community living.
- Video: "Inclusive Education with Kids My Age."
- Reading assignment: Shapiro (1992), chapters 5 & 6.

Session 3, June 9

- Site visit at the Special School District's Family and Community Resource Center with Judy Presberg, Administrative Liaison—Family Services. A tour and a parent perspective presentation will be given.
- Reading assignment: Shapiro (1992), chapters 7 & 8.

Session 4, June 16

- Community resource visits.

Session 5, June 23

- Discussion of reading assignment and journals.
- Assistive technology, disability simulations, recreation, sexuality, and other social benefits issues: Guest Speaker—Paraquad Independent Living Center.
- Children's book reviews orally presented to class.
- Reading assignment: Shapiro (1992), chapters 9, 10, & Epilogue.
- Gay Lesbian Straight Education Network (GLSEN): Guest Speakers—Disability and Sexual Orientation.

Session 6, June 30

- Day will be set aside for interviews and disability simulations.

Session 7, July 7

- Community resource presentations. Legislative processes will be discussed. Review appropriate methods when interacting with legislators for educational and lobbying purposes.
- Guest Speaker—National Alliance for The Mentally Ill (NAMI).

Session 8, July 14

- Interviews with legislator.

Session 9, July 21

- Discussion of reading assignment and journals.
- Exploring the Internet and disability related issues video: "Max and the Magic Pill."

Session 10, July 28

- Open book exam—all projects due.

Disability through the Life Cycle: Practice, Policy, and Research Issues for Social Workers

A proposed elective course in the MSW program

DESCRIPTION

The Americans with Disabilities Act of 1990 acknowledged that there are 43 million Americans who have one or more mental or physical disabilities, which means that it is essential that all social workers become knowledgeable about the laws, current policy issues, clinical approaches, and community resources as they begin to encounter this fast growing, diverse, minority population. This course is intended to be an introduction to some of the key issues impacting on the lives of people with disabilities and their families from birth to retirement. Historical issues, current policy issues, social work inteventions, and research findings from the literature will be addressed. Case examples of successful contemporary people with disabilities will be utilized. The course is organized around a developmental approach, addressing issues that impact families at birth, school age, adolescence, transition from school to adult life, adult life, and aging. Particular attention will be given to issues surrounding education and employment. Using a strengths approach, this course will provide a framework of how social workers can become involved in the challenge of helping people with disabilities to become independent, productive, and integrated into society through clinical practice, policy, and research initiatives.

OBJECTIVES

1. Students will identify and be able to describe the five competing ideologies that have impacted the treatment of people with disabilities throughout history.

2. To identify and be able to describe several key pieces of contemporary social policy legislation that impact on the lives of people with disabilities and to describe some of the debates about these policies from different viewpoints.

3. To be able to describe a strengths approach and to write a strengths-based assessment.

4. To describe the life cycle tasks at each stage of development and to describe at least ten disabilities that can impact people at different stages in the life cycle.

5. To identify a variety of social work interventions for working with people with disabilities.

6. To describe ways in which racial, ethnic, class, and gender differences relate to disability.

7. To identify the struggles and accomplishments of well-known contemporary people with disabilities and their contributions to society to provide role models for change.

8. To identify areas where research has been done, the impact of social policy and clinical practice, and what areas need to be researched in the future.

9. To compile a list of disability resources in the local area and national resources that can be used when working with families as students or professional social workers.

10. To identify several areas of social work practice with people with disabilities where employment opportunities are likely for new MSW graduates.

REQUIREMENTS

Students are expected to attend and participate in all classes to demonstrate an understanding of the readings and class discussion. Students need to leave a telephone message or email the instructor if unable to attend class. More than two absences will lower the course grade. Students are expected to read and familiarize themselves with the readings prior to class so they will be able to make relevant contributions to the class discussion.

REQUIRED TEXTBOOKS

Mackelprang, R.W. and R.O. Salsgiver. (1999). *Disability: A diversity model approach in human service practice.* Pacific Grove, CA: Brooks/Cole. (Note: Both authors are social workers; one author has a disability.)

McMahon, B.T. and L.R. Shaw. (Eds.). (2000). *Enabling lives: Biographies of six prominent Americans with disabilities.* Boca Raton, FL: CRC Press. (1-800-272-7737)

SUPPLEMENTARY TEXTBOOKS

Olkin, R. (1999). *What psychotherapists should know about disability.* New York: Guilford Press.

RECOMMENDED RESOURCES

Batshaw, M.L. and Y.M. Perrett. (1992). *Children with disabilities: A medical primer, 2nd edition.* Baltimore, MD: Paul H. Brooks. (Note: the second author is a social worker.)

Blotzer, M.A. and R. Ruth. (1995). *Sometimes you just want to feel like a human being: Case studies of empowering psychotherapy with people with disabilities.* Baltimore, MD: Paul H. Brooks. (Note: the first author is a social worker.)

Miller, N.B. and C.C. Sammons. (1999). *Everybody's different: Understanding our changing reactions to disabilities.* Baltimore, MD: Paul H. Brooks. (Note: both authors are social workers.)

Seigelman, M. and R.B. Benjamin. (1997). *Ordinary families: Special children: A systems approach to childhood and disability, 2nd edition.* New York: Guilford Press.

Turnbull, A., J.M. Patterson, S.K. Behr, D.L. Murphy, J.G. Marquis, and M.J. Blue-Banning. (1993). *Cognitive coping, families, and disability.* Baltimore, MD: Paul H. Brooks.

Turnbull, A. and R. Turnbull. (2001). *Families, professionals, and exceptionality: Collaborating for empowerment, 4th edition.* Upper Saddle River, NJ: Merrill Prentice Hall.

Required readings are available in the library at the front desk in a folder with the name and number of this course. You will need your student ID card to access these reserve items. It is necessary to do these readings prior to class so that students can participate in class.

Supplementary readings are available on reserve at the library. The purpose of these readings is to allow for further exploration on a particular area of student interest for class discussions. These readings may be used to fulfill the ten reference requirements of the written assignment and class presentation (also see page 3).

COURSE GRADE

1. Written Assignment (Book critique, Movie critique, or Life cycle issue): 40%
2. Class Presentation: 40%
3. Class Participation and attendance: 20%

ASSIGNMENTS

A. Written Assignment

Due Session 10. Late papers will not be accepted. Double-spaced, one inch margins, 12 pt. font size, white paper, APA style, no fancy covers. Select (1) or (2):

(1) A 15-20 page critique of a fiction novel, play, or recent movie about people with disabilities, or a auto/biographical book written by a person with a disability about their life. (Be sure to name the author, title, publisher, date.)

Begin with a brief plot summary of the work consisting of 1-2 pages maximum.

Address all of these issues in any order that you like:

- What was the historical context of the work? (Include any debates about the work.)
- What was the author's purpose/views/ideology and how was this conveyed?
- What was the connection between the issues raised and the stage of the life cycle?
- What was your reaction to the work? Feelings? Thoughts?
- How were people with disabilities portrayed? Main character or not? Is portrayal accurate?
- How do you think an audience/reader who has a disability would have reacted to this work?
- How did issues of race, class, ethnicity, and gender impact this work?
- If you had a chance to edit the work, what would you like to change about it and why?
- What does the social work literature mention about the issues in this work? (This is critical.)
- Using the social work literature on this course bibliography, information in this course, and other courses, how might a social worker intervene on a practice, research, and/or policy level? (This question is also critical.) (Use 10 references from this class and other classes.)

The book needs to be brought to class or discussed with instructor in the second class.

(2) A 15-20 page paper about a particular life cycle issue or policy debate.

Address all of these in any order:

- What is the issue? Describe it.
- How many people are affected? (Statistics/numbers.)
- What is the connection between the issue and the relevant stage in life cycle development?
- When and how long has this issue been seen as a "problem"?
- What are some of the current debates about this issue in the news today?
- Why is the issue important to you? To social work? To people with disabilities?
- What has been done about it? Policies? Practices? Research findings?
- How do race, class, gender, and ethnicity impact this issue?
- What does the literature suggest are the roles of the social worker regarding this issue?
- Using information from this course and other courses, how might a social worker intervene on a policy, clinical, or research level? (Key question.) (Use at least 15 different references from social work journals or newspapers; it is fine to use the ones on this syllabus.)

B. Class Presentation

Presentation will be on the same topic that you selected in the written assignment (either 1 or 2), or the student may take full responsibility for a detailed discussion of a particular case study from the textbook *Enabling Lives.*

If you wish to do the case study, you need to inform the instructor in advance, or else it will be assumed that your presentation will be on the same topic as your final paper.

The goal of the presentation is to get feedback on your topic from the class and the instructor prior to submitting your final paper for the semester.

Time/Length: To be determined based upon number of students in the class, (15-30 minutes each).

Please provide a handout to the class, if possible. Several students may present together, but this needs to be discussed with instructor in advance; presentation time will be longer for groups.

(Author's Note: Students are then given suggestions of films and movies in a handout. See the list compiled for this volume in the Annotated Bibliography.)

SUGGESTED AGENDA FOR EACH CLASS SESSION

(Assumes that class will meet once a week for 2 hours.)

First half-hour: brief review of prior session and lecture; second half-hour: case study discussion; 10 minute break; final 50 minutes: class activities, debates, and student presentations.

HINTS FOR LOCATING BOOKS ON DISABILITY ISSUES IN THE LIBRARY

HD 7256: Disability and Rehabilitation   HV 1568: Disability and Social Work

HQ 759: Disability and Parents/Families   KF 480: Disability and Law

HV 1552: Disability and Research   RC 394: Learning Disabilities and Therapy/Mental Health Issues

HV 1553: Disability and Social Policy   RC 451: Disability and Psychotherapy

OUTLINE

SESSION ONE. INTRODUCTION AND OVERVIEW

Learning objectives:

- To describe the many different definitions of disability and their implications.
- To appreciate well-known theories of human development and developmental tasks.
- To learn how disabilities impact on life development tasks and transitions through the life span.
- To examine the stereotypes that society creates about people with disabilities through the media and to prevent these stereotypes from being brought into practice situations.

Suggested Classroom Exercises (after the usual first day introductions)

1. Ask students to discuss their fears about people with disabilities and how they might be played out in everyday life. How to prevent this from happening?

2. Discuss the research findings of Bricout and Bentley (2000) of employer perceptions of people with disabilities. What are the independent and dependent variables in the study? Who were the participants? What were the findings of the study? What is the generalizability? How does this study reflect larger societal attitudes? What are the implications of this study for social work practice, policy, and future research?

Required Reading

Bricout, J.C. and K.J. Bentley. (2000, June). Disability status and perceptions of employability by employers. *Social Work Research,* 24, (2), 87-95. (Article to be distributed in class).

Byrd, K.E. (1989, Summer). A study of depiction of specific characteristics of characters with disability in film. *Journal of Applied Rehabilitation Counseling*, 20, (2), 43-45.

Mackelprang and Salsgiver (1999). Chapter 1: Societal and Professional Stereotypes. Chapter 4: Life Stage Development.

Recommended Reading

Miller and Sammons (1999). Chapter 1: Differences in everyday life. Chapter 2: About disability differences. Chapter 3: Understanding your reactions to disability differences. Chapter 4: The 4-D approach (to disability awareness).

Olkin (1999). Chapter 1: Who are people with disabilities? Definitions, the disability community, categorization, severity, functioning, statistics. Chapter 3: The disability experience: stereotypes and attitudes.

Turnbull and Turnbull (2001). Chapter 7: The impact of exceptionality on family functions—affection needs self-esteem, spiritual, economic, care, socialization, recreation, education. Chapter 8: Family life cycle: theory, stages, and transitions.

SESSION 2. HISTORY: MOVING FORWARD

Learning objectives:

- To trace a brief history of societal responses to people with disabilities in the United States.
- To describe the ideological differences reflected in the Moral Model, the Medical Model, Social Darwinism and Eugenetics, the Social Minority Model, and the Independent Living Model.
- To critically evaluate key pieces of contemporary social policies affecting people with disabilities such as deinstitutionalization or the Americans with Disabilities Act.
- To examine the impact of race, ethnicity, class, and gender on the lives of people with disabilities and on the growing disability movement.
- To trace the history of the social work profession in working with people with disabilities.

Suggested Classroom Exercises

1. Discuss the findings of a recent study by Bell and Stoneman (2000) of prenatal testing and the decision to continue or abort the pregnancy if the fetus was diagnosed with a disability. Or discuss the findings of Lin's (2000) study on coping and families of children with cerebral palsy. What are the independent and dependent variables in the study? Who were the participants? What were the findings of the study? What is the generalizability? How does this study reflect larger societal attitudes? What are the implications of this study for social work practice, policy, and future research?

2. Have students debate the issue of abortion and disability. Should the same or different legal rights apply if testing has found that the fetus has a disability?

Required Reading for Classroom Exercise

Bell, M. and Z. Stoneman. (2000). Reactions to prenatal testing: Reflection of religiousity and attitudes toward abortion and people with disabilities. *American Journal on Mental Retardation*, 105, (1), 1-13.

Lin, S.L. (2000). Coping and adaption in families of children with cerebral palsy. *Exceptional Children*, 66, (2), 201-218.

Required Reading for Class Discussion

Asch, A. and N.R. Murdick. (1995). Disability. *Encyclopedia of Social Work, 19th edition* (pp.752-761). Washington, DC: National Association of Social Workers.

Mackelprang and Salsgiver (1999). Chapters 2: Disability culture. Chapter 3: Disability history in the United States.

Olkin (1999). Chapter 2: The minority model of disability. Chapter 6: Laws and social history: ADA.

Recommended Reading

Cole, B.S., C.C. Christ, and T.R. Light. (1995, Spring/Summer). Social work education and students with disabilities: Implications of Section 504 and the ADA. *Journal of Social Work Education, 31*(2), 261-268.

DeWeaver, K.L. (1983, Nov.-Dec.). Deinstitutionalization of the developmentally disabled. *Social Work,* 28, (6), 435-439.

Ell, K. (1985). The role of social work in rehabilitating people with disabilities. *Annual Review of Rehabilitation,* 4, 145-179.

Fine, M. and A. Asch. (1981). Disabled women: Sexism without the pedestal. *Journal of Sociology and Social Welfare,* 8, 233-248.

Gordon, E.B. (1994). Promoting the relevance of policy to practice: Using the ADA to teach social policy. *Journal of Teaching in Social Work,* 10, (2), 165-176.

Hanley, B. and C.B. Parkinson. (1994, Dec.). Position paper on social work values: Practice with individuals who have developmental disabilities. *Mental Retardation,* 32, (6), 426-431.

Hanna, W. and B. Rogousky. (1996). Women and disability: Two handicaps plus. *Disability, Handicap and Society,* 6, (1), 49-63.

Gilson, S.F., J.C. Briocut, and F.R. Baskind. (1998, March-April). Listening to the voices of individuals with disabilities. *Families in Society,* 79, (2), 188-196.

Jimenez, M.A. (1988, Dec.). Chronicity in mental disorders: Evolution of a concept. *Social Casework,* 627-633. (Traces a history of mental disorders.)

Kopels, S. (1995, Fall). The Americans with Disabilities Act: A tool to combat poverty. *Journal of Social Work Education,* 31, (3), 337-346.

Longmore, P.K. (1987, Sept.). Uncovering the hidden history of people with disabilities. *Reviews in American History,* 15, 355-364.

Mackelprang, R.W. and R.O. Salsgiver. (1996). People with disabilities and social work: Historical and contemporary issues. *Social Work,* 41, (1), 7-14.

Mary, N.L. (1998, Spring/Summer). Social work and the support model of services for people with developmental disabilities. *Journal of Social Work Education,* 34, (2), 247-260.

Moxley, D. (1992, May). Disability policy and social work practice. *Health and Social Work,* 17, (2), 99-103.

Owen, M.J. (1985, Summer). One last bastion of segregation: It is time to integrate people with disabilities into our society. *Public Welfare, 43,* 25-30.

Pardeck, J.T. (1998). *Social Work After the Americans with Disabilities Act: New Challenges and Opportunities for Social Service Professionals.* Westport, CT: Auburn House.

Pardeck, J.T. and W.S. Chung (1992). An analysis of the Americans with Disabilities Act. *Journal of Health and Social Policy*, 4, (1), 47-56.

Pardeck, J.T. (1997). Americans with Disabilities Act of 1990: Implications for human service agencies. *The Clinical Supervisor*, 15, (2), 147-161.

Quinn, P. (1994, Spring). America's disability policy: Another double standard? *Affilia: Journal of women and social work*, 9, (1), 45-59.

Quinn, P. (1995). Social work education and disability: Benefiting from the impact of the ADA. *Journal of Teaching in Social Work*, 12, (1/2), 55-71.

Thompson, R.G. (1994). Redrawing the boundaries of feminist disability studies. *Feminist Studies*, 20, (3), 583-597.

Todd, A.D. (1984). Women and the disabled in contemporary society. *Social Policy*, 14, (4), 44-46.

Wendell, S. (1997). Toward a feminist theory of disability. In L. Davis (Ed.), *The Disability Studies Reader* (pp. 260-278). New York: Routlage.

SESSION 3. FINDING STRENGTHS: A CLINICAL APPROACH

Learning objectives:

- To describe the basic concepts of a strengths approach in social work practice.
- To discuss the benefits of a strengths approach in working with people with disabilities.
- To construct and use various assessment tools, including an eco-map, using case examples.
- To write a strengths-based assessment using a variety of individual and environmental factors.
- To identify effective social work skills for working with people with disabilities.

Suggested Classroom Exercises

1. Have students practice writing an eco-map of themselves in order to emphasize that people with disabilities are also part of a larger family, environment, and community.

2. Using case examples provided by the instructor, or from students, have students practice creating a strengths-based assessment. They can work in small groups or individually. Compare this strengths-based assessment to the more traditional way that assessments have been done.

3. Have students discuss the obstacles that might be faced in terms of managed care issues if all assessments were done this way, and discuss how this method can be utilized effectively.

Required Reading

DeJong, P. and D. Miller. (1995, Nov.). How to interview for client strengths. *Social Work*, 40, (6), 729-736.

Mackelprang and Salsgiver (1999). Chapters 11: Assessment. Chapter 12: Models of professional practice. Chapter 13: Guidelines for practice with persons with disabilities.

Weick, A., C. Rapp, W.P. Sullivan, and W. Kisthardt. (1989, July). A strengths perspective for social work practice. *Social Work*, 34, 350-354.

Recommended Reading

Blotzer and Roth (1995). Chapter 1: Toward basic principles. Chapter 2: On sitting with uncertainty: treatment considerations for people with disabilities.

Cowger, C.D. (1994, May). Assessing client strengths: Clinical assessment for client empowerment. *Social Work*, 39, (3), 262-268.

Hartman, A. (1978, Oct.). Diagrammatic assessment of family relationships. *Social Casework, 59*, 465-476.

McQuaide, S. and J.H. Ehrenreich. (1997, March-April). Assessing client strengths. *Families in Society*, 78, (2), 201-212.

Olkin (1999). Chapter 7: Beginning treatment: Guidelines for clinical work with people with disabilities. Chapter 8: Etiquette with clients with disabilities. Chapter 9: Interviews, assessment, evaluation, and diagnosis.

Russo, R. (1999, Jan.-Feb.). Applying a strengths-based practice approach in working with people with developmental disabilities and their families. *Families in Society*, 80, (1), 25-33.

Saleebey, D. (1992 or 1997). *The Strengths Perspective in Social Work Practice.* (1st or 2nd ed.) New York: Longman.

SESSION 4. FROM BIRTH TO SCHOOL AGE: AN AGE OF EARLY INTERVENTION

Learning objectives:

- To describe a variety of reactions and coping patterns in family responses to having a disabled child, including ethnic and cultural differences, and sibling adjustment, that have been found among clinical practice and research literature findings.

- To develop a list of resources and to be able educate caregivers and families about the variety of available cost and no-cost services, such as respite, recreation, early intervention, etc.

- To understand some of the factors that contribute to disability (prenatal care, drugs, HIV, genes.)

- To review the developmental tasks associated with the early years of life.

- To continue to identify roles of social workers in early intervention.

Suggested Classroom Exercises

1. Case study discussion of Judy Heumann (from *Enabling Lives* textbook). Although she used a wheelchair since childhood, she overcame many obstacles in education and employment to become successful in life. Have students discuss the following items: What can we learn from her life? What were her contributions to the disability movement? How is her struggle related to the social work profession? In this regard, what are the roles for social workers in practice, research, and policy?

Required Case Study Reading

McMahon and Shaw (2000). Judy Heumann, pp. 87-106.

Required Reading

DeWeaver, K.L. (1995). Developmental disabilities: Definitions and policies. *Encyclopedia of Social Work, 19th edition* (pp. 712-719). Washington, DC: National Association of Social Workers.

Ellis, J.B. (1989, Winter). Grieving for the loss of the perfect child: Parents of children with handicaps. *Child and Adolescent Social Work*, 6, (4), 259-269.

Heller, T., R. Markwardt, and L. Rowitz. (1994). Adaptation of Hispanic families to a member with mental retardation. *American Journal on Mental Retardation*, 99, (3), 289-300.

Ryan, A.S. and M.J. Smith. (1989, Winter). Parental reactions to developmental disabilities in Chinese American families. *Child and Adolescent Social Work*, 6, (4), 283-299.

Shapiro, J. and D. Simonsen. (1994, Dec.). Educational/Support group for Latino families of children with Down Syndrome. *Mental Retardation*, 32, (6), 403-415.

Wikler, L., M. Walow, and E. Hartfield. (1983). Seeking strengths in families of developmentally disabled children. *Social Work*, 28, (4), 313-315.

Recommended Reading

Atkins, S.P. (1989, Winter). Siblings of handicapped children. *Child and Adolescent Social Work*, 6, (4), 271-282.

Batshaw and Perrett (1992). Chapters: 8, 10, 3, 29: alcohol, cocaine, AIDS, genetics, birth defects, prenatal diagnosis, caring & coping. Chapter 1, 2, 4, 5, 6, 7: chromosomes, heredity, birth process, first weeks of life, prematurity.

Bernier, J.C. (1990, Dec.). Parental adjustment to a disabled child: A family-systems perspective. *Families in Society*, 589-596.

Booth, C.L. and J.F. Kelly. (1999). Child care and employment in relation to infants' disabilities and risk factors. *American Journal on Mental Retardation*, 104, (2), 117-130.

Davis, B.H. (1987, June). Disability and grief. *Social Casework*, 68, 353-357.

Families and Disability Newsletter, Vol. 9, Number 1, Summer 1998. Entire Issue. "Strengthening Families." Published by Beach Center on Families and Disability, University of Kansas. (www.isi.ukans.edu/beach/beachhp.htm.)

Fujiura, G.T. and K. Yamaki. (2000, Winter). Trends in demography of childhood poverty and disability. *Exceptional Children*, 66, (2), 187-199.

Herman, S.E. and L. Thompson. (1995, April). Families' perceptions of their resources in caring for children with developmental disabilities. *Mental Retardation*, 33, (2), 73-83.

Johnson, H.C., E.F. Renaud, D.T. Schmidt, and E.J. Stanek. (1998, March-April). Social workers' views of parents of children with mental and emotional disabilities. *Families in Society*, 79, (2), 173-187.

Kratocchvil, M.S. and S.A. Devereux. (1988). Counseling needs of parents of handicapped children. *Social Casework*, 69, 420-426.

Olkin (1999) Chapter 5: Families with disabilities: children, siblings, partners, parents.

Park, J., A.P. Turnbull, H. Rutherford Turnbull III. (2002, Winter). Impacts of poverty on quality of life in families of children with diabilities. *Exceptional Children*, 68, (2), 151-170.

Rounds, K.A. (1991, Dec.). Early intervention services for very young children and their families under P.L. 99-457. *Child and Adolescent Social Work*, 8, (6), 489-499.

Seligman, M. and R.B. Darling. (1997). Chapter 2: Becoming the parent, pp. 36-56. Chapter 7: Cultural reactions to childhood disability and subcultural variation, pp. 167-197.

Skinner, D.G., V. Correa, M., Skinner, and D.B. Bailey, Jr. (2001). Role of religion in the lives of Latino families of young children with developmental delays. *American Journal on Mental Retardation*, 106, (4), 297-313.

Smith, P.M. (1984, March). You are not alone: For parents when they learn that their child has a handicap. Washington, DC: National Information Center for Handicapped Children and Youth (NICHCY).

Starkey, J. and P. Sarli. (1989, Winter). Respite and family support services: Responding to the need. *Child and Adolescent Social Work*, 6, (4), 313-326.

Turnbull and Turnbull (2001). Chapter 1: Historical and current roles of families and parents: Parents as source of child's disability, organization members, recipients of professionals decisions, advocates, education decision makers, collaboration.

Warfield, M.E. (2001, August). Employment, parenting, and well-being among mothers of children with disabilities. *Mental Retardation*, 39, (4), 297-309.

Werrbach, G.B. (1996, April). Family-strengths-based child case management. *Families in Society*, 77, (4), 216-226.

SESSION 5. CHILDHOOD, PART II: CHILDHOOD DISABILITIES

Learning Objectives are the same as prior lesson, plus

- To describe the major types of disabilities that affect children in the early years.
- To continue to identify roles for social workers.

Suggested Classroom Exercises

1. Case study discussion of Frank Bowe (from *Enabling Lives* textbook). Although he became deaf at age 2, he became successful in life. Have students discuss the following items: what can we learn from his life? What were his contributions to the disability movement? How is his struggle related to the social work profession? In this regard, what are the roles for social workers in practice, research, and policy?

2. Discuss the findings of a recent study by Scorgie, Wilgosh, and McDonald (1999). Compare this qualitative/quantitative study with the quantitative studies discussed earlier in terms of reader interest, clarity, details, and validity and reliability. Is this more effective or not? What are the independent and dependent variables in the study? What are the roles for parents of children with disabilities? Who were the participants? What were the findings of the study? What is the generalizability?

Required Case Study and Class Exercise Reading

McMahon and Shaw (2000). Fred Bowe, pp. 101-32.

Scorgie, K., L. Wilgosh, and L. McDonald (1999). Transforming partnerships: Parent life management issues when a child has mental retardation. *Education and Training in Mental Retardation and Developmental Disabilities*, 34, (4), 395-405.

Required Reading

Mackelprang and Salsgiver (1999). Chapters: 5, 6, 7, 8, 9: People with mobility, hearing, visual, developmental, cognitive, and learning disabilities.

Recommended Reading

Batshaw and Perrett. (1992). Chapters 16: People with mental retardation. Chapter 17: Vision disabilities. Chapter 18: Hearing disabilities. Chapter 19: Language communication disabilities. Chapter 20: Learning disabilities. Chapter 21: Attention deficit/hyperactivity. Chapter 22: Autism. Chapter 24: Cerebral palsy. Chapter 25: Neural tube defects. Chapter 26: Seizures.

Bessell, A.G. (2001, Spring). Children surviving cancer: Psychosocial adjustment, quality of life, and school experiences. *Exceptional Children*, 67, (3), 345-359.

Miller and Sammons (1999). Chapter 5: People who look different. Chapter 6: People who move different. Chapter 7: People who communicate different. Chapter 8: People who behave different. Chapter 9: People who learn different. Chapter 10: People who have non-visible disabilities.

Raines, J.C. (1989, Winter). Social work practice with learning disabled children. *Social Work in Education*, 89-105.

Turnbull and Turnbull (2001). Chapter 11: Referring and evaluating for special education.

SESSION 6. FROM SCHOOL AGE TO ADOLESCENCE

Learning objectives:

- To review the developmental tasks associated with the school age and early adolescent years.
- To describe the provisions of PL 94-142: Education for Handicapped Children Act of 1975.
- To trace the special education process: referral, evaluation, recommendation, and placement, with a particular focus on how it happens in the local area.
- To examine current debates about special education and inclusion.
- To examine the impact of race, culture, and gender in special education.
- To describe the Individualized Education Plan (IEP), its vocabulary, and the services provided.
- To review life cycle developmental tasks for persons from school age to adolescence.
- To identify the variety of roles for the social worker.

Suggested Classroom Exercises

1. Case study discussion of Evan Kemp and Tony Coelho (from *Enabling Lives* textbook). Although Mr. Kemp had muscular dystrophy since age 12, he became successful in life. Mr. Coelho had epilepsy, he became successful in life. Have students discuss the following items: what can we learn from their lives? What were their contributions to the disability movement? How are their struggles related to the social work profession? In this regard, what are the roles for social workers in practice, research, and policy?

2. Discuss the findings of a recent qualitative study by Boyce, Marshall, and Peters (1999). Compare this qualitative study with the quantitative studies discussed earlier in terms of reader interest, clarity, details, and validity and reliability. Is this more effective or not? What are the independent and dependent variables in the study? What are the areas of struggle for adolescents? How can social workers be involved? Who were the participants? What were the findings of the study? What is the generalizability?

Required Case Study Reading

Boyce, G.C., E.S. Marshall, and M. Peters. (1999). Daily stressors, coping responses and uplifts of adolescents with disabilities. *Education and Training in Mental Retardation and Developmental Disabilities*, 34, (4), 406-417.

McMahon and Shaw (2000). Evan Kemp, pp. 39-64, and Tony Coelho, pp. 139-149.

Required Reading

Gruber, C. (1987, Spring). Repairing ego deficits in children with developmental disorders. *Child and Adolescent Social Work*, 4, (1), 50-63.

Individuals with Disabilities Education Act Amendments of 1997 (IDEA): Implications for social workers [brochure]. (1997, June). Washington, DC: National Association of Social Workers.

Mackelprang and Salsgiver (1999). Chapter 9: Persons with psychiatric disabilities. Chapter 10: Cognitive disability.

Nelson, M., S. Rush, Z. Jackson, L. Bloom, and R. Part. (1992). Towards an understanding of families with physically disabled adolescents. *Social Work in Health Care*, 17, (4), 1-25.

Recommended Reading

A Parent's Guide to Special Education for Children Ages 5-21. New York: Board of Education of the City of New York.

Batshaw and Perrett (1992). Chapter 23: Dual diagnosis: Psychiatric disorders and mental retardation. Chapter 27: Traumatic brain injury.

Cohen, J. (1985). Chapter 13: Learning disabilities and adolescence: Developmental Considerations, pp. 177-195. Title Unknown. Chicago: The University of Chicago.

Cole, B.S., L.F. Pearl, and M.J. Welsh. (1989, Winter). Education of social workers for intervention with families of children with special needs. *Child and Adolescent Social Work*, 6, (4), 327-338.

Diblasio, F.A. (1989, Oct.). Behavorial program for hyperactive students. *Social Work in Education*, 12, 45-52.

Early, T.J. and L.F. GlenMaye. (2000, March). Valuing families: Social work practice with families from a strengths perspective. *Social Work*, 45, (2), 118-128.

Fiene, J.I. and P.A. Taylor. (1991, July). Serving rural families of developmentally disabled children: A case management model. *Social Work*, 36, (4), 323-327.

Marcenko, M. and L.K. Smith. (1992). The impact of a family-centered case management approach. *Social Work in Health Care*, 17, (1), 87-99.

McCallion, T. and R.W. Toseland. (1993, Dec.). Empowering families of adolescents with developmental disabilities. *Families in Society*, 74, (10), 579-589.

Ornstein, M. (2000). *Smart but stuck: What every therapist needs to know about learning disabilities and imprisoned intelligence.* Binghamton, NY: Haworth Press.

Rousso, H. (1984). Disabled yet intact: Guidelines for work with cogenitally physically disabled youngsters and their parents. *Child and Adolescent Social Work*, 254-269.

Seligman, M. and R.B. Darling. (1997). *Ordinary families: Special children: A systems approach to childhood disability, (2nd ed.).* New York: Guilford Press. Chapter 3: Childhood and adolescence: Continuing adaptation, p. 57-88.

Turnbull and Turnbull (2001). Chapter 12: Individualizing for appropriate education. Chapter 13: Extending learning into home and community.

Whitney-Thomas, J. and M. Moloney. (2001, Spring). "Who I am and what I want": Adolescents' self-definition and struggles. *Exceptional Children*, 67, (3), 375-389.

SESSION 7. LATE ADOLESCENCE/TRANSITION TO ADULT LIFE FOR PEOPLE WITH DISABILITIES

- To review developmental issues associated with adolescence, including the separation process from school and family, and the growing influence of the peer group.
- To discuss college and work issues for people with disabilities.
- To describe life cycle issues for people with disabilities.
- To understand particular concepts in the field, such as inclusion, quality of life.
- To discuss the impact of drug addiction and mental illness in adolescence.
- To acknowledge that people with disabilities are also susceptible to peer pressure.
- To identify the social worker's role in prevention and treatment of drugs and alcohol.
- To examine the impact of crime and violence in the lives of people with disabilities.
- To develop a list of community resources for working with adolescents with disabilities.

Suggested Classroom Exercise

1. Case study discussion of Justin Dart (from *Enabling Lives* textbook). Although he had polio since age 18, he became successful in life. Have students discuss the following items: what can we learn from his life? What were his contributions to the disability movement? How is his struggle related to the social work profession? In this regard, what are the roles for social workers in practice, research, and policy?

2. Discussion of recent legal cases involving individuals with mental retardation. Should people with mental retardation go to jail? Receive a death sentence? What does it mean to be competent? Examples: Craig Godineaux: The killing at Wendy's fast food in Flushing, Queens, NY. Antonio Richardson: The Missouri Case involving rape and murders—still pending at this time. John Paul Perry: The Texas Case—still pending at this time.

Required Case Study and Classroom Exercises Reading

McMahon and Shaw (2000). Justin Dart, pp. 65-86.

One of the following:

> Ballard, M.B. and S. Austin. (1999). Forensic interviewing: Special considerations for children and adolescents with mental retardation and developmental disabilities. *Education and Training in Mental Retardation and Developmental Disabilities*, 34, (4), 521-525.

> Grubb-Blaubaugh, V., B.J. Shire, and M.L. Balser. (1994, June). Behavior management and offenders with mental retardation: The jury system. *Mental Retardation*, 32, (3), 213-217.

> Perske, R. (1994, Oct.). Thoughts on the police interrogation of individuals with mental retardation. *Mental Retardation*, 32, (5), 377-380.

> Smith, S.A. and S.F. Broughton. (1994, Aug.). Competency to stand trial and criminal responsibility: An analysis in South Carolina. *Mental Retardation*, 32, (4), 281-287.

> Stricker, H.L. (2001, December). Interaction between family violence and mental retardation. *Mental Retardation*, 39, (6), 461-471.

Required Reading

Ell, K.O. and K.R. Reardon. (1990, Nov.). Psychosocial care for the chronically ill adolescent: Challenges and opportunities. *Health and Social Work*, 15, (4), 272-282.

Families and Disability Newsletter. Volume 8, Number 1, Spring, 1997. Entire Issue: "Life after high school". Published by Beach Center on Families and Disability, University of Kansas.

Kraemer, B.R. and J. Blacher. (2001, December). Transition for young adults with severe mental retardation: School preparation, parent expectations, and family involvement. *Mental Retardation*, 39, (6), 423-435.

McNair, J. and F. Rusch. (1991, April). Parent involvement in transition programs. *Mental Retardation*, 29, (2), 93-101.

Palumbo, J. (1979). Perceptual deficits and self-esteem in adolescence. *Clinical Social Work Journal,* 7, (1), 34-61.

Thoma, C.A. (1999, May-June). Supporting student voices in transition planning. *Teaching Exceptional Children*, 31, (5), 4-14

Recommended Reading

Anderson, J. (1999). Chapter 30: Special needs offenders. In P.M. Carlson and J.S. Garrett (Eds.), *Prison and jail administration: Practice and theory*. Gaithersburg, MD: Aspen Publications.

Appell, A. (1999). Chapter 48: Accommodating inmates with disabilities. In P.M. Carlson and J.S. Garrett (Eds.), *Prison and jail administration: Practice and theory*. Gaithersburg, MD: Aspen Publications.

Bennett, L.W. (1995, Nov.). Substance abuse and the domestic assault of women. *Social Work*, 40, (6), 760-771.

Brier, N. (1986, Oct.). The mildly retarded adolescent: A psychosocial perspective. *Developmental and Behavorial Pediatrics*, 7, (5), 320-323.

Chernus, L.A. (1985, Jan.). Clinical issues in alcoholism treatment. *Social Casework*, 66, 67-75.

Daniels, V.I. and S. Vaughn. (1999, May). A tool to encourage "best practice" in full inclusion. *Teaching Exceptional Children*, 31, (5), 48-62.

Garvin, C. (1992). A task centered group approach to work with the chronically mentally ill. *Social Work with Groups*, 15, 67-80.

Goldberg, M.E. (1995, Nov.). Substance-abusing women: False stereotypes and real needs. *Social Work*, 40, (6), 789-798.

Halpern, A.S. (1993, May). Quality of life as a conceptual framework for evaluating transition outcomes. *Exceptional Children*, 59, (6), 486-498.

Hasazi, S. B., L.R. Gordon, and C.A. Roe. (1985, April). Factors associated with the employment status of handicapped youth exiting high school from 1979-1983. *Exceptional Children*, 51, (6), 455-469.

Katch, M. (1988, Spring). Acting out adolescents: The engagement process. *Child and Adolescent Social Work*, 5, (1), 30-40.

Libassi, M.F. (1988, Feb.). The chronically mentally ill: A practice approach. *Social Casework*, 69, 89-97.

Leikin, C. (1986, Jan.). Identifying and treating the alcoholic client. *Social Casework*, 67, 67-73.

Morehouse, E.R. (1989, June). Treating adolescent alcohol abusers. *Social Casework*, 70, (6), 355-363.

Morrell, C. (1996, May). Radicalizing recovery: Addiction, spirituality, and politics. *Social Work*, 41, (3), 306-312.

Norman, J.S. (1980, Feb.). Short-term treatment with adolescent clients. *Social Casework*, 61, 74-82.

Pharis, M.E. (1967, Feb.). The use of adolescents' creative writing in diagnosis and treatment. *Social Casework*, 48, 67-74.

Plasse, B.R. (1995, Jan.). Parenting groups for recovering addicts in a day treatment center. *Social Work*, 40, (1), 65-74.

Rapp, R.C., C.W. Kelliher, J.H. Fisher, and F.J. Hall. (1994, Winter). Strengths-based case management: A role in addressing denial in substance abuse treatment. *Journal of Case Management*, 3, (4), 139-144.

Rubenstein, E. (1991, April). An overview of adolescent development, behavior, and clinical intervention. *Families in Society*, 72, 220-225.

Sherraden, M. and M. Adamek. (1985, Oct.). Treating unemployed adolescents. *Social Casework*, 66, 467-474.

Stewart, C. S. and M.M. Zaengllein-Senger. (1982, Oct.). The parent-adolescent power contest. *Social Casework*, 63, 457-459.

Szymanski, E.M., J. King, R.M. Parker, W.M. Jenkins. (1989, Sept.). The State-Federal rehabilitation program: Interface with special education. *Exceptional Children*, 56, (1), 70-77.

Thomma, C.A. and P. Rogan. (2001, March). Student voices in transition planning: Unheard voices. *Education and Training in Mental Retardation and Developmental Disabilities*, 36, (1), 16-29.

Warren, P. (1987). The social therapeutic club: A collectivity for ex-psychiatric patients. *Social Work with Groups*, 91-101.

SESSION 8. ADULT LIFE

Learning objectives:

- To review the developmental tasks associated with adult life: to live, love, and work.
- To discuss issues for people with chronic disability and the new onset of disability.
- To learn about the variety of services provided by the State Vocational Rehabilitation Agency to people with disabilities in areas of education and employment.
- To learn about issues for people with disabilities in higher education and college.
- To discuss the barriers to employment such as transportation, accessibility, etc., and what the current debates are in this area.
- To describe the role of employee assistance programs with people with disabilities at work.
- To discuss a diversity of adult needs of people with disabilities (love, marry, have children, etc.).
- To describe a variety of social worker interventions with adults who have disabilities.
- To appreciate program evaluation and the concept of "consumer satisfaction" with services.

Suggested Classroom Exercises

1. Case study discussion of Harold Russell (from *Enabling Lives* textbook). Although he lost limbs during war, he became successful in life. Have students discuss the following items: w hat can we learn from his life? What were his contributions to the disability movement? How his struggle is related to the social work profession? In this regard, what are the roles for social workers in practice, research, and policy?

Required Case Study Reading

McMahon and Shaw (2000). Harold Russell, pp. 1-38.

Required Reading

Andrews, S. and L. Wikler. (1981, Summer). Developmental disabilities. *Health and Social Work*, 62-67.

Jordan, B. and G. Dunlap. (2001, August). Construction of adulthood and disability. *Mental Retardation*, 39, (4), 286-296.

Olkin (1999). Chapter 10: Dating, romance sexuality, pregnancy, birthing, and genetic testing. Chapter 11: Special issues in therapy with clients with disabilities: living with a progressive disorder, living with pain, advocacy and discrimination.

Murdick, N.R. (1991, Nov.). An underdeveloped role for occupational social work: Facilitating employment of people with disabilities. *Social Work*, 36, (6), 490-495.

Whitman, B.Y. , B. Graves, and P.J. Accardo. (1989, Sept.). Training in parenting skills for adults with mental retardation. *Social Work*, 34, 431-434.

Recommended Reading

Carlson, B.E. (1997, Jan.). Mental retardation and domestic violence: An ecological approach to intervention. *Social Work*, 42, (1), 79-89.

Dattilo, J. and S.J. Schleien. (1994, Feb.). Understanding leisure services for individuals with mental retardation. *Mental Retardation*, 32, (1), 53-59.

Hall, J.A., D.J. Schlesinger, and J.P. Dineen. (1997, April). Social skills training in groups with developmentally disabled adults. *Research on Social Work Practice*, 7, (2), 187-201.

Hayden, M.F. and J. Goldman. (1996, Nov.). Families of adults with mental retardation: Stress levels and need for services. *Social Work*, 41, (6), 657-667.

Kendall, E. and N. Buys. (1998, July-Aug.). An integrated model of psychosocial adjustment following acquired disability. *Journal of Rehabilitation*, 64, (3), 16-20.

Krauss, M.W., M.M. Seltzer, and S.J. Goodman. (1992). Social support networks of adults with mental retardation who live at home. *American Journal on Mental Retardation*, 96, (4), 432-441.

Kurzman, P.A. and S.H. Akabas. (1993). *Work and well-being*. Washington, DC: National Association of Social Workers. (A great source of information about disability in the workplace, employee assistance.)

Magana, S.M. (1999). Puerto Rican families caring for an adult with mental retardation: Role of familism. *American Journal on Mental Retardation*, 104, (5), 466-482.

Pitman, J.A. (1994, Summer). Students' familiarity with and attitudes toward the rights of students who are disabled. *Journal of Applied Rehabilitation Counseling*, 25, (2), 38-40.

Satcher, J.F. and K. Dooley-Dickey. (1991, July-Aug.-Sept.). Helping college bound clients with learning disabilities. *Journal of Rehabilitation*, 57, 47-50.

Smith, J.O. (1992, March-April). Falling through the cracks: Rehabilitation services for adults with learning disabilities. *Exceptional Children*, 24, 451-461.

Soyer, D. (1963, July). The right to fail. *Social Casework*, 44, 72-78.

Thurer, S. and E.S. Rogers. (1984). The mental health needs of physically disabled persons: Their perspective. *Rehabilitation Psychology*, 29, (4), 239-249.

West, M., J. Kregel, F. Getzel, M. Zhu, S.M. Ipsen, and E.D. Martin. (1993, March-April). Beyond Section 504: Satisfaction and empowerment of students with disabilities in higher education. *Exceptional Children*, 59, (5), 456-467.

SESSION 9. AGING: RETIREMENT AND BEYOND

Learning objectives:

- To discuss the needs of a growing group of elders with disabilities who have been able to live longer due to improvements in living conditions and new medical technologies.
- To describe the life cycle issues facing people at the retirement stage, elderly persons with disabilities, and long-term care.
- To examine the needs of caregivers of people with disabilities.

Suggested Classroom Exercises

1. Have students discuss the Essex, Seltzer, and Krauss (1999) article. What are the independent and dependent variables in the study? Who are the participants? What are the findings? What is the generalizability of the findings? What are the implications for social work practice, policy, and research?

2. Discuss "physician-assisted suicide." Should it be allowed in certain cases for people with disabilities? When and why? Or why not?

Required Reading for Classroom Exercise

Essex, E.L., M.M. Seltzer, and M.W. Krauss. (1999). Differences in coping effectiveness and well-being among aging mothers and fathers of adults with mental retardation. *American Journal on Mental Retardation*, 104, (6), 545-563.

McMahon and Shaw (2000). Appendix C: Assisted suicide: A disability perspective (by R.L. Burgdorf).

Required Reading for Class Discussion

Gibson, J.W., J. Rabkin, and R. Munson. (1992). Critical issues in serving the developmentally disabled elderly. *Journal of Gerontological Social Work*, 19, (1), 35-49.

Olkin (1999). Chapter 10: Aging and long-term care, "physician-assisted suicide," and "right to die."

Perkins, K. and C. Tice. (1995). A strengths perspective in practice: Older people and mental health challenges. *Journal of Gerontological Social Work*, 23, (3/4), 83-97.

Selzer, M. and G. Seltzer. (1985). The elderly mentally retarded: A group in need of service. *Journal of Gerontological Social Work*, 8, (3 & 4), 99-119.

Sullivan, W. and Fisher, B. (1994). Intervening for success: Strengths based case management and successful aging. *Journal of Gerontological Social Work*, 22, (1/2), 61-74.

Recommended Reading

Fast, B. and R. Chapin. (1996, Summer). The strengths model in long-term care: Linking cost containment and consumer empowerment. *Journal of Case Management*, 5, (2), 51-57.

Heller, T. and A. Factor. (1993). Aging family caregivers: Support resources and changes in burden and placement desire. *American Journal on Mental Retardation*, 98, (3), 417-426.

Lifshitz, H. (2001, March). Aging phenomena among people with mental retardation in community residence in Israel. *Education and Training in Mental Retardation and Developmental Disabilities*, 36, (1), 30-41.

McCarthy, M.G. and L.M. Stough. (1999). The qualifying game: A search for services by individuals with disabilities. *Education and Training in Mental Retardation and Developmental Disabilities*, 34, (4), 485-498.

National Family Caregivers Association. (1996). *The resourceful caregiver: Helping family caregivers help themselves.* St. Louis, MO: Mosby-Year Book. (An excellent collection of national resource organizations for many disabilities.)

Parry, R.J. (1993). Acute psychiatric hospital admissions of adults and elderly adults with mental retardation. *American Journal on Mental Retardation*, 98, (3), 434-436.

Schreiber, M. (1990, Spring). Aged parents of disabled and dependent adults. *The Jewish Social Work Forum*, 26, 38-43

Valentine, D., and S. McDermott. (1998, Nov.-Dec.). Mothers of adults with mental retardation: Is race a factor in perceptions of burdens and gratifications? *Families in Society*, 79, 577-584.

SESSION 10. SUMMARY OF COURSE AND CAREERS IN WORKING WITH PEOPLE WITH DISABILITIES

Learning Objective 1:

- To discuss the changes that have happened since the Americans with Disabilities Act of 1990.
- To discuss the future roles of social workers and people with disabilities.
- To discuss implications for future social work practice, research, and policy.

Suggested Classroom Exercise

1. Discuss the findings of Abakas and Gates' (2000) study. Let's review the ADA. It's 10 years since the ADA; according to this study, is it working or not? Why? What else can be done? Do the findings apply to other disability groups? What are the roles for social work in employment of people with disabilities? What are the implications for future social work practice, research, and policy?

Suggested Reading For Classroom Exercise

Abakas, S.H. and L.B. Gates. (2000). A social work role: Promoting equity for people with serious and persistent mental illness. *Administration in Social Work,* 23, pp. 163-184. Special section on Broadening the Occupational Social Work Domain.

Learning Objective 2:

- To identify the diversity of social work opportunities for MSW graduates who are interested in working with people with disabilities.

Required Reading

Ash, A. and N.R. Murdick. (1995). Disability. *Encyclopedia of Social Work, (19th ed.).* (pp. 752-761). Washington, DC: National Association of Social Workers.

Kobe, F.H. and D. Hammer. (1993). Who is interested in careers in mental retardation and developmental disabilities? *Mental Retardation,* 31, (5), 316-319.

Recommended Reading

Bogo, M., J.H. Mischalski, D. Raphael, and R. Roberts. (1995, Spring/Summer). Practice interests and self-identification among social work students: Changes over the course of graduate education. *Journal of Social Work Education,* 31, (2), 228-246.

Bogo, M. and R. Roberts. (1993, Fall). Interests, activities, and self-identification among social work students: Towards a definition of social work identity. *Journal of Social Work Education,* 29, (3), 279-192.

Butler, A.C. (1990, Winter). A re-evaluation of social work students' career interests. *Journal of Social Work Education,* 26 (1), 45-56.

Dane, B.O. and B.L. Simon. (1991, May). Resident guests: Social workers in host settings. *Social Work,* 36, (3), 208-213.

DeWeaver, K.L. (1982, Spring). Producing social workers trained for practice with the developmentally disabled. *Arete: Journal of the College of Social Work of the University of South Carolina,* 7, (1), 59-62.

Ell, K. (1985). The role of social work in rehabilitating people with disabilities. *Annual Review of Rehabilitation,* 4, 145-179.

Gibelman, M. (1995). *What social workers do.* Washington, DC: National Association of Social Workers. (See section on developmental disabilities, pp. 293-296.)

Grobman, L.M. (Ed.). (1999). *Days in the lives of Social Workers: 50 professionals tell "real-life" stories from social work practice, (2nd ed.).* Harrisburg, PA: White Hat Communications. (See section on disabilities, pp. 123-136.)

Iverson, R.R. (1998, Nov.). Occupational social work for the 21st century. *Social Work,* 43, (6), 551-566.

Miller and Sammons (1999). Chapter 12: Expanding our vision (of people with disabilities).

Rubin, A., P.J. Johnson, and K.L. DeWeaver. (1986, Spring/Summer). Direct practice interests of MSW students: Changes from entry to graduation. *Journal of Social Work Education,* 22, (2), 98-108.

Rubin, A. and P.J. Johnson. (1984, Spring). Direct practice interests of entering MSW students. *Journal of Social Work Education,* 20, (2), 5-16.

Developmental Disabilities: Supports and Services

SW 420 (Spring 2001)

INTRODUCTION

Social workers operate within the ethical guidelines prescribed by the National Association of Social Workers Code of Ethics and utilize the problem-solving model to intervene with all levels of client systems (individuals, families, groups, organizations, communities, and institutions). Social work practice is grounded in a systems and person-in-environment framework with the goal of identifying multiple potential points for intervention, thereby helping solve difficulties within the functioning of client systems as well as enhancing and strengthening the inherent capacities of a wide range of diverse client systems.

This course presents knowledge, explores values, and addresses issues important for successful social work practice with individuals with developmental disabilities, their families, and their communities. Social workers increasingly are entering the disabilities field in a variety of positions. Social workers are integral members of a team of professionals working in the disabilities field. In addition, social workers in other practice settings are frequently serving individuals with disabilities in areas such as child welfare, corrections, health and mental health, adoptions, and aging. Knowledge about the special needs and strengths of people with developmental disabilities, their families, and intervention strategies that enhance social functioning in the community enable social workers to better perform their jobs.

DESCRIPTION

This course is an overview of developmental disabilities from social work's person-in-environment perspective. In contrast to the moral or medical model, a minority model of disability is emphasized.

STUDENT LEARNING OBJECTIVES

Students will demonstrate knowledge about

- Developmental disabilities and laws pertaining to people with disabilities;
- The effect of labeling and the role of social work practice in the disabilities field;
- The special needs and strengths of persons with developmental disabilities, especially as they relate to family and community life and social work intervention strategies to meet these needs;
- Forms and mechanisms of oppression and discrimination against people with developmental disabilities;
- Service systems, current policies, structures, and programs serving people with developmental disabilities and their families;
- The special needs and strengths of the family system with an emphasis on parents, siblings, and grandparents of people with developmental disabilities; and
- The social services, agencies, and community resources available to persons with developmental disabilities and their families.

Students will have skills to

- Enhance the problem solving, coping, and developmental capacities of individuals with developmental disabilities and their families;
- Link individuals with disabilities and their families with resources, services, and opportunities;

- Advance social and economic justice by improving the effective and humane operation of the systems that provide services, resources, and opportunities to individuals with disabilities and their families;

- Advocate with and on behalf of individuals with disabilities and their families; to encourage the development of systems that are equitable, just, and responsive to consumers of service; and to work with others to eliminate those systems that are unjust; and

- Participate actively with professionals across disciplines, as well as individuals with developmental disabilities and their families, increasing new, modified, or improved services and resources.

Students will also

- Adhere to social work values, such as self-determination and confidentiality, that are embodied in the NASW Code of Ethics, and address ethical issues regarding all clients but especially as these values apply to people with developmental disabilities, colleagues, employers, the profession, and society;

- Value the need to address social and economic inequities as they pertain to people with developmental disabilities; and

- Value diversity, such as race, ethnicity, culture, class, gender, sexual orientation, religion, physical or mental ability, age, and national origin as it coexists with people with developmental disabilities.

POLICIES

Academic Dishonesty

University Regulation 802, revision 2 (1992) prohibits any form of academic dishonesty. An act is academically dishonest when it is an act attempted or performed which misrepresents one's involvement in an academic task in any way, or permits another student to misrepresent the latter's involvement in an academic task by assisting in the misrepresentation. (See entire text of UniReg 802 in Appendix of *Student Handbook*.)

Nondiscrimination Statement

The department's educational programs, activities, and services offered to students are administered on a nondiscriminatory basis subject to the provisions of all civil rights laws and statutes. It is the policy of the Social Work Department to accommodate students with disabilities, pursuant to federal and state law. Any student who needs accommodation because of a disability should inform the instructor at the beginning of the course. Students with disabilities are also encouraged to contact Student Education Opportunity Services.

Attendance

Attendance at each class is expected of all students. Any student absent from 25% or more of class sessions is subject to failing the course.

Preparation for each class (i.e., reading scheduled chapters and articles or completing homework assignments) is necessary for optimal learning and relevant participation.

REQUIRED TEXTS

Hughes, R. C., & Rycus, J. S. (1998). *Developmental disabilities and child welfare.* Washington DC: CWLA Press.

Olkin, R. (1999). *What psychotherapists should know about disability.* New York: Guilford.

Nagler, M. (1993). *Perspective on disabilities.* Palo Alto, CA: Health Markets Research.

A bibliography of recommended readings will be distributed as a separate handout in class. This list will be updated throughout the course as necessary.

ASSIGNMENTS

1. Site Visit *or* Interview (25%)
2. Annotated Bibliography (25%)
3. Paper *or* Book Critique (25%)
4. Final Examination (25%)

CONTENT OUTLINE

Unit One	Introductions, grading, and expectations
	Definitions and context of developmental disabilities
	Language and labeling
Unit Two	Discrimination and oppression of people with developmental disabilities
Unit Three	Ethics and values as applied to the developmental disabilities field
Unit Four	Specific developmental disabilities
Unit Five	Context of developmental disabilities: Historical, legal, political, and cultural
Unit Six	Assessment and intervention: Individuals with a developmental disability
Unit Seven	Assessment and intervention: The family
Unit Eight	Assessment and intervention: Organizations
Unit Nine	Assessment and intervention: Communities
Unit Ten	Professional issues

READINGS

Unit One

Hughes & Rycus (1998). Understanding developmental disabilities and myths and misconceptions about developmental disabilities. pp. 1-28.

In Olkin (1999):

Introduction and overview. pp. 1-8.

Chapter 1: Who Are People with Disabilities? pp. 9-32

In Nagler (1993):

Zola, I. K. Self, identity and the naming question: Reflections on the language of disability. pp. 15-23.

Blaska, J. The power of language: Speak and write using "person first." pp. 25-32.

Pointdexter, C., Valentine, D., & Conway, P. (1999). Chapter 15: Developmental disabilities. In *Essential Skills for Human Services*. Belmont, CA: Wadsworth. pp. 259-290.

Unit Two

In Olkin (1999):

Chapter 2: The minority model of disability. pp. 24-53.

Chapter 3: The disability experience: Stereotypes and attitudes. pp. 54-75.

Chapter 4: The disability experience: Affect and everyday experiences. pp 76-89.

Schwartz, D. B. (1992). What really keeps people with disabilities safe in society? In *Crossing the River: Creating a Conceptual Revolution in Community and Disability*. Cambridge, MA: Brookline Books. pp.149-184.

In Nagler (1993):

>   Nagler, M. The disabled: The acquisition of power. pp. 33-36.

>   Hahn, H. The politics of physical differences: Disability and discrimination. pp. 37-42.

>   Hanna, W. J., & Rogovsky, B. Women with disabilities: Two handicaps plus. pp. 109-120.

Unit Three

In Nagler (1993):

>   Baker, D. Human rights for persons with disabilities. pp. 483-494.

>   Kaeser, F. Can people with severe mental retardation consent to mutual sex? pp. 247-253.

>   Held, K. R. Ethical assets of sexuality of persons with mental retardation. pp. 255-259.

Unit Four

In Hughes & Rycus (1998):

>   Mental retardation, pp. 51-68:

>   - *Genetics*: Down Syndrome, Fragile X, Neurofibromatosis, Rett Syndrome, Turner Syndrome, Klinefelder Syndrome
>   - *Trauma during pregnancy*: Violence during pregnancy, birth trauma
>   - *Congenital infection*: Influenza, rubella, syphilis, toxoplasmosism, AIDS
>   - *Nutrition and malnutrition during pregnancy*: Poverty, eating disorders, spina bifida, iodine deficiency
>   - *Childhood infections:* Meningitis, encephalitis, measles
>   - *Childhood trauma*: Child abuse and neglect, environmental factors (lead-based paint, environmental toxins)
>   - *Unknown causes*: Prader-Willi Syndrome

>   Cerebral palsy, pp. 29-40.

>   Epilepsy, pp. 41-50.

>   Spina bifida, pp. 69-74.

>   Autism and other pervasive developmental disorders, pp. 75-84.

>   Attention deficit hyperactivity disorder (ADHD) and learning disabilities, pp. 85-90.

>   Prenatal exposure to alcohol and other drugs, pp. 91-98.

Unit Five

In Olkin (1999):

>   Chapter 6: Laws and social history. pp. 137-153.

In Nagler (1993):

>   Gent, P. J., & Mulhauser, M. B. Public integration of students with handicaps: Where it's been, where it's going, and how it's getting there. pp. 397-409.

>   Hamre-Nietupski, S., Nietupski, J., & Maurer, S. A comprehensive state education agency plan to promote the integration of students with moderate/severe handicaps. pp. 411-421.

>   Schnorr, R.F. "Peter? He comes and goes…": First graders' perspective on a part-time mainstream student. pp. 423-435.

Unit Six

In Hughes & Rycus (1998):

Services for children with developmental disabilities and their families. pp. 99-128.

In Olkin (1999):

Chapter 7: Beginning treatment. pp. 154-189.

Chapter 8: Etiquette with clients with disabilities. pp. 190-200.

Chapter 9: Interviews, assessment, evaluation, and diagnosis. pp. 201-222.

Chapter 10: Dating, romance, sexuality, pregnancy, birthing, and genetic testing. pp. 223-240.

Chapter 11: Special issues in therapy with clients with disabilities. pp. 241-271.

Pfadt, A. (1991). Group psychotherapy with mentally retarded adults: Issues related to design, implementation, and evaluation. *Research in Developmental Disabilities, 12,* 261-285.

In Nagler (1993):

O'Toole, C. J., & Bregante, J. L. Disabled lesbians: Multi-cultural realities. pp. 261-271.

Tharinger, D., Horton, C. B., & Millea, S. Sexual abuse and exploitation of children and adults with mental retardation and other handicaps. pp. 235-245

Sobsey, D., & Mansell, S. The prevention of sexual abuse of people with developmental disabilities. pp. 283-292.

Wilkins, S., & Cott, C. Aging, chronic illness and disability. pp. 363-377.

Unit Seven

Valentine, D. P. (1993). Children with special needs: Sources of support and stress for families. In R. Mackelprang & D. Valentine (Eds.), *Sexuality and disabilities: A guide for human services practitioners* (pp. 107-129). Binghamton, NY: Haworth.

In Olkin (1999):

Chapter 5: Families with disabilities. pp. 90-136.

In Nagler (1993):

Traustadottir, R. Mothers who care: Gender, disability and family life. pp. 173-183.

Ziolko, M. E. Counseling parents of children with disabilities: A review of the literature and implications for practice. pp. 185-193.

Phillips, R. S. (1999). Intervention with siblings of children with developmental disabilities from economically disadvantaged families. *Families in Society, 80*(6), 569-577.

Seligman, M., Goodwin, G., Paschal, K., Applegate, A., & Lehman, L. (1997). Grandparents of children with disabilities: Perceived levels of support. *Education and Training in Mental Retardation and Developmental Disabilities, 32*(4), 293-303.

Valentine, D. (1990). Double jeopardy: Child maltreatment and mental retardation. *Child and Adolescent Social Work Journal, 7*(6), 487-500.

Unit Eight

In Olkin (1999):

Chapter 12: Assistive technology and devices. pp. 272-294.

In Nagler (1993):

Bryant, M. D. Religion and disability: Some notes on religious attitudes and views. pp. 91-95.

Hamre-Nietupski, S., Krajewski, L., Nietupski, J., Ostercamp, D., Sensor, K., & Opheim, B. Parent/professional partnerships in advocacy: Developing integrated options within resistive systems. pp. 437-448.

Unit Nine:

Sullivan, P. M., & Knutson, J. F. (2000). Maltreatment and disabilities: A population-based epidemiological study. *Child Abuse and Neglect, 24*(10), 1257-1273.

Fletcher, R. J., & Poindexter, A. R. (1996). Current trends in mental health care for persons with mental retardation. *Journal of Rehabilitation, 193*(1), 23-25.

Nahom, D., Richardson, M. L., Romer, L., & Porter, A. (2000). Family support and community guiding. *Families in Society, 81*(6), 629-633.

Unit Ten

Stoneman, Z., & Malone, D. M. (1995). The changing nature of interdisciplinary practice. In B. A. Thyer & N. P. Kropf (Eds.), *Developmental disabilities: A handbook for interdisciplinary practice.* Cambridge, MA: Brookline Books. pp. 234-247.

In Olkin (1999):

Chapter 13: The personal, the professional, and the political. pp. 294.

Chapter 14: Research on disability: Shifting the paradigm from pathology to policy. pp. 308-321.

ASSIGNMENTS

Site Visit Assignment

Guidelines

1. Locate an agency or institution that provides services to people with developmental disabilities or their families. Make an appointment with the director of the organization or a staff member to interview him or her and to visit the facility. After your interview and visit, write a thank you note to the person you interviewed.

2. Write a paper that answers the following questions:

   a. Identify in the first paragraph the name of the organization and the name and title of the person you interviewed. State the date and time of your visit.

   b. What is the mission and philosophy of the organization?

   c. Who is the client population served?

   d. What are the eligibility requirements to receive services?

   e. Identify where the organization received its sanction. How is funding obtained?

   f. Is there a Board of Directors? Parent Advisory Board? What is the composition of these boards? Are people with developmental disabilities represented on policy-making boards and committees?

   g. What major social services does the organization provide?

h. Does the organization hire social workers? What activities do the social workers perform? If the organization does not hire social workers, would they benefit from social work services?

i. In your opinion, what are the strengths and limitations of this organization?

j. What did you learn from making this site visit and conducting this interview?

k. Attach the thank you note that you sent to the interviewee.

Interview Assignment

Guidelines

1. Select an individual with a developmental disability or a family member of a person with a developmental disability (Mother, father, sibling, grandparent, aunt, uncle, cousin). Invite this person to participate in an interview that is designed to help you better understand developmental disabilities and the family. Inform the interviewee that participation is completely voluntary and that they can stop the interview at any time. Let the person know that there will be no penalty or consequences if he or she does not want to talk to you. Assure the interviewee that you will maintain confidentiality. Let the interviewee know that you will be writing a paper about the interview for your professor, but that you will change the names and any identifying characteristics. (Sometimes people like to select an alias.) Make sure you get verbal consent to conduct the interview.

2. Based on the individual that you are interviewing, develop an "interview protocol." An interview protocol is usually a list of open-ended questions that will help you better understand an individual or a group of individuals. You will probably want to start by asking some basic demographic questions: name, age, education, living arrangements, diagnosis, family composition, etc. Afterward, you will probably want to ask about 5-7 open-ended questions. Examples include: "Would you tell me what school was like for you when you were growing up?" (for an adult with developmental disabilities); "Would you tell me what it was like when you first heard that your son/daughter had a developmental disability? (for a parent); "I wonder how you think your life is different from other people because you have a brother/sister with a developmental disability? (sibling); "Do you ever worry about the future? In what ways?"

   Use your class readings to help you formulate your questions. Type the questions up and let the instructor approve them before you proceed with your interview.

3. Conduct your interview. Review with the interviewee the fact the participation is voluntary and confidential.

4. Write a summary of the interview. The paper should contain the following elements.

   a. A paragraph description (disguised, of course) of the demographic characteristics of the interviewee.

   b. A copy of the interview protocol.

   c. A narrative describing the content of the interviews. What did the interviewee say to answer the questions?

   d. Provide a personal reaction to the interview. What did you learn? What strengths did you identify in the interviewee? What is your personal reaction to hearing about the interviewee's life?

5. Attach a copy of a thank you note that you sent to the interviewee. Blank out the true name and address.

Annotations Assignment

Directions and Example

Select a specific developmental disability. The instructor will approve your topic. After you select and get your paper topic approved, I would like you to locate at least eight journal articles published in the past ten years that pertain to your topic. The student should write the annotation her/himself. (Do not copy the abstract at the beginning of the article.) I would like the annotation to include two paragraphs. The first paragraph should summarize the content of the article in your own words. The second paragraph should be a critique of the article. The critique should include your thoughts and opinions about the strengths of the article, the weaknesses, the usefulness of the article for working with the topic you selected, etc. The journal article should not be ones that are required reading for this course or any other social work course.

Please attach your actual journal articles to your packet of annotations. The journal articles and annotations will be returned to you.

Be sure the citation is in APA (American Psychological Association) reference style. Some examples follow.

Topic: Williams Syndrome

Finn, R. (1991). Different minds: People with Williams Syndrome. *Discover, 12*(6). 55-58.

This article describes the mysterious and rare genetic disorder called Williams Syndrome. The author describes people with Williams Syndrome as having distinct physical characteristics including an "elfin-face," a narrowing of the aorta, and high blood pressure. People with Williams Syndrome typically have limited spatial skills and motor control. Most have very limited ability to perform arithmetic. Although the onset of language is delayed in most children with Williams Syndrome, once language begins, it develops faster than in a typical child. The author states that the child with Williams Syndrome "tests like a retarded child, talks like a gifted child, behaves like a disturbed child, and functions like a learning-disabled child" (p. 58). The article concludes with suggestions to families and communities for meeting the needs of adults with Williams Syndrome.

This article effectively uses a case illustration to describe Williams Syndrome. Pictures drawn by people with Williams Syndrome are included to illustrate the difficulty these children have with spatial skills. I appreciate the way the author considers the strengths as well as the limitations of people with Williams Syndrome. The author does not use person-first language, however. Overall, this was an excellent article to begin my research on Williams Syndrome.

Topic: Autism

Cesaroni, L., & Garber, M. (1991). Exploring the experience of autism through firsthand accounts. *Journal of Autism and Developmental Disorders, 21*(3), 303-312.

This article describes the first-person accounts of a 27 year-old man and a 13 year-old boy with autism. The authors briefly provided background information about the participants and reported the results of in-depth interviews. The authors emphasized the following themes: sensory processing; memory; stereotypical behavior; and social interaction and empathy. The article contains numerous quotations from the interviewees. For example, with regard to stereotypical behaviors, the 13 year-old stated "It feels funny to be autistic. Like riding a truck around really fast, riding through a whole house fast, excited. I smell something really strange I get excited from it. I smell something really strange I ride my truck really fast and spin around" (p. 308).

The authors provide a fascinating opportunity to hear how two people with autism think about their disability and their lives. Based on the insight that was gained from these interviews, I think that more qualitative research should be conducted. I am disappointed that females with autism were not interviewed. I wonder if the experiences of girls and women with autism are different than the male views.

Book Analysis

Guidlelines

1. Select one of the following two books listed.

    Lefkowitz, B. (1997). *Our Guys.* New York: Vintage Books.

    Fadiman, A. (1997). *The Spirit Catches You and You Fall Down.* New York: Farrar, Straus and Giroux.

2. After reading the book, write a 7-10 page book analysis. The book analysis should include the following components.

   a. A complete citation in American Psychological Association referencing style. Include a statement about the author of the book that includes the professional affiliation, state of residence, and any other pertinent information. Comment on the year that the book was published and discuss its historical context.

   b. Summarize the book in no more than three pages.

   c. Write a critique of the book and analyze its content using the concepts you learned from your reading and class discussions. A critique is a critical review that examines the strengths and limitations of a subject. An analysis requires that you combine and apply ideas in new ways. Some examples of criteria from which to critique and analyze the book follow. Feel free to select your own criteria.

      • How does the book portray people with disabilities?

      • How does the book portray family interaction?

      • How does the book portray communities in which people with disabilities and their families live?

      • Are the characters with developmental disabilities in the book portrayed in a multidimensional way or are they stereotyped?

      • Discuss how developmental disabilities are understood from a multi-system level perspective?

      • What are the overall messages of the book with regard to attitudes, respect, inclusion, etc.?

      • What does the book teach the reader about developmental disabilities?

      • Describe ways that the book presents disabilities from the perspective of the moral model, medical model, and minority model.

      • Discuss ways the book illustrates the effects of gender, race or ethnicity, and social class on people with disabilities and their families.

      • Using the NASW Code of Ethics as a framework for analysis, how are ethics and values reflected in the book?

   d. Write a personal reaction to the book. This discussion should include how the information you acquired from the book will inform your social work practice.

Paper Assignment

Guidelines

The student will write a 7-10 page paper based on the topic selected and approved by the instructor for the annotated bibliography assignment. This paper should be written in a manner that is consistent with the American Psychological Association referencing style.

The paper should include the following subheadings.

a. A description of the nature, etiology, and characteristics of the disability selected;

b. A discussion of the special needs that people with the selected developmental disability might have;

c. A discussion of the impact of the disability on family members;

d. A description of the social services and intervention strategies recommended to meet the special needs of people with the selected disability (these services might be ones that already exist or might be suggestions that you propose);

e. A personal reaction to your investigation of this topic. This section should include a discussion on how the information you acquired writing this paper will inform your social work practice.

Introduction to Developmental Disabilities
SW f311K (Fall 2001)

INTRODUCTION

The Introduction to Developmental Disabilities course is designed to enhance the student's understanding of the unique issues impacting the lives of individuals with developmental disabilities and their families. The course content is derived from the philosophy of humanization, an ideology based on the principles of individual worth and uniqueness and the concomitant rights of individuals with developmental disabilities.

As a journey throughout the life cycle, the course begins with an exploration of the continuum of national and international definitions and classifications of developmental disabilities. The course continues with an overview of various historical perspectives, an examination of disability paradigms from which to explore the definition of disability, and a study of disability as a culture. The impact of the media, societal attitudes and barriers, oppression, discrimination, stigmatization, and abuse are introduced. An in-depth examination of life span issues ranging from early childhood intervention to aging and disability are reviewed and analyzed from social, cultural, political, and economic discourses. Life cycle issues including school, transition, employment, sexuality, impact on parents and siblings, and healthcare are presented. A strong emphasis on culturally relevant and responsive practice is infused within the course curriculum, in addition to a class period dedicated to disability and diversity. An overview of human rights issues and controversial topics allows for discussion and debate on ethical dilemmas, quality of life issues, genetics, parenthood, and consent. The course concludes by focusing on a range of topics including law and disability, self-advocacy, case management, clinical interventions, self-injurious behavior, dual diagnosis, Social Security, Medicaid, and future legislation.

DESCRIPTION

This is an introductory social work course in which students are provided with a broad base of knowledge and a professional awareness concerning individuals with developmental disabilities and their families. The course places disability in a political, social, cultural, and economic context to increase awareness and understanding of the needs of and societal barriers for individuals with developmental disabilities throughout their life cycle.

OBJECTIVES

By the end of the course, students will be able to demonstrate knowledge of the following:

1. historical and social perspectives of societal treatment of individuals with developmental disabilities
2. the range of developmental disabilities, their causes, prevalence, and associated behaviors
3. oppression, social injustice, stigmitization, discrimination, and abuse of people with developmental disabilities
4. the structure and organization of the MR/DD service delivery system
5. supports and services for individuals with developmental disabilities and their families
6. social work case management and clinical approaches to enhancing the lives of individuals with developmental disabilities

7. culturally relevant and responsive practice with diverse families who have one or more members with a developmental disability

8. human rights concerns and controversial issues facing the disability community

9. communication strategies and terminology for effective interaction with individuals with developmental disabilities

10. the challenges affecting persons with developmental disabilities and their families across the life span

11. legal issues and legislation impacting the lives of individuals with developmental disabilities

TEACHING METHODS

This course will integrate a variety of teaching methods, including lecture, group discussion, audio-visual materials, experiential exercises, collaborative learning, and guest speakers. Numerous case examples will be used to provide opportunities for critical analyses of service delivery and life span issues for people with developmental disabilities.

REQUIRED TEXT

McLaughlin, P., & Wehman, P. (Eds.). (1996). *Mental retardation and developmental disabilities* (2 ed.). Austin, TX: Pro-ed.

ADDITIONAL REQUIRED READINGS

Alford, J., Aruffo, J. F., Thompson, R. G., & Dobbins, W. N. (1994). HIV and psychiatric clients with a developmental disability. *Psychosocial Rehabilitation Journal, 17* (4), 41-49.

Ball, M. S. (1999). *Kiss of God: The wisdom of a silent child.* Deerfield Beach, FL: Health Communications Inc.

Ballan, M. S. (2001, February/March). Parents as sexuality educators for their children with developmental disabilities. *SIECUS Report, 29* (3), 14-19.

Ballan, M. S., Onken, S., Batchelder, M., Manaster, J., & McRoy, R. (1998). *Persons with disabilities: Cultural diversity curriculum for social workers and health practitioners.* Austin, TX: Texas Department of Health.

Blacher, J. (2001). Transition to adulthood: Mental retardation, families and culture. *American Journal of Mental Retardation, 106* (2), 173-188.

Bogdan, R., & Biklen, D. (1993). Handicapism. In M. Nagler (Ed.), *Perspectives on disability* (2 ed., pp. 69-76). Palo Alto, CA: Health Markets Research.

Bradley, V. J., Ashbaugh, J. W., & Blaney, B. C. (1994). *Creating individual supports for people with developmental disabilities: A mandate for change at many levels.* Baltimore, MD: Paul H. Brookes Publishing.

Covey, H. C. (1998). People with developmental disabilities. *Social perceptions of people with disabilities in history.* Springfield, IL: Charles C. Thomas Publisher.

Davis, L. (1997). Constructing normalcy: The bell curve, the novel and the invention of the disabled body in the nineteenth century. In L. J. Davis (Ed.), *The disability studies reader* (pp. 9-28). New York: Routledge.

Edgerton, R. B. (1994). Quality of life issues: Some people know how to be old. In M. M. Seltzer, M.W. Krauss, & M. P. Janicki (Eds.), *Life course perspectives on adults and aging* (pp. 149-160). Washington, DC: American Association on Mental Retardation.

Everson, J. & Reid, D. (1997, September). Using person-centered planning to determine vocational preferences. *Supported Employment Infolines, 10,* 4-5.

Foelker, G. A., Jr. & Luke, E. A., Jr. (1989). Mental health issues for the aging mentally retarded population. *The Journal of Applied Gerontology, 8* (2), 242-250.

Harris, A. (1997, September). Gay man with disabilities troubled by life's barriers. *TASH Newsletter,* 17-18.

Heal, L. W., Borthwick-Duffy, S. A., & Saunders, R. R. (1996). Assessment of quality of life. In J. W. Jacobson & J. A. Mulick (Eds.), *Manual of diagnosis and professional practice in mental retardation* (pp. 199-209). Washington, DC: American Psychological Association.

Held, K. R. (1992). Ethical aspects of sexuality of persons with mental retardation. *Sexuality and Disability, 10* (4), 237-243.

Hollander, R. (1989). Euthanasia and mental retardation: Suggesting the unthinkable. *Mental Retardation, 27* (2), 53-61.

Housewright, E. (1999, June 10). Into the mainstream. *The Dallas Morning News,* pp. A1, A17.

Howell, M. C. (1989). Working with people who are old and mentally retarded. In M. C. Howell & G. B. Seltzer (Eds.), *Serving the underserved: Caring for both people who are old and mentally retarded* (pp. 11-17). New York: Exceptional Parent Press.

Hubbard, R. (1997). Abortion and disability: Who should and should not inhabit the world. In L. J. Davis (Ed.), *The disability studies reader* (pp. 187-200). New York: Routledge.

Hunsberger, M. B. (1997, Winter). Having children. *Families, 7,* 32-40.

Hurley, A. D., Pfadt, A., Tomasulo, D., & Gardner, W. I. (1996). Counseling and psychotherapy. In J. W. Jacobson & J. A. Mulick (Eds.), *Manual of diagnosis and professional practice in mental retardation* (pp. 371-378). Washington, DC: American Psychological Association.

Kempton, W., & Gochros, J. S. (1986). The developmentally disabled. In H. L. Gochros, J. S. Gochros, & J. Fischer (Eds.), *Helping the sexually oppressed* (pp. 224-237). Englewood Cliffs, NJ: Prentice-Hall.

Livneh, H. (1991). On the origins of negative attitudes toward people with disabilities. In R. P. Marinelli & E. Dell Orto (Eds.), *The psychological and social impact of disability* (3 ed., pp. 181-196). New York: Springer Publishing.

Mackelprang, R., & Salsgiver, R. (1998). *Disability: A diversity model approach in human services.* Pacific Grove, CA: Brookes/Cole Publishing.

McGee, J. J., & Menolascino, F. J. (1992). The evaluation of defendants with mental retardation in the criminal justice system. In W. W. Conley, R. Luckasson, & G. N. Bouthilet (Eds.), *The criminal justice system and mental retardation* (pp. 55-77). Baltimore, MD: Paul Brookes Publishing.

Orlin, M. (1995). The Americans with Disabilities Act: Implications for social services. *Social Work, 40* (2), 233-239.

Pelka, F. (1997). *The disability rights movement.* Santa Barbara, CA: ABC-CLIO Inc.

Perske, R. (2001). A joint statement: Stop the execution of persons with mental retardation. *Mental Retardation, 39* (4), 327-328.

Pfeiffer, D. (1994). Eugenics and disability discrimination. *Disability and Society, 9* (4), 481-499.

Ramey, C. T., Mulvihill, B. A., & Ramey, S. L. (1996). Prevention: Social and educational factors and early intervention. In J. W. Jacobson & J. A. Mulick (Eds.), *Manual of diagnosis and professional practice in mental retardation* (pp. 215-227). Washington, DC: American Psychological Association.

Rittelmeyer, H. (2000, April). My special sister. *Parents*, 83-88.

Rock, P. (1996). Eugenics and euthanasia: A cause for concern for disabled people, particularly disabled women. *Disability and Society, 11* (1), 121-127.

Ronai, C. R. (1997). On loving and hating my mentally retarded mother. *Mental Retardation, 35* (6), 217-232.

Rounds, K. A., Weil, M., & Bishop, K. K. (1994). Practice with culturally diverse families of young children with disabilities. *Families in Society: The Journal of Contemporary Human Services, 75* (1), 3-15.

Schilling, R. F., Kirkham, M. A., & Schinke, S. P. (1986). Do child protection services neglect developmentally disabled children? *Mental Retardation, 21* (1), 21-26.

Schnorr, R. F. (1993). Peter? He comes and goes: First graders perspective on a part-time mainstream student. In M. Nagler (Ed.), *Perspectives on disability* (2 ed., pp. 423-435). Palo Alto, CA: Health Markets Research.

Searight, H. R., & Noce, J. J. (1991). The psychiatrically disturbed developmentally disabled adult: A behaviorally-oriented inpatient program to facilitate community integration. *Psychotherapy in Private Practice, 9* (1), 115-129.

Seligman, M., & Darling, R. B. (1989). *Ordinary families, special children: A systems approach to childhood disability*. New York: Guilford Press.

Shapiro, J. P. (1993). *No pity: People with disabilities forging a new civil rights movement*. New York: Random House.

Shapiro, J. P., Loeb, P., Bowermaster, D., Wright, A., Headden, S., & Toch, T. (1993, December 13). Separate and unequal. *U.S. News & World Report*, 46-60.

Sobsey, D., & Mansell, S. (1992, Fall). Teaching people with disabilities to be abused and exploited. *Active Treatment Solutions, 4* (3), 6-11.

Stavis, P., & Walker-Hirsch, L. (1999). Consent to sexual activity. In R. D. Dinerstein, S. S. Herr, & J. L. O'Sullivan (Eds.), *A guide to consent* (pp. 57-65). Washington, DC: American Association on Mental Retardation.

Sundram, C. J., & Stavis, P. (1994). Sexuality and mental retardation: Unmet challenges. *Mental Retardation, 32* (4), 255-264.

Wehmeyer, M., Bersani, H., Jr., & Gagne, R. (2000). Riding the third wave: Self-determination and self-advocacy in the 21st century. *Focus on Autism & Other Developmental Disabilities, 15* (2), 106-115.

Ziolko, M. E. (1993). Counseling parents of children with disabilities: A review of the literature and implications for practice. In M. Nagler (Ed.), *Perspectives on disability* (2 ed., pp. 185-193). Palo Alto, CA: Health Markets Research.

All readings will be on reserve in the LRC. I reserve the right to add or delete any readings from the course syllabus and will inform you of such changes in writing. The textbook is on reserve at the Perry-Castenada Library.

COURSE REQUIREMENTS

Students will be evaluated on the following written and oral assignments:

1. **Oral Report.** Students will select a developmental disability and provide an oral presentation to the class either individually or in conjunction with a peer. The content of the oral presentation should address the following information:

a. What is the disability? How did the disability receive its name? Who is the disability named for? When was the disability discovered?

b. Thoroughly describe the disability. How does the disability impact an individual's appearance, behavior, movement, functioning, etc.? Are there specific features affiliated with the disability? What is the range of severity for the disability? Are there different types of the disability?

c. How is the disability diagnosed? Are there specific tests to indicate the disability? Are the tests administered to the unborn fetus or once the infant is born?

d. At what point in the individual's life span is the disability most likely to occur? Who does the disability typically affect (race, ethnicity, religion, gender, etc.)?

e. What are the incidence rates and prevalence of the disability throughout the United States?

f. What causes the disability? Are there additional disabilities or diagnoses commonly associated with the disability? Are there ways to prevent the disability?

g. How is the disability managed? Are there specific services or supports needed to assist families with a child who has the disability?

h. What are the expected outcomes of the disability?

The oral presentations should be 10-12 minutes in duration and address the questions and requested information in letters a-h. Please provide additional information pertinent to your topic. Use visual aids including pictures or tables and charts. If you will be using an overhead projector or video, please provide me with advance notice so that I may schedule the audio-visual equipment. Please provide your classmates with handouts. You should prepare 20 copies of all handouts. Please provide me with a list of the references (minimum of five) used to prepare your presentation. Oral reports will be presented from September 26 through December 5.

2. **Research Paper.** Select a service or support provided to people with developmental disabilities or their families. Examples include early intervention, inclusive education, supported employment, respite care, family support, and case management. Present a critical analyses of the service by addressing each of the following:

a. Provide a complete description of the service or support model, including intended outcome, eligibility, length of time in receipt of service or support, funding situation, etc. Information can be depicted at the state or national level.

b. Who uses this support? Describe demographics including race, ethnicity, gender, age, disability type, etc.

c. What is the value base of this service or support?

d. What are the primary goals of the service or support model?

e. What is the role of the social worker in providing or interacting with this service or support?

f. Reflect upon the strengths and weaknesses of this service or support. What could be done differently to improve its outcome?

g. Summarize the results of at least three research studies that have examined the effectiveness of this service or support for people with developmental disabilities. What criteria are used to determine effectiveness?

h. Discuss unanswered questions for service delivery and avenues for future research.

The research paper should be a minimum of 8 pages and a maximum of 10 pages, not including the references. You are required to use a minimum of 10 sources, at least 3 of which should be government documents or journal articles. Please address the questions and suggestions in letters a-h within the context of your paper. The order of information can be presented at your discretion. Please provide any additional information you find interesting or relevant to the assignment topic. The research paper is due on October 24.

3. **Field Project.** Volunteer to work with individuals with developmental disabilities for a minimum of ten hours. Variations of the volunteer experience are acceptable, including observing two different Life Skills classes, taking tours of an independent living center and a group home, etc. Present a reflective paper concentrating on your experiences and interactions with people with developmental disabilities by addressing each of the following:

    a. Describe your volunteer experience. Where did you volunteer? With whom did you interact? Why did you select this activity?

    b. How did the experience affect you? What are your reactions to this experience? What have you learned from it? What is different about this experience than you may have anticipated?

    c. How did this experience support or negate class discussions and readings? Incorporate information provided in class by the instructor and guest speakers, as well as the topics addressed by videos and readings.

    The field project should focus on the questions and suggestions in letters a-c. The paper should be a minimum of 5 pages and a maximum of 10 pages. Students who volunteer to work with individuals with developmental disabilities in excess of 20 hours during the semester (i.e., Best Buddies) will have one point added to their final grade. The field project is due November 28.

4. **Final Exam.** Students will complete a final examination addressing the course content for the entire semester, including information from lectures, readings, guest speakers, and videos. The final will consist of multiple choice and essay questions. This exam will be administered on December 10.

GRADING

1. Grades will be earned as follows:

•	Oral presentation	15%
•	Research paper	30%
•	Field project	15%
•	**Final exam**	**40%**
	Total	100%

2. Grades will be assigned as follows:

    A   90-100

    B   80-89

    C   70-79

    D   65-69

    F   0-64

CRITERIA FOR EVALUATING ASSIGNMENTS

All graded assignments will be evaluated based on evidence of careful, systematic, reasoned thought as demonstrated by (a) critical analyses of course readings, (b) understanding of lecture material, and (c) attention to guest speakers and videos. The following criteria are used in grading as appropriate to the specific assignment:

1. Is the writing style professional and technical?

2. Is the information presented comprehensive and well-ordered?

3. Are underlying assumptions clearly stated and justified?

4. Are major points clearly thought-out and adequately emphasized?

5. Are alternative explanations considered and understood?

6. Are conclusions supported by appropriate and sufficient evidence?

7. Does the work meet the criteria specified by the guidelines for the assignment?

8. Does the work reflect sensitivity to people with developmental disabilities?

9. Does the work use people-first language?

10. Is the work well-written and free from spelling, punctuation, and grammatical errors?

11. Is the APA format used, including non-sexist language and appropriately cited references?

POLICIES

A. **Attend class regularly.** Materials covered on the final exam will be taken from the lectures as well as from the readings, videos, and guest speakers. After the second class missed, students are required to submit abstracts (one page in length each) on each topic discussed during the class period in which they were absent. The abstracts should be turned in to the instructor during the class period following the class missed. Failure to complete this task will result in a three point deduction (per class missed) from the final grade (excluding the two class periods each student is permitted to miss without penalty).

B. **Complete the assigned readings.** You are expected to have read the assigned chapters and articles and to raise questions to demonstrate analytical skills. Not all readings will be reviewed in class, but the content from assigned readings will be included on the final exam.

C. **Take the final as scheduled.** You must be present for the examination on the date indicated unless special circumstances make this impossible and prior arrangements have been formalized.

D. **Turn assignments in on time.** Late assignments will have 10 points deducted from the assignment grade per class period unless prior approval has been obtained or a catastrophic event has occurred.

E. **Be honest.** Assignments or examinations which show evidence that they have not been completed directly by the student will not be accepted and may result in automatic failure for the course. Scholastic dishonesty, including cheating and plagiarism, constitutes academic misconduct and makes the student subject to possible expulsion from the university.

F. **Participate.** Social workers strive to be team players, jointly working with the people they serve, their colleagues, and other members of the community. Class participation is expected in order to facilitate a learning experience for all students.

G. **Express differences respectfully.** Social workers aim to understand, value, and respect the uniqueness, worth, and diversity of other people. Differences in values, opinions, and ideas are encouraged, yet refinement is necessary to ensure a respectful discourse with other students, guest speakers, and the instructor.

H. **Seek feedback.** Social workers try to provide and use constructive feedback to improve themselves and their services. Students are encouraged to seek feedback on initial drafts of their research and field papers and on the organization of their oral presentation.

I. **Offer feedback.** Your feedback about the course and the teaching methods used is welcomed on a one-to-one basis. The course is a joint effort between the students and the instructor.

J. **Seek assistance.** If you are experiencing difficulty with the course content, assignments, or teacher expectations, please talk to me as soon as possible during the semester.

Accommodations for students with disabilities. The instructor is committed to providing a safe and comfortable classroom for students with disabilities. Modifications will be made to instructional materials, methods, tests, or the classroom environment upon confirmation that the individual has been deemed eligible for academic adjustments by the Office for Students with Disabilities at the University of Texas at Austin. Whenever possible, and at the student's discretion, individual modifications will be kept confidential.

COURSE SCHEDULE

SESSION 1

- Introduction and overview of the course
- Prelude to developmental disabilities
- Who are people with developmental disabilities?
- Definition and causes of developmental disabilities
- Communicating with people who have developmental disabilities
- **Video:** *Ten Commandments for Interacting with People with Disabilities*
- **Exercise:** Perspective on Disabilities
- **Exercise:** Dear Ann Landers

Readings

- Syllabus
- Ball (1999). My harmony prevails to free (pp. 2-3)
- Ball (1999). Remember rooms rest (pp. 22-25)

SESSION 2

- Historical perspectives of the treatment of individuals with developmental disabilities: eugenics, sterilization, marriage restriction laws, and segregation by institutionalization.
- Social perceptions of people with developmental disabilities throughout history
- Historical trends in service delivery after World War II and the disability rights movement: parents' movement, civil rights movement, deinstitutionalization, independent living movement, and legislation
- Choose a developmental disability as the topic for your oral report and sign-up. Please do not duplicate disability choices. Select the date of your presentation on the sign-up sheet from the designated choices.
- **Visit:** Austin State School

Readings

- Covey (1998). Chapter 7: People with developmental disabilities (pp. 235-272)
- Davis (1997). Constructing normalcy: The bell curve, the novel and the invention of disabled body in the nineteenth century (pp. 9-28)
- Hollander (1998). Euthanasia and mental retardation (pp. 53-61)
- Pfeiffer (1994). Eugenics and disability discrimination (pp. 481-499)
- McLaughlin & Wehman (1996). Chapter 1: Service Delivery (pp. 3-27)

SESSION 3

- Heartshare Presentation by individuals whose siblings were institutionalized in Willowbrook
- **Video:** *Unforgotten, 25 Years After Willowbrook*
- **Exercise:** Moving to an institution

Readings

- Bradley, Ashbaugh, & Blaney (1994). Chapter 18 by Gagne: A self-made man (pp. 327-334)
- Shapiro (1993). Chapter 6: No pity: People with disabilities forging a new civil rights movement (pp. 184-210)

SESSION 4

- Negative attitudes toward people with developmental disabilities. Oppression, discrimination, stigmatization, and abuse of individuals with developmental disabilities.
- The media and people with disabilities
- History and application of service paradigms to people with developmental disabilities
- **Video:** *Norman Kunce*
- **Exercise:** Glen Ridge Case
- **Exercise:** Alligator River Story

Readings

- Sobsey & Mansell (1992, Fall). Teaching people to be abused and exploited (pp. 6-11)
- Bogdan & Biklen (1993). Handicapism (pp. 69-76)
- Livneh (1991). On the origins of negative attitudes toward people with disabilities (pp. 181-196)
- Schilling, Kirkham, & Schinke (1986). Do child services neglect developmentally disabled children? (pp. 21-26)

SESSION 5

- Early childhood intervention services and inclusive preschool
- **Guest Lecturer:** Joy Dillman "Cultural Competency in the Delivery of Early Childhood Intervention Services"
- **Video:** *ECI-Parents Speak Out*

Readings

- McLaughlin & Wehman (1996). Chapter 2: Early Intervention (pp. 29-47)
- Ramey, Mulvihill, & Ramey (1996). Chapter 16: Prevention: Social and educational factors and early intervention (pp. 215-227)

SESSION 6

- Services to children and their families during the school years
- Transition to adulthood: Transition planning
- **Guest Lecturer:** Steve Haman "Promoting Inclusion"
- **Video:** *Educating Peter*
- **Exercise:** Creating a Transition Plan

Readings

- Shapiro, Loeb, Bowermaster, Wright, Headden, & Toch (1993, December 13). Separate and unequal (pp. 46-60)
- McLaughlin & Wehman (1996). Chapter 3: Going To School (pp. 49-67)
- Seligman & Darling (1989). Chapter 3: Childhood and adolescence: Continuing adaptation (pp. 52-82)
- Schnorr (1993). Peter? He comes and goes (pp. 423-435)
- Blacher (2001). Transition to adulthood: Mental retardation, families and culture (pp. 173-188)
- McLaughlin & Wehman (1996). Chapter 4: Transition from School to Adulthood (pp. 69-84)

SESSION 7

- Residential and employment services for adolescents and adults with developmental disabilities
- Assistive technology
- **Guest Lecturer:** Deborah Halleck "Supported Employment at Goodwill"
- **Video:** *Unlocking Tomorrow*

Readings

- McLaughlin & Wehman (1996). Chapter 17: Supported Employment (pp. 317-338)
- McLaughlin & Wehman (1996). Chapter 18: Supported Living and Collaborative Transition (pp. 339-369)
- Everson & Reid (1997, September). Using person-centered planning to determine vocational preferences (pp. 4-5)
- Housewright (1999, June 10). Into the mainstream (A1, A17)

SESSION 8

- The impact of disability on the family-parental focus
- **Guest Lecturers:** Panel of parents, Susan Prior, Carlos Guitterez, Jan Dimare, and Henry McMahon
- **Exercise:** The Cross Family

Readings

- Ziolko (1993). Counseling parents of children with disabilities: A review of the literature and implications for practice (pp. 185-193)
- Hunsberger (1997, Winter). Having children (pp. 32-40)

SESSION 9

- The impact of disability on siblings
- **Guest Lecturers:** Panel of siblings, Sophia Guitterez, Yolanda Montoya, and Summer M'Conley
- Services for aging persons with developmental disabilities
- **Exercise:** Sibshops
- **Exercise:** Here today, gone tomorrow

Readings

- Seligman & Darling (1989). Chapter 5: Effects on siblings (pp. 111-133)
- Rittelmeyer (2000, April). My special sister (pp. 83-84, 86-87)
- McLaughlin & Wehman (1996). Chapter 5: Growing Older (pp. 85-109)
- Foelker & Luke (1989). Mental health issues for the aging mentally retarded person (pp. 242-250)
- Edgerton (1994). Some people know how to be old (pp. 149-160)

SESSION 10

- Psychosexual development, sexuality, sex education, sexual function and dysfunction, and sexual offenders
- **Video:** Excerpts from *Sexuality Reborn* and *Choices in Sexuality with Physical Disability*
- **Exercise:** Just Like Everyone Else
- **Presentation:** Staying Safe Program

Readings

- Ballan (2001, February/March). Parents as sexuality educators for their children with developmental disabilities (pp. 14-19)
- Harris (1997, September). Gay man with disabilities troubled by life's barriers (pp. 17-18)
- Held (1992). Ethical aspects of sexuality of persons with mental retardation (pp. 237-243)
- Kempton & Gochros (1986). The developmentally disabled (pp. 224-237)
- Sundram & Stavis (1994). Sexuality and mental retardation: Unmet challenges (pp. 225-264)

SESSION 11

- Disability and diversity: focusing on culturally relevant and responsive practice
- Emphasis on the special issues related to women and disabilities
- **Video:** PBS Series-*Mending Spirits*, *Pathways*, and *Full Circle*

- **Exercise:** Ethnic Identity Development

Readings

- Ballan, Onken, Batchelder, Manaster, & McRoy (1998). Unit 6: Disability and cultural diversity (pp. 85-93)
- Rock (1996). Eugenics and euthanasia: A cause for concern for disabled people, particularly disabled women (pp. 121-127)
- Rounds, Weil, & Bishop (1994). Practice with culturally diverse families of young children with disabilities (pp. 3-15)

SESSION 12

- Federal legislation
- The law and disability, specific focus on offenders with developmental disabilities, competency to stand trial, and the death penalty
- Self-Advocacy
- **Guest Lecturer:** Jan Hannah "The Cleburne Decision"
- **Guest Lecturers:** Panel of Self-Advocates, Kevin Tracy, Beth Holt, and Jonas Schwartz
- **Exercise:** Hate Crimes

Readings

- Chapter 3 by McGee & Menolascino (1992). The evaluation of defendants with mental retardation in the criminal justice system (pp. 55-77)
- Orlin (1995). The Americans with Disabilities Act: Implications for social services (pp. 233-239)
- Perske (2001). A joint statement: Stop the execution of persons with mental retardation (pp. 327-328)
- Wehmeyer, Bersani, & Gagne (2000). Riding the third wave: Self-determination and self-advocacy in the 21st century (pp. 106-115)

SESSION 13

- Human rights issues and controversial topics pertaining to individuals with developmental disabilities. Topics include quality of life issues, genetic screening and testing, individuals with disabilities as parents, and consent regulations
- **Exercise:** What is Quality of Life?

Readings

- Hubbard (1997). Abortion and disability: Who should and who should not inhabit the world (pp. 187-200)
- Heal, Borthwick-Duffy, & Saunders (1996). Assessment of quality of life (pp. 199-209)
- Pelka (1997). Sandra Jensen (pp. 171)

- Ronai (1997). On loving and hating my mentally retarded mother (pp. 417-432)
- Stavis & Walker-Hirsch (1999). Consent to sexual activity (pp. 57-67)
- Packet: The Arc on genetics and disability and quality of life statement

SESSION 14

- Social work case management services and clinical interventions for working with people with developmental disabilities
- Behavior modification, emphasis on self-injurious behavior
- **Guest Lecturer:** Dr. Bruce Weinheimer "The Truth about Maladaptive and Self-injurious Behaviors"
- **Exercise:** Interdependence—A Real Paradigm

Readings

- McLaughlin & Wehman (1996). Chapter 15: Case Management (pp. 283-295)
- Mackelprang & Salsgiver (1998). Chapter 13: Guidelines for practice with persons with disabilities (pp. 241-258)
- Hurley, Pfadt, Tomasulo, & Gardner (1996). Counseling and psychotherapy (pp. 371-378)
- McLaughlin & Wehman (1996). Chapter 12. Self-Injurious Behavior (pp. 217-240)

SESSION 15

- Social Security, Medicaid, and other human services affecting individuals with developmental disabilities
- Future directions of legislation and services for individuals with developmental disabilities and their families
- Dual diagnosis, psychological and developmental disabilities

Readings

- McLaughlin & Wehman (1996). Chapter 19: Social Security (pp. 371-381)
- Packet: handouts on Medicaid and SSDI
- Searight & Noce (1991). The psychiatrically disturbed developmentally disabled adult: A behaviorally-oriented inpatient program to facilitate community integration (pp. 115-129)
- Alford, Aruffo, Thompson, & William (1994). HIV and psychiatric clients with a developmental disability (pp. 41-49)

SESSION 16

- Final Exam

WASHINGTON UNIVERSITY IN ST. LOUIS
GEORGE WARREN BROWN SCHOOL OF SOCIAL WORK | ST. LOUIS, MO
JEFFREY J. BASSIN

Intervention Approaches in Working with Families Who Have Children with Developmental Disabilities

530-7817.01 (Summer 2002)

INTRODUCTION

The initial impetus for the development of this course came from the recognition on the part of the Children, Youth, and Family Concentration Committee at the George Warren Brown School of Social Work of the need for a specialized course focusing on social work practice with families who have children with developmental disabilities. This course was developed with the awareness that today's social work practice involves intervention with persons who have disabilities and that a set of specific skills are needed to be effective with their immediate as well as extended families. Some students may have a specific interest in specializing in this field. Others may not, yet will undoubtedly encounter work with such families in schools, mental health settings, community agencies, etc.

Many social work practitioners have found themselves working with persons with developmental disabilities, as well as their family members, without adequate preparation. As a social work practitioner in the field of developmental disabilities, I have witnessed both inappropriate "caretaking" interventions and judgmental approaches to families based upon the perceived inability of families, and family members with disabilities, to act on their own initiative. Our profession is not always viewed in a positive light by persons with disabilities and their families. This course has been designed to provide students with the needed self-awareness, sensitivity, skills, and knowledge to enter the practice arena with strength-based and empowering approaches to practice with families who have children with developmental disabilities.

The self-advocacy and self-determination movement of persons with disabilities has been paralleled with strong parent activism. Parents of children with disabilities have long advocated for services and supports for their children. Aging parents vividly remember the years of minimal or no services for their children. Decades of exclusion and segregated services (when available at all) have been replaced with the development of inclusive approaches to the delivery of services and supports. Many families now desire full participation for themselves and their children and actively advocate for such. Freedom of choice in services and supports is desired and often demanded by both consumers with disabilities and family advocates. When viewed as partners, collaborators, advocates, and facilitators, social workers can positively affect the lives of persons with developmental disabilities and their families by supporting them in achieving their vision for the present and future.

COURSE DOMAIN AND BOUNDARIES

This course will provide students with the knowledge and skills needed for social work practice with families who have children with developmental disabilities. The focus will be on the application of theoretical models and practice concepts for intervening with family systems, siblings, and in situations where the parent is an individual with a developmental disability. Students will gain an understanding of the impact of disability on the family unit, family coping-skills, and current evidence-based practice approaches to family support, empowerment, and self-advocacy. Emphasis will be placed on the development of assessment and intervention skills for practitioners that are family-strength based as relevant to working with this specialty population.

Practice models for family interventions over the life span, service coordination, and types of social support systems (family, school, community) available for effective service delivery will be presented. Students will apply the classroom learning in an experiential community-based context. Throughout the course, the transactions between groups and their environments (e.g., communities, organizations, economic, technological, cultural, physical, and political environments) are presented. The role of race, ethnicity, culture, class, gender, sexual orientation, physical or mental disability or illness, age, and national origin in social work practice will be an integral part of this course.

COURSE OBJECTIVES

At the end of the course students should be able to

1. Demonstrate an understanding of the psychosocial impact of developmental disability on the family system and its environment.

2. Identify and describe the values and ethics underlying social work practice that include work with oppressed and disempowered populations and constituencies as related to families with children with developmental disabilities.

3. Demonstrate an understanding of the current definitions (federal, state, and local) of developmental disability and how these definitions influence service delivery.

4. Conceptualize and demonstrate an understanding of the impact of family empowerment and self-advocacy for social and economic justice as capacity building strategies for working with families with children with developmental disabilities.

5. Identify and understand personal attitudes, values, beliefs, ethical issues, and biases regarding developmental disabilities and utilize this information in social work practice.

6. Identify the role of community-based family support services for families who have children with developmental disabilities.

7. Apply principles of ethnic and cultural sensitivity when working with families and disability.

8. Demonstrate practice skills in assessing and intervening with families who have children with developmental disabilities using a solution-focused, strength-based approach.

9. Describe how federal, state, and local social service delivery systems affect families who have a child or children with developmental disabilities.

10. Demonstrate an understanding of the unique impact of the various life stages (early childhood, school age, adolescence, and adulthood) and related transitions for families who have children with developmental disabilities.

11. Demonstrate evidence-based practice skills needed in developing a person- or family-centered support plan.

12. Apply knowledge of race, ethnicity, culture, class, gender, sexual orientation, physical or mental disability or illness, age, and national origin in social work practice with families with children with developmental disabilities.

RELATIONSHIP TO PRACTICUM LEARNING OBJECTIVES

Knowledge gained in this course will prepare students for meeting the following practicum objective: utilizing information obtained from a multidimensional assessment of families, individuals, and community needs (as applicable), the student will learn about the development of an appropriate intervention plan for families with children with developmental disabilities, taking into account multiple levels of influence on a particular client or client system. Students will develop a professional understanding and use of self in the context of practice with populations with developmental disabilities.

TEXTS AND REQUIRED READINGS

Required class texts

- Singer, G. S. H., Powers, L. E., & Olson, A. L. (1996). *Redefining Family Support: Innovations in Public – Private Partnerships.* Baltimore, MD: Paul H. Brooks.
- Gill, B. (1997). *Changed by a Child: Companion Notes for Parents of a Child with a Disability.* New York: Doubleday.

On Reserve
- Readings as assigned in course outline

Course Packet

COURSE ASSIGNMENTS AND GRADING CRITERIA

CLASS DISCUSSION

Class discussion and attendance is highly valued and expected in this course. Many class sessions will be based upon a lecture and discussion format. Participation in classroom activities will include class presentations and case discussions. Assigned readings should be read prior to the class session and students should come prepared to talk about the readings and to participate in discussion. Class participation will account for 5% of the final grade.

Please Note: Please contact the instructor if you feel you may need special assistance with lectures, reading assignments, or testing because of a learning, sensory, or physical disability, or if English is your second language.

SAMPLE ASSIGNMENT

Group Discussion – Scenario

Inclusion Scenario: You are a social worker intervening with a family whose nine-year-old son, Alex, has autism. At times, his behavior causes real challenges for his parents and two teenage sisters. This mom and dad disagree about including their son in family events as well as inclusive social and educational opportunities. Dad wants Alex included in everything possible. Mom has observed Alex exhibit behaviors both at home and in public that lead her to be extremely cautious. She feels Alex needs to be protected from society. The parents have agreed to work on building stronger consensus on this issue.

- How would you approach and work with this family? How might your views about inclusion affect your work here?

GROUP PROJECT

A group project is a required assignment. This group project will focus on the portrayal of persons with disabilities in the popular media. Persons with disabilities are portrayed in various media, including newspapers, magazines, television, radio, film, etc. These portrayals continue to define and influence societal views of persons with developmental disabilities and their families. This group project will include a written report (2-3 pages) and a class presentation of current issues and themes. This report should include current clippings and examples. The group project will account for 15% of the final grade. The group project is due on class session 5.

SAMPLE ASSIGNMENT

Group Project – Instructions

The group project will focus on conducting a review of the way that persons with developmental disabilities and their families are portrayed in the popular media. Include current news clippings and examples. This group project shall include a short paper (2 to 3 pages) and a class presentation of currents themes and issues that will include the following:

- How were individuals with developmental disabilities and their families portrayed? Were portrayals positive or negative? Were myths and stereotypes dispelled or supported? Was "people first" language utilized? (5 points)

- What impact might these messages have on families who have children with developmental disabilities? How can social workers be of support to families who read and see these messages? (5 points)

- How can social workers positively influence the manner in which persons with developmental disabilities and their families are portrayed in the media? (5 points)

INTERVENTION PAPER

An intervention paper is a required assignment. This paper shall focus on an intervention or treatment strategy for social work practice with families who have children with a developmental disability. We will identify and review numerous strategies over the course of the semester. Your paper should provide an in-depth analysis of the chosen intervention. This paper will include a review of the current literature and a discussion of the effectiveness of the strategy as well as possible limitations. Papers should be double-spaced. There is no page limit on this assignment, although the paper must be a complete and comprehensive review and analysis of the strategy chosen. The intervention paper will account for 40% of the final grade. The intervention paper is due on class session 10.

SAMPLE ASSIGNMENT

Intervention Paper – Instructions

Write a research-based paper that focuses on an intervention or treatment strategy for social work practice with families who have children with developmental disabilities.

- Define and describe in detail the social work intervention or treatment strategy. (5 points)

- What is the effectiveness of this intervention as related to the family and child with developmental disabilities? (5 points)

- Evaluate the research or other relevant literature (conduct a literature review) that supports or challenges this social work intervention or treatment strategy and its impact on the family. (5 points)

- Describe the barriers (including controversy) or limitations for this intervention. (5 points)

- Identify alternative strategies (historic or current) and compare them to the social work intervention you have chosen. (5 points)

- This intervention must focus on the family. What role does the family play in the chosen intervention or treatment strategy? How does this strategy fit into the concept of family support? Describe the specifics of social work interaction with the family in the implementation of this intervention or treatment strategy. (10 points)

- What are the implications for social work practice? Examples include the need for additional social work education around this intervention, the need for additional research, staff training, and technical assistance needs. (5 points)

FINAL EXAM

There will be a comprehensive final exam, covering the fifteen weeks of class lectures and assigned readings. The format will include essay and short answer questions. The final exam will account for 40% of the final grade. The final exam will be administered at the last meeting of the course, class session 16.

GRADING CRITERIA

Each project and assignment noted will contribute to a percentage of your final grade, as described below. Student performance will be evaluated based on the following criteria:

- Group Project   15%
- Intervention Paper   40%
- Class Participation   05%
- Final Exam   40%

COURSE OUTLINE

SESSION I

Topics

- Organization of class and course expectations
- Nature of developmental disability
- Historical trends in the field of developmental disability
- Myths and stereotypes
- Disability and bias
- Attitude assessment

Objectives

Students will develop an understanding of

1) The variety of approaches used to define developmental disability
2) The historical patterns of treatment of persons with disabilities
3) The manner in which myths and stereotypes impact intervention with persons who have developmental disabilities as well as their families
4) How social workers' attitudes about disability can impact and bias intervention

Format

- Lecture
- Class discussion
- Video: *A credo for support* (1995). Produced by Norman Kunc and Emma Van der Klift.

Readings

Reserve

- Stainton, T. (1994). *Autonomy and social policy.* Burlington, VT: Ashgate Publishing. Part 2, Section 8: Autonomy, rights and rhetoric: Present realities (pp. 135 – 159)

Reading Packet

- Zastrow, C. (1996). *Introduction to social work and social welfare.* (6th ed.). Pacific Grove, CA: Brooks/Cole Publishing. Chapter 15: History of rehabilitation practices, developmental disabilities, cognitive disabilities, & society's reactions to disabilities. (pp. 512 – 521)
- Mackelprang, R. W. & Salsgiver, R. O. (1996). People with disabilities and social work: Historical and contemporary issues. *Social Work, 41*(1), 7-13.
- Fujiura G. T. & Yamaki, K. (1997). Analysis of ethnic variations in developmental disability prevalence and household economic status. *Mental Retardation, 35*(4), 286 – 294.

SESSION 2

Topics

- Identification of professional roles played by social workers in the lives of people with developmental disabilities and their families
- Social work values
- Use of appropriate terminology in written and oral communication
- Use of "People First" language
- Professional and social etiquette used when intervening with persons with developmental disabilities and their families

Objectives

Students will have knowledge of

1) A minimum of five distinct professional roles social workers play in the lives of persons with developmental disabilities and their families
2) A social work value system appropriate for working with persons who have developmental disabilities and their families
3) The tools needed to professionally interact with, discuss, and write about persons with developmental disabilities and their families

Format

- Lecture
- Class discussion

Readings

Reserve

- Petr, C. G. (1998). *Social work with children and their families.* New York: Oxford University Press. Chapter 7: Introduction to social work in child welfare settings. (pp. 125–156)

Reading Packet

- DePoy, E. & Miller, M. (1996). Preparation of social workers for serving individuals with developmental disabilities: A brief report. *Mental Retardation, 34*(1), 54–57.
- Hanley, B. & Parkinson, C. B. (1994). Position paper on social work: Practice with individuals who have developmental disabilities. *Mental Retardation, 32*(6), 426–431.
- Zastrow, C. (1996). *Introduction to social work and social welfare.* (6th ed.). Pacific Grove, CA: Brooks/Cole Publishing. Chapter 15: Roles of social workers. (pp. 525–526)

SESSION 3

Topics

- Psychosocial issues
- Grief and loss
- Circles of support
- Natural supports

Objectives

Students will develop an understanding of

1) Psychosocial issues and their impact on the family

2) The significance of loss and grief work with families

3) The usefulness of developing circles of support and the role social workers play in their development

Format

- Lecture

- Class discussion

- Video: *When miracles hide: Children with down syndrome* (1995). Produced by St. Charles, Missouri Down Syndrome Group.

- Guest speakers: Mothers from St. Louis Chapter Down Syndrome Association

Readings

Class Text

- Gill, B. (1997).

Reserve

- Seligman, M. (1991). *The family with a handicapped child.* Boston: Allyn & Bacon. Chapter 3: Initial and continuing adaptation to the birth of a disabled child. (pp. 55–89)

Reading Packet

- Zastrow, C. (1996). *Introduction to social work and social welfare.* (6th ed.). Pacific Grove, CA: Brooks/Cole Publishing. Chapter 15: The grieving process. (pp. 527–536)

SESSION 4

Topics

- Family support model as an approach to intervention

- Family preservation and developmental disability

- Taxonomy of family support

Objectives

Students will

1) Understand the concept of family support as it pertains to serving persons with developmental disabilities and their families

2) Increase knowledge of and familiarity with current trends in service provision for families who have children with developmental disabilities

3) Be able to apply knowledge by demonstrating the ability to connect families with needed services

Format

- Lecture

- Class discussion

Readings

Class Text

- Singer, G. S. H., Powers, L. E., & Olson, A. L. (1996). Section I: The concept of family support for families of people with special needs, (pp. 3 - 112). Recommended readings are found in Section II: Family support across populations, (pp. 115 – 290). Omit Chapters 6 & 11, as they are assigned later.

SESSION 5

Topics

- The social history and current status of the parent and self-advocacy movements
- Choice and consumer control of services and supports
- The self-determination movement
- Individualized funding and citizenship as a driving philosophy

Objectives

Students will gain an understanding of

1) The impact of empowerment on persons with developmental disabilities
2) The "People First" self-advocacy movement and its effect on the system
3) The effectiveness of parents as advocates for themselves and their children as well as the role played by social workers in parent and consumer advocacy

Format

- Lecture
- Class discussion
- Guest speakers: Individuals from local parent and self-advocacy group

Readings

Reading Packet

- Amado, A. N. (1996). Two views on self-advocacy: How self-advocates can support national and local organizations. *Mental Retardation, 34*(4), 254–255.
- Dudley, J. R. (1996). Seeking a closer partnership with the self advocacy movement. *Mental Retardation, 34*(4), 255-256.
- Miller, A. & Keys, C. B. (1996). Awareness, action, and collaboration: How the self-advocacy movement is empowering for persons with developmental disabilities. *Mental Retardation, 34*(5), 312–319.
- Tease, C. (October 1997). Self-determination: A family perspective. *TASH Newsletter, 23*(10), 12 –14.

SESSION 6

Topics

- Helping families access the service delivery maze: federal, state, and local services and supports designed for families and family members with developmental disabilities

Objectives

Students will gain an understanding of

1) The complex nature of these systems and its impact on the family

2) The emotional toll families may encounter when accessing services and supports as well as the supportive and clinical role of social workers

3) The benefits common in these systems

Format

- Lecture
- Class discussion

Readings

Reserve

- Seligman, M. (1991). *The family with a handicapped child*. Allyn & Bacon. Chapter 4: Families and the community service maze. (pp. 91–118)

Reading Packet

- Forest, M. & Pearpoint, J. (May 1997). Practical and useful tools for change. *TASH Newsletter, 23*(5), 13–15.

SESSION 7

Topics

- Current public policy issues and trends affecting families with children who are developmentally disabled

Objectives

Students will have an understanding of

1) Current funding methodologies

2) Trends that influence service delivery

3) Social work intervention in supporting families affected by public policy and current service trends

Format

- Lecture
- Class discussion

Readings

Class Text

- Singer, G. S. H., Powers, L. E., & Olson, A. L. (1996). Section III: Issues and innovations in public policy. (pp. 313–463)

SESSION 8

Topics

- Service and support needs for the caregivers
- Sensitivity and skills related to race, culture, and ethnicity
- Peer support
- Role of support groups
- Respite care services as critical family supports

Objectives

Students will have knowledge of

1) Assessing for critical support needs of caregivers

2) Race, culture, and ethnicity and related skill-building in working with families who have children with developmental disabilities

3) Support options, such as self-help groups, that have arisen on a grassroots level

4) Respite care service delivery options and related outcomes for families

Format

- Lecture
- Group discussion
- Case studies

Readings

Reading Packet

- Hanneman, R. & Blacher, J. (1998). Predicting placement in families who have children with severe handicaps: A longitudinal analysis. *American Journal on Mental Retardation, 102*(4), 392-408.

- Valentine, D., McDermott, S., & Anderson, D. (1998). Mothers of adults with mental retardation: Is race a factor in perceptions of burdens and gratifications? *Families in Society, 79*(6), 577-584.

- Bruns, D. A. (2000). Leaving home at an early age: Decisions about out-of-home placement for young children with complex medical needs. *Mental Retardation, 38*(1), 50-60.

- Wituk, S., Shepherd, M. D., Slavich, S., Warren, M. L., & Meissen, G. (2000). A topography of self-help groups. *Social Work, 45*(2), 157-165.

SESSION 9

Topics

- Impact of developmental disability on parents
- Family support
- Family life education

Objectives

Students will gain knowledge of

1) Psychosocial impact of developmental disability on parents

2) The impact of community and peer support on parents of children with developmental disabilities

3) Approaches to involve fathers in care-giving and family support

Format

- Lecture
- Group discussion
- Video: *Dads and kids out together: An organization for children with disabilities and their families* (1996). Produced by the DAKOTA organization.
- Guest speaker: The father of a child with developmental disabilities

Readings

Reserve

- Seligman, M. (1991). *The family with a handicapped child.* Allyn & Bacon. Chapter 6: Fathers of children with special needs. (pp. 151–179)

Reading Packet

- Willoughby, J. & Glidden, L. M. (1995). Fathers helping out: Shared care and marital satisfaction of parents who have children with disabilities. *American Journal on Mental Retardation,* 9(4), 399-406.
- Hayden, M. F., & Goldman, J. (1996). Families of adults with mental retardation: Stress levels and need for services. *Social Work, 41*(6), 657-667.

SESSION 10

Topics

- Supporting siblings as an integral part of the family with a child who has developmental disabilities

Objectives

Students will gain knowledge of

1) Psychosocial impact on siblings
2) Intervention strategies, sibshops for example, for siblings who have a brother or sister with a developmental disability

Format

- Lecture
- Group discussion
- Guest speakers: Siblings who have brothers and sisters with developmental disabilities

Readings

Reserve

- Seligman, M. (1991). *The family with a handicapped child.* Allyn & Bacon. Chapter 7: Siblings of disabled brothers and sisters. (pp. 181–201)

Reading Packet

- Krauss, M. W., Seltzer, M. M., Gordon, R., & Freidman, D. H. (1996). Binding ties: The roles of adult siblings of persons with mental retardation. *Mental Retardation, 34*(2), 83–93.
- Wolf Heller, K., Gallagher, P. A., & Fredrick, L. D. (1999). Parents' perceptions of siblings' interactions with their brothers and sisters who are deaf-blind. *Journal of the Association for Persons with Severe Handicaps, 24*(1), 33-43.

SESSION 11

Topics

- Adolescence and disability
- Sexuality
- Sexuality education
- Family involvement

Objectives

Students will gain knowledge of

1) The impact of adolescence on the family
2) Sexuality and developmental disability
3) Sexuality education in the field of developmental disability
4) Family life education as an effective intervention

Format

- Lecture
- Group discussion
- Case studies

Readings

Reserve

- Stefan, S. (1994). Dancing in the sky without a parachute: Sex & love in institutional settings. In C. J. Sundram, (Ed.), *Choice and responsibility: Legal & ethical dilemmas in services for persons with mental disabilities* (pp. 219–243). Albany, NY: The New York State Commission on Quality of Care For the Mentally Disabled.

Reading Packet

- Ames, T. R. H. & Samowitz, P. (1995). Inclusionary standard for determining sexual consent for individuals with developmental disabilities. *Mental Retardation, 33*(4), 264 - 268.
- Harris, A. (1997). Gay man with disabilities troubled by life's barriers. *TASH Newsletter, 23*(9), 17-18.

CLASS SESSION 12

Topics

- Transition into adulthood as a crossroads for the individual with developmental disability and the family
- Adult service delivery system
- Employment opportunities
- Community living options

Objectives

Students will understand

1) The need for transition planning
2) The principals of transition
3) The role of social work in transition planning

Format

- Lecture
- Group discussion
- Guest speaker: A parent experiencing the process of transition

Readings

Reserve

- McLaughlin, P. J. & Wehman, P. (1992). *Developmental disabilities: A handbook for best practices.* Boston: Andover Medical Publishers. Chapter 15, Community living, Section on Transition, collaboration and advocacy. (pp. 259–267)

Reading Packet

- President's Committee on Mental Retardation, U. S. Department of Health and Human Services, Administration for Children and Families (1995). *The journey to inclusion: A resource for state policymakers.* Washington, DC: U.S. Government Printing Office. Section on Transition. (pp. 49–52)

- Center for Innovations in Special Education. (1999). *Did you know...Parent's role in transition to adult life, 2*(1) [Brochure]. Columbia, MO: Author.

SESSION 13

Topics

- Aging and developmental disability
- Impact on service delivery
- Impact on the family and older adult service delivery system

Objectives

Students will develop an understanding of

1) The aging process and developmental disability

2) An emerging collaboration among the fields of geriatrics and developmental disability service delivery

3) The application of generic resources to this population

Format

- Lecture
- Group discussion
- Case studies
- Guest speakers: Family members experiencing the aging process of a person with developmental disabilities

Readings

Class Text

- Singer, G. S. H., Powers, L. E., & Olson, A. L. (1996). Section II, Chapter 6: The aging family in a multigenerational perspective. (pp.135–149)

Reserve

- McLaughlin, P. J. & Wehman, P. (1992). *Developmental disabilities: A handbook for best practices.* Andover. Chapter 17: Gerontology. (pp. 277–297)

Reading Packet

- Rinck, C. (1993). *Fast facts on aging #9: Assessment for choosing work or retirement options.* [booklet]. Kansas City, MO: University of Missouri–Kansas City Institute for Human Development.

- Lehr Essex, E., Mailick Seltzer, M., Wyngaarden Krauss, M. (1999). Differences in coping effectiveness and well-being among aging mothers and fathers of adults with mental retardation. *American Journal on Mental Retardation, 104*(6), 545-563.

SESSION 14

Topics

- Treatment approaches
- Case management and service coordination
- Brief treatment model as an effective social work intervention tool

Objectives

Students will

1) Be able to identify effective clinical intervention models
2) Demonstrate practice skills by using brief treatment approaches in working with families

Format

- Lecture
- Group discussion
- Case studies

Readings

Reserve

- McLaughlin, P. J. & Wehman, P. (1992). *Developmental disabilities: A handbook for best practices.* Andover. Chapter 12: Case management. (pp. 172–183)
- Seligman, M. (1991). *The family with a handicapped child.* Allyn & Bacon. Chapter 12: Counseling parents with children with disabilities: Rationales and strategies, (pp. 337 – 368). Chapter 13: Family therapy. (pp. 369 – 406)

SESSION 15

Topics

- Person- or family-centered planning as a critical intervention in the lives of persons with developmental disabilities and their families

Objectives

Students will

1) Demonstrate knowledge of the basic principles of person- or family-centered planning
2) Demonstrate practice skills in the planning process

Format

- Lecture
- Group discussion
- Video: *Common threads: Key themes in person centered planning* (1997). Produced by the Missouri Department of Health with the Missouri Medicaid Waiver Certification Project.

Readings

Class Text

- Singer, G. S. H., Powers, L. E., & Olson, A. L. (1996). Section II, Chapter 11: Developing Family-Centered Care for Families of Children with Special Health Care Needs. (pp. 239 – 257)

Reading Packet:

- O'Brien, C. L., O'Brien, J., & Mount, B. (1997). Person centered planning has arrived...or has it? *Metal Retardation, 35*(6), 480-483.
- Lubetsky, M. J., Mueller, L., Madden, K., Walker, R., & Len, D. (1995). Family centered/ interdisciplinary team approach to working with families of children who have mental retardation. *Mental Retardation, 33*(4), 251-256.
- Budzinski-McMullen, V. (1999). Moving to Italy. *Journal of Positive Behavior Interventions, 1*(1), 59-61.

SESSION 16

Topic

- Final exam

Objectives

Students will

1) Be evaluated on their knowledge and understanding of the materials presented during the semester

Disability: Social and Health Issues

SW 466 (Fall 2001)

INTRODUCTION

This course is the product of years of university and community collaboration. It represents the collective answer to a single question: *"What do social workers need to know about disability?"* My answer was influenced by half a lifetime of first-hand experience. I had also learned some remarkable lessons over the years as a medical and clinical social worker. Realizing that my own perspective was still limited, however, I asked the question to friends with disabilities and professional colleagues. I asked people from major disability groups and family organizations. There was an outpouring of support and ideas. The greatest challenge was, and still is, how to find time within a 15-week semester for all of the content that should be included.

Guest experts representing different aspects of the disability community are invited to visit the classroom (e.g., consumers, family members, human service providers, advocates, and wheelchair athletes). Both guests and students are "primed" in advance to ask and answer difficult or personal questions. The class is a favorite among students with disabilities, so we always have a few "resident experts" in our midst. All students are engaged in experiential learning, including reality-based exercises, class discussions, and direct service to individuals with disabilities. Oppression and injustice are examined with special attention to current political issues. We debate controversial topics that divide the disability community (e.g., cochlear implants, "Jerry's kids"). It is a highly spirited class that combines consciousness-raising with practical social work knowledge.

This course is currently taught as an integrative capstone course for seniors. All seniors at this university must take two capstone electives in order to graduate. It is listed as a social work course, however it is open to other majors. There is usually a mix of about 50/50 social work students and majors from other health-related disciplines. The class has been a good opportunity for future social workers to network with other helping professions (e.g., medicine, nursing, special education, physical therapy, speech pathology). This cross-fertilization of perspectives and knowledge has led to some exciting transdisciplinary teamwork.

Although the course was designed for undergraduate seniors, it could be used as an elective at the graduate level. Some portions of the class may also be useful as disability content in a more generalized diversity course.

COURSE DESCRIPTION

Understanding disability requires a willingness to critically examine long-held personal beliefs. Misperceptions and stereotypes are barriers to effective social work practice. Throughout this course, the emphasis will be on demystifying disability by examining the lived experiences of people with a variety of developmental, traumatic, and acquired disabilities. Students will explore disability from bio-psycho-social and cultural perspectives. They will gain knowledge of the disability community's common language, norms of conduct, economic concerns, political issues, and struggles with stigmatization. This course is designed to prepare students for generalist practice with emphasis on social and health issues that impact on people with disabilities across the life span. Theories of human behavior, best-practice models, important government policies, and current research studies that are relevant to professional service to individuals with disabilities are presented. A number of specific disabilities will be discussed with attention to the needs associated with each.

OBJECTIVES COMMON TO ALL CAPSTONE COURSES

As an integrative capstone course, this class is designed to

1. Build upon the core curriculum by providing the opportunity for students to bring to bear knowledge gained in core courses and knowledge derived from major and elective courses.

2. Promote integration, multi- and transdisciplinary cooperation, and cross-cultural competency.

3. Focus on ethical and substantive issues, problems, and themes that affect the world community and broad cross-sections of humankind.

4. Encourage critical thinking and reaching beyond traditional approaches and perspectives.

5. Improve and enhance writing ability through a rigorous writing component.

EDUCATIONAL OUTCOMES

Upon successful completion of this course, the student should be able to demonstrate competency in the following areas:

1. Improved awareness-of-self with regard to common fears and myths about disability.

2. Increased sensitivity to the perspectives of people with disabilities and their families.

3. Understanding of the resources that exist to promote the inclusion of people with disabilities through adaptations, technology, and public awareness. Students will gain knowledge of state and federal programs and examine the proliferation of private rehabilitation services. Students will increase their awareness of the role of professionals in accessing, implementing, and developing resources.

4. Knowledge of practice strategies used with persons with disabilities including case management, advocacy, family and group work, and some clinical interventions.

5. Knowledge of the characteristics, etiology, and demographics of the most common disabilities.

6. Awareness of the cultural aspects of disability, including contemporary disability culture and disability and race or ethnicity.

7. Understanding of the major federal laws and policies that impact on children and adults with disabilities.

8. Comprehension of the dynamic nature of rehabilitation and medical practices and awareness of the limitations of the medical/rehabilitation model.

9. Understanding of the influence of disability on the behavior of the individual and the family within the context of their environment.

10. Utilization of professional literature and research methodologies in disability-related practice.

11. Understanding disability as a form of human diversity that is susceptible to oppression and injustice on micro/meso/macro system levels.

REQUIRED READING:

Mackelprang, R. & Salsgiver, R. (1999). *Disability: A diversity model approach in human service practice.* Pacific Grove, CA: Brookes/Cole Publishing.

An additional study packet of materials on developmental disabilities will be available for purchase ($5.00) through the School of Social Work.

COURSE ASSIGNMENTS

Group presentation 50 points

This assignment reflects social work's commitment to action and service. It is also intended to improve awareness, sensitivity, and cross-cultural communication skills. Students will work on a project throughout the semester that contributes to the welfare of people with disabilities. Groups shall consist of 5-6 students who agree on an issue of particular interest to the members. Students are welcome to choose a project that benefits an individual or an entire group of persons with disabilities. All of the groups will present their projects on the last regularly scheduled night of class (see Course Outline). Supportive material about the project should be prepared (e.g., charts, photographs, drawings, videos, invited guests) for a presentation that may last for *no longer than 15 minutes.* One written summary of the project should also be submitted to describe the steps taken to accomplish the group's goals (may be the major contribution of one of the group members. Hint: a working parent with limited time).

Here are a few examples of projects that previous groups accomplished:

- Elimination of architectural barriers that kept wheelchair users from enjoying a public park.
- Creation of the first annual "Walk-a-Thon for Cystic Fibrosis" in Northern Nevada.
- Development of adaptive clothing for a woman with severe arthritis.
- Construction of a 25-foot long sidewalk for children in wheelchairs to get to a petting zoo.
- Production of a video expose of inaccessibility problems of a major airline.
- A study of accommodations for wheelchair users at a major shopping mall.
- Participation in adaptive sporting events: adaptive skiing, wheelchair basketball, tennis (Note: more than just observing...participating!).
- Creation of an integrated haunted house (Halloween) for children with and without disabilities.

Finding a project

People within the group may already have ideas about an individual or group of people with disabilities that could be served by this assignment. It is important that the group find consensus about the selected issue and the feasibility of the project. If members do not have a direct link to an issue, consider similar projects to those presented above or take one of these suggestions:

- Contact the Northern Nevada Center for Independent Living to ask about a volunteer activity that your group could engage in this semester.
- Ask the Washoe County School District (Office of Special Education) about an activity that you could do to benefit children with disabilities.
- Help existing organizations that serve people with disabilities (e.g., MS Society, Northern Nevada Amputee Support Group, Cancer Society, Headway, Nevada Alliance for the Mentally Ill, Bridges in Consciousness, United Cerebral Palsy, Nevada Parent Network).
- Help the UNR Cooperative Extension and Moana Nursery establish a community garden with accessible plots for people with disabilities.
- Study accessibility issues at public facilities, such as the new downtown development project, *and* make appropriate recommendations to public officials about improving access.
- Follow a legislative issue, such as funding for independent living, *and* make your opinions known to appropriate legislators or administrators.
- Volunteer to improve access for recreational opportunities at parks, playgrounds, camping and fishing facilities, etc.
- Create something through the arts (e.g., art, music, video) to promote the lives of people with disabilities and reduce stigmatization.

These projects may be as simple as helping a single person solve a disability-related problem (like getting a ramp to the front door) or as grand as changing public policy. Grading for this assignment will be in two parts: a group grade and an individual grade.

Group grade: 10 points = Conceptualization of a useful project
                       10 points = Value of the project to the individual or group
                       10 points = Ability of the group to collaborate and cooperate
                       10 points = Presentation of the project to the class

Individual grade: 10 points = Individual members' participation in the project
                       (This will be judged from class presentation, written materials,
                       and self-report)

Extra credit: The professor reserves the right to add up to 10 points of additional credit on those projects that demonstrate the greatest creativity or effort. These extra credit points will be given only to those students who do extraordinary work.

Awareness exercise 50 points

The purpose of this assignment is to raise the level of students' consciousness about the realities of everyday life with a physical disability. Students will spend a 12-hour period living with an assigned disability. Two partners will pair-up to participate in this assignment. The pairs will sign-up for specified disabilities and each student will participate in the experience. The pairs will determine a particular day in which they will be able to assume the characteristics of a person with a disability (e.g., SCI, blind, deaf). During the 12 hours, one student will engage in typical daily activities and the other will maintain a log with hourly entries. The other will also serve to protect the student with a "new" impairment from harm. The students' grades will be heavily weighted on the authenticity and richness of the experiences. For instance, the student who goes into the community, uses public transportation, and encounters real-life barriers will receive a higher grade than those who stay in a "safe" setting. Fakers will be obvious.

After the experience, the log should be typed for submission. Each of the participants should engage in introspection about the experience and write a separate summary of their feelings and insights. The papers should then be combined and submitted as a single document.

Grading criteria: Log with hourly entries   30 points
                       Individual summaries of the experience   20 points

INDIVIDUAL ASSIGNMENTS

Literature review 50 points

This assignment serves several purposes, including helping students develop a deeper understanding of one particular area of disability. It is also designed to foster students' use of current research to inform future practice. Capstone courses require a rigorous writing component, and this assignment is designed to meet that expectation.

Students will conduct a library search about an approved topic related to disability. You must locate recent articles from *professional journals* that are directly related to your topic. The articles should have publication dates no later than 1990 (more recent is preferable). The Internet and other resources may be used for **Parts 1** and **2**, but be certain to use legitimate professional journal articles for **Part 3**. Don't use abstracts. Don't confuse website information with published articles. Avoid references from popular magazines (e.g., Reader's Digest, People, Time, Newsweek). Journals are recommended from social work, psychology, sociology, nursing, medicine, health education, rehabilitation (including speech, physical, or occupation therapy), or other professions associated with disability issues. In **Part 4** focus on writing succinctly yet with sufficient detail to convey the essence of the articles.

Procedures for this review

Introduction (**Parts 1** and **2** are your introduction)

1. Briefly describe the cause, prevalence, and demographics of the assigned disability. (Locate at least one reliable source of data about the disability and summarize the information within one paragraph.) Prevalence: How many people are affected by the disability? Demographics: Who is affected? (male/female, age, vulnerable groups). Actual numbers or percentages will suffice. If the cause is not known, just report that information with a reference.

2. Briefly describe (within one or two paragraphs) the characteristics of the disability. (Use one or more references to explain the nature of the disability.) So far, you should have everything from **1** and **2** summarized within one or two pages.

Synthesis (Notice: These parts are worth 60% of your grade)

3. Locate and copy five recent journal articles that pertain to your specific topic. Do not cite more than two articles from the same journal.

4. Copy the author's name, date, complete title of the article, journal title, volume number, and page numbers. Under the citation, write a brief summary of article. Be critical in your thinking about the research methodologies that you see. Discuss the strengths and weaknesses of the article. Discuss the implications for social workers or other helping professionals.

Criteria for grading this paper: Part 1 = 10 points
Part 2 = 10 points
Part 3 = 10 points
Part 4 = 20 points

Papers should be typed, using double-spacing, font size 12 points, with 1" margins. Points for each section may be reduced by excessive spelling, grammar, and punctuation errors. Points are given for selecting appropriate articles, synthesizing the most relevant information, and demonstrating clarity of expression.

Reading and Reflection Log 25 points

The purpose of this assignment is to increase the students' awareness-of-self in relationship to disability. It also serves to guarantee that students will complete their assigned readings.

Students must begin keeping a journal in which they reflect on their feelings and impressions about the weekly readings, lectures, discussions, and guest speakers. There must be some evidence that the student has grasped the key concepts presented in each chapter. Of the 15 weeks of content presented this semester, students must have entries from no less than 12 weeks. At the end of the semester, the students are asked to summarize the course by spending some time thinking about what they learned from the experience and what they will carry with them.

CLASS ATTENDANCE AND PARTICIPATION

Attendance and participation are expected from students in this course. The professor reserves the right to reduce a student's grade by as much as 10% for unexcused absences (particularly during the last half of class) or poor participation.

ACCOMMODATIONS

The professor will gladly make reasonable accommodations that are necessary for students with disabilities. Please notify the instructor as soon as possible about making adaptations in instruction or scheduling.

COURSE OUTLINE

Unit 1: Historical and contemporary perspectives on disability

- Week 1
  - Introduction
  - Self-awareness exercises
  - Video: "Full Circle"
- Week 2
  - Language of disability
  - Disability etiquette
  - John Callahan cartoons
  - Guests: Panel of individuals with SCI
  - Reading: Chapter 1
- Week 3
  - Disability throughout history
  - Debate: Pros and cons of telethons
  - Reading: Chapter 2
- Week 4
  - Contemporary disability culture
  - Disability in diverse cultures
  - Video: "Mending Spirits: Native Americans with Disabilities"
  - Reading: Chapter 2

Unit 2: Developmental disabilities (DD)

- Week 5
  - Pre-test knowledge of DD (relax, it's ungraded)
  - Overview of developmental disabilities
  - Introduction to DD concepts
  - Reading: Chapter 3, Study packet
- Week 6 (Literature Review Due)
  - Major categories of developmental disabilities
  - Video clips of children with disabilities
  - Implications for practitioners
  - Debate: Cochlear implants for deaf children
  - Reading: Chapter 4, Study packet
- Week 7
  - Special education policies
  - Guests: Nevada Parent Network panel
  - Post-test on DD (it's ungraded too)
  - Reading: Chapter 10, Study packet

- Week 8
  - Class competition: "The Case of Molly B."
  - Working with families
  - What families need
  - What families don't need (or want!)

Unit 3: Disability in Adulthood

- Week 9
  - Meaning and medicine
  - Existential/phenomenological issues
- Week 10 (Awareness Exercise Due)
  - Adapting to disability
  - Disability and substance abuse
  - Video: "When Billy Broke His Head"
  - Reading: Chapter 13
- Week 11
  - Sexuality and disability
  - Video clips: "Sexuality and SCI"
  - Reading: Chapter 9
- Week 12
  - Women with disabilities
  - Guests: Panel of women with disabilities
  - Aging with disability
  - Chapter 11

Unit 4: The Great Equalizers: Advocacy, Policy, and Technology

- Week 13
  - Discrimination and oppression
  - Advocacy issue: Olmstead case
  - Guests: Panel of disability rights advocates
- Week 14
  - Individuals with Disabilities Education Act
  - Americans with Disabilities Act
  - Reading: Chapter 12, Study packet
- Week 15 (Reflection log due)
  - Assistive technology
  - Exhibit: Technology specialist will display high and low tech devices
  - Video: "People in Motion"
  - Chapter 7
- Finals week (Group presentations due)

BIBLIOGRAPHY

Unit I: Introduction and Overview

Alle-Corliss, L. & Alle-Corliss, R. (1999). *Advanced practice in human service agencies: Issues, trends, and treatment perspectives.* Belmont, CA: Brooks/Cole Publishing.

Condeluci, A. (1995). *Interdependence: The route to community.* Winter Park, FL: GR Press.

Corbet, B. (2000). *Spinal Network: The total wheelchair resource book.* (3rd ed.). Malibu, CA: New Mobility Publications.

Callahan, J. (1989). *Don't worry, he won't get far on foot: An autobiography of a dangerous man.* New York: Morrow Publishing.

Cousins, N. (1976). Anatomy of an illness. *New England Journal of Medicine, 295,* 1458-63.

Eisenberg, M., Griggins, C., & Duval, R. (1982). *Disabled people as second-class citizens.* New York: Springer Publishing.

Goffman, E. (1963). *Stigma.* Englewood Cliffs, NJ: Prentice Hall Publishing.

Greif, E. & Matarazzo, R. (1982) *Behavioral approaches to rehabilitation.* New York: Springer Publishing.

Kaye, H. S., LaPlante, M., & Wenger, B. L. (1996). Trends in disability rates in the United States, 1970-1994. *Disability Statistics Abstracts, 17,* 1-6.

Kenyatta, M., & Tai, R. H. (Eds.). (1997). Ethnicity and education forum: What difference does difference make? *Harvard Educational Review, 67*(2), 169-187.

Kraus, L., Stoddard, S., & Gilmartin, D. (1996). *Chartbook on disability in the United States.* Washington, DC: National Institute on Disability and Rehabilitation Research.

Lathrop, D. (1999). Finding the art and soul of disability. *New Mobility, 10,* 24-27.

Lee, M. & Greene, G. (1999). A social constructivist framework for integrating cross-cultural issues in teaching clinical social work. *Journal of Social Work Education, 35*(1), 21-38.

Luey, H. S., Glass, L., & Elliott, H. (1995). Hard-of-hearing or Deaf: Issues of ears, language, culture, and identity. *Social Work, 40,* 177-181.

Mackelprang, R. & Salsgiver, R. (1996). Persons with disabilities and social work: Historical and contemporary issues. *Social Work, 41,* 7-14.

Mackelprang, R. & Salsgiver, R. (1999). *Disability: A diversity model approach in human service practice.* Pacific Grove, CA: Brookes/Cole Publishing.

Maddox, S. (1990). *Spinal network: The total resource manual for the wheelchair community.* Boulder, CO: Spinal Network Publishing.

Marinelli, P. & Dell Orto, A. (1992). *The social and psychological impact of disability.* New York: Springer Publishing.

McMillen, J. (1999). Better for it: How people benefit from adversity. *Social Work, 44,* 455-468.

Medgyesi, V. (1996). The chrome ceiling. *New Mobility, 37,* 26-30.

Phillips, M. (1985). Try harder: The experience of disability and the dilemma of normalization. *The Social Science Journal, 22,* 47-57.

Pinderhughes, E. (1989). *Understanding race, ethnicity, and power: The key to efficacy in clinical practice.* New York: Free Press.

Pitzele, S. (1986). *We are not alone: Learning to live with chronic illness.* New York: Workman Publishing.

Shapiro, J. (1993). *No pity: People with disabilities forging a new civil rights movement.* New York: Times Books.

Tower, K. (1992). Culture shock: Native American's wake up in a strange land. *Spinal Network, Winter,* 25-26.

Turnbull, H. R. & Turnbull, A. P. (1996). *Families, professionals, and exceptionality: A special partnership.* (2nd ed.). New York: Merrill Publishing.

Turner, F. (1986). *Social work treatment: Interlocking theoretical approaches.* (2nd ed.). New York: Free Press.

Vash, C. L. (1995). From transcendence to transformation. *New Mobility, 6,* 36-37.

Wade, C. (1992). Disability culture rap. *The Disability Rag, Sept/Oct,* p.37.

Wang, C. (1993). Culture, meaning and disability: Injury prevention campaigns and the production of stigma. In M. Nagler, (Ed.), *Perspectives on disability.* (2nd ed., pp. 77-90). Palo Alto, CA: Health Markets Research.

Weaver, H. (1999). Indigenous people and the social work profession: Defining culturally competent services. *Social Work, 44,* 217-225.

White, B. (1999). Quality in social work education. *CSWE Reporter, 47,* 1.

Unit II: Developmental Disabilities

Anderson, B. (1997, July 08). Reno mother questions state program for disabled children. *Reno Gazette-Journal,* pp. 1A-3A.

Arias, R. (1994). Group work with women who have a child with a developmental disability. *Australian Social Work, 47,* 37-42.

Baumeister, A., Kupstas, F., & Klindworth, L. (1990). New morbidity: Implications for prevention of children's disabilities. *Exceptionality, 1,* 1-16.

Bennett, T., DeLuca, D., & Allen, R. (1996). Families of children with disabilities: Positive adaptation across the life cycle. *Social Work in Education, 18,* 31-44.

Bradley, R., Rock, S., Whiteside, L., Caldwell, B., & Brisby, J. (1991). Dimensions of parenting in families having children with disabilities. *Exceptionality, 2,* 41-61.

Court backs option for mentally disabled. (1999, September). *NASW News, 44(6),* 6.

Cruickshank, W. M. (1990). Definition: A major issue in the field of learning disabilities. In M. Nagler (Ed.), *Perspectives on disability* (pp. 389-406). Palo Alto, CA: Health Markets Research.

Fergusson, D. M. & Horwood, L. J. (1995). Early disruptive behavior, IQ, and later school achievement and delinquent behavior. *Journal of Abnormal Child Psychology, 23,* 183-199.

Mackelprang, R. & Salsgiver, R. (1999). *Disability: A diversity model approach in human service practice.* Pacific Grove, CA: Brookes/Cole Publishing.

Meecham, M. J. (1996). *Cerebral palsy.* (2nd ed.). Austin, TX: Pro-Ed Publishing.

Petr, C. & Barney, D. (1993). Reasonable efforts for children with disabilities: The parent's perspective. *Social Work, 38,* 247-258.

Public Law 94-142. (1977). Education for All Handicapped Children Act of 1975. *Federal Register* (August 23, 1977).

Public Law 101-476. (1990). Individuals with Disabilities Education Act of 1990. *Federal Register* (October 30, 1990).

Rousey, A., Best, S., & Blacher, J. (1992). Mothers' and fathers' perceptions of stress and coping with children who have severe disabilities. *American Journal on Mental Retardation, 97,* 99-109.

Turnbull, A. P. & Turnbull, H. R. (1996). *Families, professionals, and exceptionalities: A special partnership.* (2nd ed.). New York: Merrill Publishing.

Unit III: Disability in Adulthood

American Psychiatric Association (1994). *The diagnostic and statistical manual of mental disorders (DSM-IV).* (4th ed.). Washington, DC: Author.

Blackerby, W. (1990). A treatment model for sexuality disturbance following brain injury. *Journal of Head Trauma Rehabilitation, 5,* 73-82.

Borysenko, J. (1987). *Minding the body, mending the mind.* Reading, MA: Addison-Wesley Publishing.

Dossey, L. (1991). *Meaning and medicine.* New York: Bantam Press.

Eisenberg, M., Sutkin, L., & Jansen, M. (1984). *Chronic illness and disability through the life span.* New York: Springer Publishing.

Hatfield, A. B. & Lefley, H. P. (1993). *Surviving mental illness: Stress, coping, and adaptation.* New York: Guilford Press.

Hillyer, B. (1993). *Feminism and disability.* Norman, OK: University of Oklahoma Press.

Levy, S. (1985). *Behavior and cancer: Lifestyle and psychosocial factors.* San Francisco: Jossey-Bass Publishing.

Mackelprang, R. & Salsgiver, R. (1996). Persons with disabilities and social work: Historical and contemporary issues. *Social Work, 41,* 7-14.

Mackelprang, R., & Salsgiver, R. (1999). *Disability: A diversity model approach in human service practice.* Pacific Grove, CA: Brookes/Cole Publishing.

Rabin, B. (1980). *The sensuous wheeler: Sexual adjustment for the spinal cord injured.* Long Beach, CA: Author.

Shapiro, C. (1993). *When part of the self is lost: Helping clients heal after sexual and reproductive losses.* San Francisco: Jossey-Bass Publishing.

Shapiro, J. (1993). *No pity: People with disabilities forging a new civil rights movement.* New York: Times Books.

Tower, K. (1994). Consumer-centered social work practice: Restoring client self-determination. *Social Work, 39,* 191-196.

Trieschmann, R. (1988). *Spinal cord injuries: Psychological, social, and vocational rehabilitation.* (2nd ed.). New York: Demos Publications.

Trieschmann, R. (1987). *Aging with a disability.* New York: Demos Publishing.

U.S. Department of Health and Human Services. (1992). *Social security handbook.* Washington, D.C.: U.S. Government Printing Office.

Wilk, R. (1994). Are the rights of people with mental illness still important? *Social Work, 39,* 167-175.

Unit IV: The Great Equalizers: Advocacy, Policy, and Technology

Alinsky, S. (1971). *Rules for radicals: A pragmatic primer for realistic radicals.* New York: Random House.

Court backs option for mentally disabled. (1999, September). *NASW News, 44(6),* 6.

Johnson, M. (1999a). Our supremely defining moment. *Ragged Edge*, May/June, 9.

Johnson, M. (1999b). Quadriplegic dies after respirator removed: Activist group denied restraining order. *Ragged Edge, September/October*, 11.

Kopels, S. (1995). The Americans with Disabilities Act: A tool to combat poverty. *Journal of Social Work Education, 31(3)*. 337-346.

Kraus, L., Stoddard, S., & Gilmartin, D. (1996). *Chartbook on disability in the United States*, Washington, DC: National Institute on Disability and Rehabilitation Research.

National Center for the Dissemination of Disability Research. (1998). How many Americans have disabilities? *The Research Exchange, 3*, p. 3.

Public Law 94-142. (1977). Education for All Handicapped Children Act of 1975. *Federal Register* (August 23, 1977).

Public Law 100-407. (1988). Technology-Related Assistance for Individuals with Disabilities Act of 1988. *Summary Report*. U.S. Department of Education, Office of Special Education and Rehabilitation Services.

Public Law 101-336. (1990). Americans with Disabilities Act of 1990, *104 Stat 327*. U.S. Government Printing Office (July 26, 1990).

Public Law 101-476. (1990). Individuals with Disabilities Education Act of 1990. *Federal Register* (October 30, 1990).

IN-CLASS EXERCISES, MATERIALS, VIDEOS

I believe in acknowledging barriers that interfere with social workers' cross-cultural relationships. Most students have been socialized not to talk about disability, at least not unless it is discussed with reverence. In this class, students examine their true feelings, talk openly about them, and learn to get over unnecessary angst and unwanted pity.

Introduction exercises

Needed: 3 x 5 cards for all students, current 1040 tax form

Immediately after my initial introduction (e.g., my name and the name of the class) and before discussing anything else, students are given cards to write down the answers to three questions:

1. What one thing do you most want to learn from this course?

2. If you had to have a disability (or a new disability), what type of disability would you dread most?

3. If you were a sales clerk at a major department store, which type of customer would you feel least prepared to serve? A person from a different race than yours, a person with a different sexual orientation, or a person with a severe disability?

I pick up the cards, finish making class introductions, then show a 30-minute video so I have time to tally Questions 2 and 3. (There is always a close race between "paralysis" and "blindness" as a response to 2. For 3, over 90% of my students consistently report that they are least prepared to work with people with disabilities). 1 is for my own information, so I check that out later.

Re: Question 2

I comment on the over-representation of blindness as an answer, especially since some other disabilities (like quadriplegia) are more costly and physically debilitating. Then, using a current 1040 tax form, I point out that blindness must indeed be the most "dreaded" disability (said in jest), since it is the only one granted an additional tax deduction. I ask students why they think this is so? I discuss how fear of the dark is a primal fear, which probably accounts for the class statistics and the support of American taxpayers. We then discuss the disparity between the reality of blindness and the myths about it. I also explain that blind people have been organized longer than any other disability group. With the influence of individuals like Helen Keller, they have been more successful politically. So, blindness isn't really the "worst" disability (there is no worst or best), however, blind people are among the most advanced disability groups.

Re: Question 3

I ask students to explain the reasons they responded as they did about feeling unprepared to serve customers with severe disabilities. This is always an interesting discussion.

John Callahan's cartoons

I have selected several of the cartoons from Callahan's book *Don't Worry, He Won't Get Far on Foot* to foster additional discussions about stereotypical responses to people with disabilities. Callahan has several cartoon books (*Do Not Disturb: Any Further* and *Digesting the Child Within*) that contain some of the most irreverent cartoons about disability. Sift through them carefully, and there are excellent cartoons for pushing students past the comfort zone. I use them to create a safe place for acknowledging their discomfort.

Debates

Twice during the semester we debate relevant disability issues. Currently, I have chosen telethons and cochlear implants as the divisive issues for discussion. I ask for volunteers from both sides of the arguments to serve on debate teams consisting of *four* members each. (Sometimes I have to appoint volunteers.) Another student is selected to be the official timekeeper. The remaining students serve as the voting judges. The teams have *five minutes* to prepare their opening arguments. Two members of each team (one member per side at a time) have *three minutes each* to make their key points. The teams are given an additional five minutes to prepare their rebuttal arguments. The last two members of each team have the same three minutes to close with their rebuttals. The class then votes on the issue.

It doesn't really matter how the decision turns out, (in fact, it usually turns out to be the side with the most charismatic speakers), but the debate gives students a chance to examine both sides of these controversial issues. During their five-minute preparation times, I listen in on *both sides* and I drop hints about issues that the teams overlooked so that the full arguments are presented. Then, I stay out of the way so I don't influence the votes.

Materials

I have developed a number of things for this class that I am glad to share including

- A list of acronyms for terms commonly used in the disability community.
- A guide to speaking and writing about disability.
- A complete training manual (120 pages) on developmental disabilities with photographs, pre-test, and post-test.
- A PowerPoint presentation to accompany the training manual.
- The "Case of Molly B.," a fictitious case used for a class competition.

For information about these unpublished, copyright materials, please contact me directly via my email address, drtower@nvbell.net.

Guests

I have an extensive network of disability-related contacts for my class, but for those who don't, I suggest contacting one of the following: Your local Center for Independent Living (CIL), Office of Protection and Advocacy, your local school district (to find parent organizations for children with disabilities), University Affiliated Program (if your university has one), an Assistive Technology Specialist (ask the school district or CIL), Department of Vocational Rehabilitation, Disabled Veterans organizations, or some of the specific disability groups (e.g., MS Society, MD Association, Cancer Society).

Videos

I use video materials that include my own productions and out-takes, as well as some excellent commercial documentaries. The KNPB productions are my own work, however they are distributed by Public Television.

Full Circle (1996).	KNPB production.	www.knpb.org
Mending Spirits (1992).	KNPB production.	www.knpb.org
When Billy Broke His Head (1994).	Fanlight Productions.	www.fanlight.com
People in Motion (1993).	Fanlight Productions.	www.fanlight.com

UNIVERSITY OF UTAH
GRADUATE SCHOOL OF SOCIAL WORK | SALT LAKE CITY, UT
JEANETTE R. DREWS

Social Work Practice with People with Developmental Disabilities and Mental Retardation

Social Work 709 (Spring 1999)

INTRODUCTION

This course is a second-year elective that provides a general introduction to social work practice with people with developmental disabilities and mental retardation. It builds on core skills offered in foundation and advanced social work classes and provides specialized knowledge, values, and skills related to individuals and families affected by disabling conditions. Students will learn about the evolution of the philosophy and theory that drives practice, the consequent array of service systems, the etiologies of disabilities, and practice issues and methods for families and individuals.

CONTEXT

The field of disabilities includes two distinct groups of people requiring quite different kinds of services. The first group includes people who have one or more physical disability but not mental retardation. The second group includes people whose primary disability is mental retardation with or without secondary physical disabilities. Disabilities have a number of different etiologies that are as different as the disabilities themselves. Some people incur disabling conditions through the course of life events such as accidental injury, violence, or illness. Others are born with disabilities due to genetic anomalies or organic intrusions such as teratagens or maternal illnesses.

The history of service and accommodation for people with disabilities varies according to the type and level of limitation. All persons with disabilities have been traditionally underserved by social work for a number of reasons. Often, helping professionals assume that the medical services provided for the individual who has a disability ensure adequate care. In fact, medical services help with very few of the everyday obstacles facing people with disabilities. The social implications of making friends, getting married, having children, getting jobs, enjoying recreational activities, and participating in the community represent much greater challenges to people with disabilities than their medical problems. This is the arena in which social workers can make a very important contribution. Public accommodations, the absence of discrimination, and the creation of positive attitudes are the top priorities for the social worker involved with disability issues. These areas require the social worker to be an advocate, a systems-change agent, a policy maker, a lobbyist, and a clinician for individuals, families, and groups.

It is reasonable for the aspiring professional to learn the full scope of social work responsibility for practice with persons with developmental or physical disabilities. Often the disabling condition of the client requires that the social work be done in a variety of creative ways with several people involved in the client's life. Also, there are no theories, as such, that directly pertain to interventions with people with disabilities because they are simply people who happen to have challenges beyond the norm. This requires accommodation for the disability while retaining appropriate respect for individual differences within the context of social work theory. Unfortunately, people who struggle with communication barriers, including some individuals with mental retardation and many with cerebral palsy, continue to be avoided by the larger mental health community whose reliance on verbal communication is obvious. It is therefore critical that social workers pursue the advancement of more meaningful and effective interventions for people with severe and multiple disabilities.

GOALS

The intention for this second-year elective is to engender enthusiasm for acquiring a knowledge base and an understanding of the issues dictating service for people with developmental and physical disabilities at every level of social work practice. To accomplish the objectives of this course, every class member will contribute their knowledge and experience to an open forum of learning and professional development that will enrich and enlarge social work participation with people who are disabled.

Your learning laboratory will consist of lecture material, reading, and meeting people. The library will be an important source for information and students will be expected to explore community resources as well. Everyone will be encouraged to recognize their personal contribution as a means of building the knowledge base that will lend credibility to social workers in this area. Assignments will reflect the broad spectrum of needs and the students' interests related to those needs. Class attendance, continuous thought and exploration, and open discussion will be essential ingredients to the success of this course.

OBJECTIVES

The knowledge base will include

1. an understanding of the definition and scope of developmental and severe physical disabilities including etiology, diagnostic implications, psychosocial prognoses, and levels of functioning;

2. clarification of individual philosophical assumptions and professional values and ethics that will impact the approach and quality of service that each student will ultimately implement professionally;

3. a knowledge of the historical evolution of public laws and services that benefit people with disabilities and an understanding of the philosophical and political debates surrounding that evolution;

4. an understanding of the rationale behind state-of-the-art services;

5. an awareness of the moral responsibility of society to afford and ensure the legal and human rights of people with disabilities;

6. an awareness of the balance between the responsibilities of people with disabilities who choose to live as citizens and their rights;

7. an understanding of the complex network of people who are served and those who are not served;

8. a conceptualization of the dilemma of knowing who "the client" is, including an appreciation for the management problems, emotional burdens, and long lasting effects of disability on the disabled, their family members, persons with whom they relate outside of the home, and the community at large;

9. intervention strategies for assisting in the adjustment and coping processes required of the client group and their family members;

10. various methods for conducting an ongoing evaluation of practice that ensures continual increase in the quality of life for the client group and their family members.

TEXTS

An anthology of readings is on reserve in the Social Work Reading Room.

EVALUATION METHODS

This course is a one-credit elective which means the student will receive a credit or no-credit grade. Students who are to receive credit for this course must complete the following requirements:

ASSIGNMENTS

1. Complete the following project:

   The goal of this assignment is to build your familiarity with people who are involved with disabling conditions and the challenges and issues that they encounter as they seek a normalized lifestyle. The professor can provide each student names of people who would be willing to participate in this experience with you. Upon your first telephone contact, you should explain the scope of the project, how it might benefit them, and that it may require 2-3 visits to complete. Plan each visit very carefully so that you are able to honor their time constraints with efficiency. Enter into this process as a learner, not a professional, understanding that you are asking them to share a very personal part of their lives with you. You will perhaps benefit far more than they, but the fulfillment of the assignment has the potential to give them useful information and experience that can be helpful to them as well. Tell them in advance that they may refuse to participate in any part of the assignment and do not have to answer any questions that they choose not to.

   a. Find and interview someone to get acquainted with the individual, his or her family, friends, and the challenges he or she lives with. This can be accomplished over one visit or several depending on the circumstances you encounter. Plan your visit in advance so you are not at a loss for material on the scene. Know what you want to know and how you might best acquire this information in as friendly a way as possible. You may want to include questions about the etiology of the condition, the diagnosis and prognosis for the person with the disabilities. How was this diagnosis arrived at? Ask the family members about their experiences with disabilities. Explore their past, understand their present, and listen to their anxieties about the future. What do they need NOW? What kind of services are they receiving, if any? What is their satisfaction level with current service provision? What have been their expectations and disappointments with the service system?

   Continue to design the interview according to your own interests with this family.

   i. Product: Write a synopsis of your experience noting what you learned about the person who has the disability, their condition, individual/family history, and challenges. Write about the family and their challenges and daily life demands. Write also about yourself. What inner issues and emotions emerged within yourself? How did it affect your response and behavior? What did you learn about you? (Can be less than 10 pages.)

   b. The second tier of the project is to explore the service system. Contact a community provider, the Utah Association of Community Services, or someone at a regional office of the Division of Services for People with Disabilities. Create a scenario that protects the confidentiality of your family but uses their circumstances as an example of a family needing services. Plan an outline of questions and topics that will guide your time with the individual you contact. You may have to make more than one contact to seek out the diversity of possibilities that are potentially available to your family or families who have similar needs. Ask about costs. Decide if your family were allotted a certain amount of money (ask your service person for a typical amount given your family's circumstances) what kind of package could/would you propose for them.

   i. Product: Develop an optimal service package within the budget that was suggested to you by whomever you spoke with in the system. Will the services change in five years? Will the person require the same level of service provision over their lifetime? Is the individual in a crisis situation today that may change over time?

PARTICIPATION (25%)

Participation is not an optional activity in this course. It is the only way you will be able to come away from this class with a useful knowledge base. So, participation is a vague way of saying: *"be there!"* Be involved in the projects set before you. *Be* in the community to explore the alternatives that really exist. *Be* with people who have disabilities. When we are talking about a certain population, such as people with disabilities, you need to be with them to get a sense of the felt needs. Go out and meet people where they live or work or play. Talk to those who work with them. The experience will have a profound effect on you, and your ability and willingness to participate in class will be significantly sharpened. *Be* in the library, finding out what is state-of-the-art practice. *Be* creative in conceptualizing services that don't already exist and prepare yourself to contribute to the future research and practice arena that needs new ideas. And, finally, *be* in class to contribute what you have learned and to learn some more.

READING

Reading is part of participation. Although the emphasis in this class is getting to know the people first, you should then let the interactions lead you to a well-grounded understanding of the knowledge base available through the literature. With every topic there are suggestions for further reading. The library has a wealth of resources in addition to those listed in the syllabus. Most of the readings listed on the syllabus are available for your convenience in the SW Reading Room. Some are not. Those with an asterisk have been put on reserve at the Marriott Library. There is no need to limit yourself to this list; many resources are available.

COMMUNITY AGENCIES

Some of the key agencies serving people with disabilities are listed below. This is by no means an inclusive list, but you should be aware of these as a bare minimum. It would be helpful for you to go to each agency and talk with someone there about their function in the community. If you are particularly interested in knowing about the agency make an appointment before you go, asking to talk with someone for a short time (approximately 30 minutes) about the purpose of the agency, its typical activities, the people they serve, current issues, etc. Prepare your questions in advance so as not to waste their time or yours. Each agency has publications that you may find useful. Ask for, or purchase, those that interest you.

1. The Arc: Utah - advocates for citizens with mental retardation
   455 East 400 South, Suite 200, SLC, Phone: 364-5060
2. Disability Law Center
   455 East 400 South, (4th Floor), SLC Phone: 363-1347
   Executive Director: Fraser Nelson, Clinical Director: Ron Gardiner
3. Utah Governor's Council for People with Disabilities
   550 East 300 South, Suite 201, Phone: 533-4128
   Executive Director: Alison Lozano
4. Utah Independent Living Center: Salt Lake County
   3445 South Main
   Executive Director: Debbie Mayer
5. Utah Association of Community Services
   455 East 400 South, Suite 301, Phone: 328-4580
6. Division of Services for People with Disabilities (DSPD)
   120 North 200 West, Suite 411, Phone: 538-4200
   Sue Geary, Executive Director
7. DSPD Regional Offices
   Central Region: Georgia Badley; Northern Region: John Schoenfield; Western Region: Judy Dixon; Eastern Region: Gerry Ulwelling

CONTENT OUTLINE

Unit I: Disabilities: A Survey of the Challenges

- Overview and discussion of course objectives.
- Describe the people and define the context of the work.

Readings

- Bogdan, R., Biklen, D., Shapiro, A. & Spelkoman, D. (1982) The disabled: media's monster. *Social Policy*. pp. 32-35; Fall.
- Bogdan, R. & Taylor, S. (1987) Toward a sociology of acceptance: The other side of the study of deviance. *Social Policy,* Fall. pp. 34-39.
- Dudley, J.R. (1987) Speaking for themselves: People who are labeled as mentally retarded. *Social Work*, 32(1), 80-82.
- Gartner, A. (1982) Images of the disabled/disabling images. *Social Policy*. p. 15; Fall.
- Feuerstein, R. (1988). Don't accept me as I am: helping "retarded" people to excel. NY: Plenum Publishing Corp.
- Goffman, E. (1963) *Stigma: Notes on the management of spoiled identity.* New York: Simon & Schuster. pp. 1-40.
- Hardman, M. (1987) Closing speech for conference focusing on the quality of life in school and community for people with disabilities. University of Utah, Special Education.
- Hauge, M. (1965) What has happened to Eugenics. *The Eugenics Review.* 56:203-205.
- Jones, E.E., Farina, A., Hastorf, A.H., Markus, H., Miller, D.T., Scott, R.A. (1984) *Social Stigma: The Psychology of Marked Relationships.* New York: W.H. Freeman and Company. pp.1-79.
- Kriegel, L. (1982) The wolf in the pit in the zoo. *Social Policy.* pp. 16-23; Fall.
- Lutfiya, Z.M. (1988) Other than clients: reflections on relationships between people with disabilities and typical people. *TASH.*

Unit II: Historical Evolution of Service Philosophy: From Medical Model to Individualized Supports and Self-Determination

Readings

- Gardner, J.F. & Chapman, M.S. (1993). Historical and contemporary trends in services (pages 37-44). *Developing staff competencies for supporting people with developmental disabilities: An orientation handbook (Second Edition)*, Baltimore, MD: Paul H. Brookes Publishing Co.
- Horne, M. (1987) *Values in Social Work.* England: Wildwood House Ltd. pp 11-31; 80-102.
- Isbel, L. (1985) A motion to adjourn. *Utah Holiday, May,* pp. 40-51.
- Keenan, M.P. & Parker, D.R. (1983) Deinstitutionalization: A policy analysis. In *Wikler, L. & Keenan, M.P. (Eds) (1983) Developmental Disabilities: No Longer a Private Tragedy.* Silver Springs, MD: National Association of Social Workers and Washington, D.C.: American Association on Mental Deficiency.
- Lakin, K.C. & Bruininks, R.H. (1985) Contemporary services for handicapped children and youth. In R.H. Bruininks & K.C. Lakin (Eds) *Living and Learning in the Least Restrictive Environment.* Baltimore, MD: Paul H. Brookes Publishing Co.
- Lutfiya, Z.M. (1988) Other than clients: reflections on relationships between people with disabilities and typical people. *TASH.*
- Pancsofar, E. & Blackwell, R. (1986) *A User's Guide to Community Entry for the Severely Handicapped.* NY: State University of New York Press.

- Peck, C.A. (1990) Linking values and science in social policy decisions affecting citizens with severe disabilities. In L.H. Meyer, C.A. Peck & L. Brown *Critical Issues in the Lives of People with Severe Disabilities.* Baltimore, MD: Paul H. Brookes Publishing Co.

- Trent, Jr. J.W. (1994). *Inventing the Feeble Mind: A history of mental retardation in the United States.* Berkeley: CA: University of California Press.

- Wright, B.A. (1982) Value-laden beliefs and principles for rehabilitation. In Alfred H. Katz and Knute Martin *A Handbook of Services for the Handicapped.* Westport, CT: Greenwood Press.

- Wright, B.A. (1988) Attitudes and the fundamental negative bias: Conditions and corrections. In Harold E. Yuker (ed) *Attitudes toward persons with disabilities.* NY: Springer Publishing Co.

Unit III: Knowing About Disabilities

- Specific types of disabilities.
- Prenatal diagnoses.
- FAS and drug abuse during pregnancy.

Readings

- Batshaw, ML (1997). Children with Disabilities, Fourth Edition. Baltimore, MD: Paul H. Brookes Publishing Co.

- Gardner, J.F. & Chapman, M.S. (1993). An introduction to developmental disabilities (pages 3-26). *Developing staff competencies for supporting people with developmental disabilities: An orientation handbook (Second Edition),* Baltimore, MD: Paul H. Brookes Publishing Co.

- Hallowell & Ratey (1994). Driven to Distraction: Recognizing and Coping with ADD from childhood to adulthood. NY: Touchstone.

- Hazelton Foundation (1993). Fetal Alcohol Syndrome and Fetal Alcohol Effects.

- Malbin, D. (1993). Fetal Alcohol Syndrome; Fetal Alcohol Effects: Strategies for Professionals. Center City, MN: Hazelden Educational Materials.

- Penso, D.E. (1993). *Perceptuo-motor difficulties: Theory and strategies to help children, adolescents and adults.* New York: Chapman & Hall.

- Stratton, Howe, & Battaglia (Eds.) (1996). Fetal Alcohol Syndrome: Diagnosis, Epidemiology, Prevention, & Treatment. Washington, DC: National Academy Press.

- Wedding, Horton, & Webster (Eds.) (1986). Neurological disorders. *The Neuropsychology Handbook:* NY: Springer Publishing Co.

- Wender, P.H. *Attention-deficit Hyperactivity Disorder in Adolescents and Adults.*

Unit IV: Genetic Implications
Readings

- Batshaw, ML (1997). Children with Disabilities, Fourth Edition. Baltimore, MD: Paul H. Brookes Publishing Co.

- Duster, Troy (1990). *Backdoor to eugenics.* New York: Routledge. [pages 112 - 162 (Includes: "Eugenics by the backdoor" and Appendices A, B & C.)]

- Modell, B. & Modell, M. (1992). *Towards a healthy baby: Congenital disorders and the new genetics in primary care.* New York: Oxford University Press.

- Schild, S. Genetics and Social Work.

Unit V: Self-determination and Choice; Rights and Responsibilities

Readings

- Bratlinger, E. (1992). Professionals' attitudes toward the sterilization of people with disabilities. *The Journal of the Association for Persons with Severe Handicaps,* Vol 17(1):4-18.

- Gardner, J.F. & Chapman, M.S. (1993). Legal rights of persons with developmental disabilities (pages 69-92). *Developing staff competencies for supporting people with developmental disabilities: An orientation handbook (Second Edition).* Baltimore: Paul H. Brookes Publishing Co.

- Guess, D., Benson, H.A., Siegel-Causey, E. (1985). Concepts and issues related to choice-making and autonomy among persons with severe disabilities. *The Association for Persons with Severe Handicaps,* Vol 10(2):79-86.

- Kelner, G. (1994). *Offenders with mental retardation in Utah: an analysis of service gaps and issues.* Utah State Division of Services for People with Disabilities.

- Mason, C.Y. (1990). *Consumer choice and satisfaction.* National Association of Rehabilitation Facilities. Washington, D.C.

- Parsons, M.B. & Reid, D.H. (1990). Assessing food preferences among persons with profound mental retardation: Providing opportunities to make choices. *Journal of Applied Behavior Analysis,* Vol.23(2): pp. 183-195.

- Shevin, M. & Klein, N.K. (1984). The importance of choice-making skills for students with severe disabilities. *The Association for Persons with Severe Handicaps,* Vol. 9(3):159-166.

- Sundram, C.J. & Stavis, P.F. (1994). Sexuality and mental retardation: unmet challenges. *Mental Retardation,* Vol 32(4):255-264.

- Wolfensberger, W. (1994). A personal interpretation of the mental retardation scene in the light of the "signs of the times." *Mental Retardation,* Vol. 32(1):19-33.

Unit VI: Clinical Needs and Issues of the Person with Disabilities

- This discussion will include the role of the social worker in working with people with disabilities and their families. Issues that emerge during the search for "appropriate services" reveal many dilemmas that reflect fundamental values, attitudes, and philosophies. Methods of creating a client-focused relationship will be key to the discussion. We will also discuss the clinical needs of the person who is developmentally disabled, and intervention strategies that encourage integration, independence, productivity, and social skills training.

Readings

- Barrett, R.P. (ed.) (1986). *Severe behavior disorders in the mentally retarded: Nondrug approaches to treatment.* New York: Plenum Press.

- Fletcher, R.J. & Dosen, A. (eds.) (1993). *Mental health aspects of mental retardation: Progress in assessment and treatment.* New York: Maxwell Macmillan International/Lexington Books.

- Gardner, J.F. & Chapman, M.S. (1993). *Developing staff competencies for supporting people with developmental disabilities: An orientation handbook (Second Edition).* Baltimore: Paul H. Brookes Publishing Co.

- Nuffield, E.J. (1986). Counseling and psychotherapy. In R.P. Barrett (Ed.) *Severe Behavior Disorders in the Mentally Retarded.* New York: Plenum Press.

- Rothenberg, E.D. (1994). Bereavement Intervention with vulnerable populations: A case report on group work with the developmentally disabled. *Social Work with Groups,* Vol 17(3):61-75.

- Sutton, E., Factor, A.R., Hawkins, B.A., Heller, T., Seltzer, G.B. (1993). *Older adults with developmental disabilities: Optimizing choice and change.* Baltimore: Paul H. Brookes Publishing Co.

Unit VII: Clinical Needs and Issues of the Family

Readings

- Baerwald, A. (1983) Case management: Defining a concept. In *Developmental Disabilities: No longer a private tragedy.* Lynn Wikler and Maryanne P. Keenan (eds). Co-published by National Association of Social Workers, MD and American Association on Mental Deficiency, Washington, D.C.

- Brown, F. & Lehr, D.H. (1989) *Persons with Profound Disabilities: Issues and Practices.* Baltimore: Paul H. Brookes Publishing Co.

- Budd, K.S. & Fabry, P.L. (1986). Parent and Family Training. In R.P. Barrett (Ed.) *Severe Behavior Disorders in the Mentally Retarded.* New York: Plenum Press.

- Buscaglia, L. (1975) *The Disabled and their Parents: A Counseling Challenge.* NJ: Charles B. Slack, Inc.

- Goldfarb, L.A., Brotherson, M.J., Summers, J.A., Turnbull, A.P. (1986). *Meeting the challenge of disability or chronic illness: A family guide.* Baltimore: Paul H. Brookes Publishing Co.

- Goldiamond, B. (1982) Families of the disabled: Sometimes insiders in rehabilitation, always outsiders in policy planning. In *Disabled people as second-class citizens, pp 152-170.* Myron G. Eisenberg, Cynthia Griggins, and Richard J. Duval (eds). NY: Springer Publishing Co., Inc.

- Hall, J.A., Ford, L.H., Moss, J.W., Dineen, J.P. (1986) Practice with mentally retarded adults as an adjunct to vocational training. *Social Work, 31(2),* 125-129.

- Hansen, J.C. (1984) *Families with handicapped members.* Rockville, MD: Aspen Systems Corporation.

- Hanvey, C. (1981) *Social Work with Mentally Handicapped People.* London: The Heinemann Educational Books, Ltd.

- Harris, S.L. (1983) *Families of the developmentally disabled: A guide to behavioral intervention.* NY: Pergamon Press.

- Lovett, H. (1985) *Cognitive Counseling and Persons with Special Needs.* NY: Praeger Publishers.

- Ludlow, B.L., Turnbull, A.P., & Lucksasson, R. (Eds) (1988) *Transition to Adult Life for People with Mental Retardation: Principles and Practices.* Baltimore, MD: Paul H. Brookes Publishing Co.

- McCarthy, W. & Fegan, L. (1984) *Sex Education and the Intellectually Handicapped.* Australia: ADIS Health Science Press.

- McGee, J.J., Menolascino, F.J., Hobbs, D.C., Menousek, P.E. (1987) *Gentle Teaching: A non-aversive approach for helping persons with mental retardation.* NY: Human Sciences Press, Inc.

- Marinelli, R.P. & Dell Orto, A.E. (1977) *The Psychological and Social Impact of Physical Disability.* NY: Springer Publishing Co.

- Mittler, P. & McConachie, H. (Eds) (1983) *Parents, Professionals, and Mentally Handicapped People.* Great Britain: Croom Helm.

- *Non-violent physical crisis intervention: A program focusing on management of disruptive, assaultive, or out of control behavior* (1982) Milwaukee, WI: Crisis Prevention Institute.

- Platt, M., Sabsay, S., et al (1985) *Social Setting, Stigma, and Communicative Competence.* Amsterdam, PA: John Benjamins Publishing Co.

- Rauch, J.B. & Tivoli, L. (1989) Social workers' knowledge and utilization of genetic services. *Social Work, 34(1),* 55-56.

- Slater, M.A. & Wikler, L. (1986) 'Normalized' family resources for families with a developmentally disabled child. *Social Work, 31(5),* 385-390.

- Thompson, C.E. (1986) *Raising a handicapped child.* NY: Ballantine Books.

- Thorin, E.J. & Irvin, L.K. (1992). Family stress associated with transition to adulthood of young people with severe disabilities. *The Journal of the Association for Persons with Severe Handicaps,* pages 31-39.

- Vash, C.L. (1981) *The Psychology of Disability.* NY: Springer Publishing Co.
- Wikler, L., Wasow, M., Hatfield, E. (1983) Seeking strengths in families of developmentally disabled children. *Social Work,* July/August, 313-315.
- Wikler, L. (1981) Chronic stresses of families of mentally retarded children. *Family Relations,* April.

Unit VIII: Behavior Supports and Interventions

- This discussion will help students understand the movement from traditional behavior interventions to a philosophy of behavioral supports that has occurred in service systems designed for people with mental retardation. We will discuss the philosophical underpinnings of an array of specific practice approaches that have evolved over the past century.

Readings

- Amado, A.N. (1994). Person-centered agency design: A three year project 1991-1994. Human services research & development center. St. Paul, MN.
- Butterworth, J., Hagner, D., Heikkinen, B., Faris, S., DeMello, S. & McDonough, K. (1993). Whole life planning: A guide for organizers and facilitators. Institute for Community Inclusion, Children's Hospital. Boston: MA.
- DaiLeo, D. (1997). It's my meeting! A family consumer pocket guide to participating in person-centered planning. Training Resource Network, Inc. St. Augustine, FL.
- Falvey, M.A., Forest, M., Pearpoint, J., Rosenberg, R.L. (1993). All my life's a circle. Using the tools: Circles, MAPS & PATH. Inclusion Press. Toronto: CN.
- Forest, M., Pierpoint, J., & O'Brien, J. (1993). PATH: A workbook for planning positive futures. Toronto: Inclusion Press. Ontario: Canada.
- Komissar, C., Hart, D. & Friedlander, R. (unpublished). Utilizing all your resources: Individuals with and without disabilities volunteering together. Institute for Community Inclusion, UAP Children's Hospital. Boston: MA.
- Mount, B. (1991). Building person-centered support. University Affiliated Program of New Jersey. Piscataway: New Jersey.
- Mount, B. & Zwernik, K. (1988). It's never too early, it's never too late: a booklet about personal futures planning. Metropolitan Council. St. Paul, MN.
- Oregon transition systems change project. (1996). Person centered planning fact sheets packet. Specialized Training Program. Eugene, OR.
- Smull, M. & Harrison, S.B. (1992). Supporting people with severe reputations in the community: Reviewing essential life style plans. National Association of State Directors of Developmental Disabilities Services, Inc. Alexandria, VA.

Unit IX: Psychotropic Medications Readings

Readings

- Bentley & Walsh (1996). The Social worker and Psychotropic Medication: Toward effective collaboration with Mental Health Clients, Families and Providers. Pacific Grove, CA: Brooks/Cole Publishing Co.
- Preston & Johnson (1997). Clinical Psychopharmacology made ridiculously simple, Edition 3. South Sacramento, CA: Kaiser Medical Ctr.
- Reiss & Aman (Eds). (1998). Psychotropic Medications and Developmental Disabilities. Ohio State University Nisonger Ctr. Unit X: Medical Issues: Managed Care; Long term care: Costs.

Unit X: From Education to Employment: Transition/Adult Planning

- This discussion will include the ramifications of P.L. 94-142 and subsequent laws and practices in the educational system. Transition and Adult Planning will address the issues and challenges associated with leaving a mandated service system under the auspices of one agency (i.e., education) to a non-mandated adult service system consisting of many agencies.

Readings

- Davis, S.B. (1994). *1994 Update on Inclusion in Education of Children with Mental Retardation* and *Plenary Speech on inclusion in education* and *Report card to the nation on inclusion of people with mental retardation in community housing.*
- Gardner, J.F., Chapman, M.S., Donaldson, G., & Jacobson, S.G. (1988) *Toward Supported Employment: A Process Guide for Planned Change.* Baltimore: Paul H. Brookes Publishing Co.
- Greenwood, R. & Johnson, V.A. (1987) Employer perspectives on workers with disabilities. *Journal of Rehabilitation*, July/August/September, 37-45.
- McCarthy, H. (1988) Attitudes that affect employment opportunities for persons with disabilities. In H.E. Yuker, *Attitudes Toward Persons with Disabilities.* NY: Springer Publishing Co.
- McDonnell, A. McDonnell,J, Hardman, M. & McCune, G. (1991). Educating students with severe disabilities in their neighborhood school: the Utah elementary integration model. *Remedial and Special Education,* Vol 12(6):32-45.
- McDonnell, J., Wilcox, B. & Hardman, M.L. (1991) *Secondary Programs for Students with Developmental Disabilities.* Needham Heights, MA: Allyn and Bacon.
- National Association on the State Boards of Education (1992). *Winners All: A call for inclusive schools.*
- Turnbull, H.R., Turnbull, A.P., Bronicki, G.J., Summers, J.A. & Roeder-Gordon, C. (1989) *Disability and the Family: A Guide to Decisions for Adulthood.*
- Weisgerber, R.A. (1991) *Quality of Life for Persons with Disabilities: Skill Development and Transitions across Life Stages.* Gaithersberg, MD: Aspen Publishers, Inc.

Unit XI: ADA: Implications of the Law; Osbourne Case

- Guest Speaker: Susan S. Behle, Executive Director of Utah Association of Community Services.
  - Ms. Behle will discuss the intent and implementation of the ADA using the implications of the recent Osbourne Case and other examples of ADA issues. Handouts will be provided by the speaker.

UNIVERSITY OF MAINE

SCHOOL OF SOCIAL WORK AND CENTER FOR COMMUNITY INCLUSION | ORONO, ME

HEATHER MACDUFFIE | ELIZABETH DEPOY | STEPHEN FRENCH GILSON

NATIONAL ASSOCIATION OF SOCIAL WORKERS

WASHINGTON, DC

EVELYN P. TOMASZEWSKI

Concentration Disability Policy Course

SWK 710 (Proposed Course, January 2002)

INTRODUCTION

The Concentration Disability Policy course has emerged from the interaction and input from the "Disabilities Awareness Curriculum for Graduate Schools of Social Work" as represented by Evelyn P. Tomaszewski, MSW Senior Staff Associate, National Association of Social Workers, in conjunction and collaboration with Heather MacDuffie and Elizabeth DePoy, University of Maine, Center for Community Inclusion, and Stephen French Gilson, University of Maine School of Social Work.

The "Disabilities Awareness Curriculum for Graduate Schools of Social Work" project was funded for three years (1990–1993) through a grant from the National Institute on Disability and Rehabilitation Research to the Washington Business Group on Health (WBGH) in Washington, DC. It was a collaborative effort between NASW, National Center for Social Policy and Practice, and WBGH. The Curriculum project established a task force that developed five syllabi for use in conjunction with the required or core foundation areas for master's level social work students. That policy syllabus provided ideas and an initial frame of reference for the Concentration Policy syllabus.

The task force—comprised of disability rights advocates, faculty of graduate schools of social work, Don Pilcher, who represented the Council on Social Work Education (CSWE), and WBGH—was convened to work on the NASW curriculum. During the second year of project (academic year 1991–92),the social work curriculum materials were pilot-tested by faculty at the University of Alabama, Catholic University of America, the University of Pittsburgh, and the University of Southern California. During the third year, (1992-93), the curriculum was disseminated to additional schools of social work (on request), and was presented at a Faculty Development Institute during the CSWE Annual Program Meeting. The input and evaluation from the "field" and the "classroom" have been incorporated into the final Disabilities Awareness Curriculum.

This Concentration Disability Policy course is a second year MSW course that mixes fundamental information on the issues of general policy formulation, development, analysis, and change with a focus on local, state, and federal disability legislation. It is also believed that aspects of this policy syllabus could readily be incorporated into or adapted for an undergraduate course.

This curriculum is based upon a full and complete appreciation of the dignity and worth of each individual; a recognition of the importance of the principles of true self-determination and empowerment; support for the practice of self-advocacy (that done by someone for themselves), where requested, and advocacy done by someone for others; and the essential need for social workers to better understand the multidimensional lived experiences of people with disabilities. The Concentration Disability Policy course recognizes that social policies, or the lack thereof, can work to marginalize persons with disabilities, creating a separation of individuals from families and communities that can range from lack of access to services to continued institutionalization.

The continued growth and recognition of the role of social work and persons with disabilities calls for course work with a concentration focused on persons with disabilities. The Concentration Disability Policy syllabus offers such a framework and provides faculty members with the opportunity to offer much needed specialized concentration content to students in pre-service training for a career in social work.

DESCRIPTION

Semester course: 3 lecture hours. 3 credits. Prerequisite: MSW concentration standing or permission of the instructor. Integrates social work disability clinical, planning and administrative practice, and policy practice in the analysis of disability policies. Extends basic knowledge and skills of policy formation, development and the impact of analysis and evaluation, as these affect clinical, planning and administrative practice, and policy practice on behalf of clients. Examines: diversity of policy sources; value, belief, political, and economic determinants; policy formation processes; the policy basis for current services; a broad range of potential need domains; and current programs and laws. Policy analysis is focused on disability and the contrasts and similarities of disability rights and experiences with those of the able-bodied world. Integrates knowledge of human behavior and the social environment relevant to the focal policy areas and pays special attention to issues of social and economic justice.

OBJECTIVES

Upon the completion of this course the student should be able to

1. articulate roles of social work in formulating, changing, and evaluating disability policies at the clinical practice, social work planning/administrative practice levels, and policy practice levels.

2. articulate in-depth knowledge about disability policy and services in the U.S.

3. understand the delivery of sources of disability policy; the value, political, and economic determinants of disability policy; and disability policy formation processes, including legislative, administrative, and judicial.

4. know and apply a variety of policy analysis frameworks and make judgements about the positive and negative impacts of these frameworks for clients affected by the disability policies under investigation.

5. demonstrate an ability to critically examine a range of disability policy need domains with emphasis on how these impact programs and clients.

6. demonstrate sensitivity to and awareness of disability policy issues at the federal, state, and local levels.

The course will focus on policies and practices in areas that address and affect social problems, vulnerable populations, marginalized groups, and service delivery systems. While the central focus of the course is that of disability, within that view numerous additional areas of focus appear.

REQUIRED TEXTS/READINGS

Albrecht, G. & Bury, M. Political economy of the disability marketplace. *Handbook of disability studies.* G. Albrecht, K. Seeleman, M. Bury (Eds.). Thousand Oaks: Sage. 585-609.

Altman, B. (2001). Disability definitions, models, classification schemes, and applications. *Handbook of disability studies.* G. Albrecht, K. Seeleman, M. Bury (Eds.). Thousand Oaks: Sage. 97-119.

Kingdon, J. W. (1995). *Agendas, alternatives and public policies.* Addison-Wesley Pub Co

National Council on Disability Policy Review Progress Report, http://www.ncd.gov/newsroom/publications/progressreport2000.html

Stone, D. A. (1997). *Policy paradox: The art of political decision making.* NY: W.W. Norton.

Turner, B. P. (1998). *Federal Disability Law in a Nutshell.* (2nd ed.). St. Paul, MN: West Group.

Wasserman, D. (1998). *Distributive justice. Disability, difference, discrimination.* A. Silvers, D. Wasserman, M. B. Mahowald, Eds. Lanham, MD: Rowman & Littlefield Publishers, Inc. 147-209.

LEARNING UNITS

Unit 1 – Policy and Social & Economic Justice

Definition of Policy. Policy as a means toward social justice for those who have experiences of discrimination, oppression, and marginalization with emphasis on persons with disabilities. There will be a focus on pertinent disability laws and their implementation.

Differential definitions of disability within diverse disability policy. Purposive formulation of definitions as they relate to and delimit the scope of policy.

- **Class 1**
  - Overview introduction to policy; introduction to value perspectives in disability policy. Self-interest vs. public interest, influence, information, and power.

- **Class 2**
  - Major federal legislation including analysis of their implementation, current implications related to original goals and solutions in an era of fluctuating and changing federal responsibility.
  - Public care policy exercise to examine current health care systems and principles.
  - Pass out research aids and web links handout.
- **Readings**
  - Kingdon – Chapter 1
  - Stone – Chapter 1
  - Wasserman – Distributive justice
  - Altman – Disability definitions

Unit 2 – Policy Sources and Development

Policy sources. Federal and state legislative/statutory law, regulatory/administrative law, judicial law, agency policy, and such.

Policy development processes with emphasis on the influence of values, economics, political power and compromise, budget, and so forth.

Case studies of the policy development process using exemplars from disability program policies.

Social work role/responsibility in the policy development process.

- **Class 3**
  - Review and reaction to Federal and State policy development. What should be the role of social work in these policy development projects?
  - Problem Mapping Exercise
- **Class 4**
  - Section 8 of the Fair Housing Act
  - Panel to discuss reasons that bar eligible persons with disabilities from living in federally subsidized, low income housing.
- **Class 5**
  - Values and Policy
  - Student debates: Four groups responding to a single piece of disability legislation, each from one of the value positions articulated by Stone.
- **Readings**
  - Kingdon – Chapters 2 and 3
  - Stone – Chapters 2, 3, 4, 5
  - Turner – 185-203

Unit 3 – Service Delivery System

Review and evaluation of different policy and programmatic bases of delivery of disability services. The influence of the "Polis" in the ways specific services are delivered, the degree to which services are accessible, and the effects on persons with disabilities.

- **Class 6**
  - Evaluation of policy
  - Video: *If I can't do it.* (1998). Fanlight Productions.
  - Development issues exercise to explore social attitudes toward, and personal experiences with, how society decides to allocate health care resources to different age groups.
- **Class 7**
  - Medicaid Community Attendant Services and Supports Act (MICASSA) and community care
  - Speaker from an independent living center
- **Readings**
  - Albrecht and Bury – Political economy of the disability marketplace
  - Kingdon – Chapter 4 and 5
  - Turner – Chapter 7: Access to Programs and Services
  - O'Day – The role of the independent living center

Unit 4 - Policy Analysis Models

Review of the policy models. Review and clarification of the identified policy analysis models, including their conceptual frameworks, value assumptions, focus on individual vs. organizational needs, and critique of how each addresses the issues of social and economic justice within disability policy.

- **Class 8**
  - Policy Analysis Models – Rational Models
- **Class 9**
  - Policy Analysis Models – "Critical" or "Non-rational" Models
- **Readings**
  - Kingdon – Chapters 3, 4, and 5
  - Stone – Chapter 10

Unit 5 - Current Policy Issues

Review of *current disability policy issues* specific to prominent service systems, social problems, or populations. Consequences and benefits of current and planned disability policies and disability policy reforms.

- **Class 10**
  - Review and reaction to Federal and State policy development. What should be the role of social work in these policy development projects?
  - Disability and research exercise
  - Review handout from session 2 "research aids"
- **Reading**
  - National Council on Disability Progress Report

Classes 11–13

  • Student study group presentations; class discussion and policy critiques

• **Readings**

  • Kingdon – Chapter 8

  • Longest – Chapters 6 and 7

Unit 6 - Regulation and Licensing

Regulation and Licensing in Disability Social Services. Review of the history of, rational for, and impact of regulation and licensing on institutions, agencies, programs, facilities, community-based services, and individuals. Review of the development process and current issues of licensing, regulation, and certification of social work in social service settings serving individuals with disabilities, including direct practice, administrative/planning practice, and policy practice.

• **Class 14**

  • Regulation and licensing and the role of the social worker as licensing agent or licensee.

  • Evaluation of the course and celebration!

ASSIGNMENTS

General Information

Written assignments will be evaluated for accomplishment of objectives of assignment, organization and clarity of discussion, demonstration of the ability to integrate and critically apply course content, and use of correct spelling, grammar, and APA style references.

Assignment 1 – (30% of course grade)

Using the "Survey on Policy Development within Agencies/Organizations" interview the executive director, board chair, board member, or other management staff of a selected disability organization. Based upon the responses, write a 3-4 page synopsis of the interview and briefly analyze the survey findings by answering the following questions:

• Do the findings reveal the existence of policies which meet the formal definition of policy? What is their level of development?

• How does the level of policy development influence the customers/consumers of the services?

• How does the level of policy development influence the structure and function of the agency/ organization?

• What recommendations would you suggest for improving the organizational structure and function through further development/revision of policy?

Assignment 2 – (30% of course grade)

For this assignment, students work in groups of 3 or 4 and select a federal or state legislated disability policy. The policy should have legislative activity within the last three years, and should have direct impact on the provision, planning, or evaluation of disability or long-term disability services in your state or the United States. Please clear all topics with the instructor to ensure their relevance to the focus of the course.

  Collaborate to develop an essay and presentation to include

1. Identity of the legislation, its name and public law number, year of enactment, year of implementation

2. Significant historical elements associated with this act's implementation (i.e., provide a brief overview of significant social, political, and economic conditions at work as this act was being developed

3. Key factors addressed by this act (i.e., who or what services are targeted; ratification of prior acts; major shifts in ideologies or practices)

4. Summary of factors that facilitated the implementation of this act

5. Intended and unintended consequences of the legislation

6. Summary of the evaluation component for this act; where there is no evaluation component, suggest the potential impact of this omission.

Length of essay: 10 pages (references are required).

Length of presentation: 1/2 hour total (20 minutes of presentation with 10 minutes for questions and discussion). Half the grade for the assignment will be based on the presentation and the other half on the grade for the essay. For access to Federal legislation on the Internet, visit http://thomas.loc.gov/

Assignment 3 – (40 % of course grade)

Each student will respond to the presentations of other student groups (Assignment 2) by preparing an individual written memorandum (no more than 3 pages double spaced) to include the following information:

1. Background of the act (one paragraph)

2. Content of the act (limit one or two paragraphs)

3. Analysis of positive and negative consequences and recommendation of changes needed to address the negative consequences that the act has/could have on individuals with disabilities, disability services, and/or resources related to disability.

Research in Disability

DIS 650 Section 900 Web-based (Spring 2001 Asynchronous)

COURSE DESCRIPTION

This course introduces the student to the spectrum of investigative strategies which can be used to answer questions and queries of concern to social workers concerned with disability knowledge and services. A conceptual framework for evaluating disability knowledge, practice, and theory will be used throughout the course to examine current research and to master basic research skills.

The course will begin with the presentation of research designs from naturalistic to experimental-type. Each design will then be analyzed through reading and evaluating current research presented in social work and disability journals. Selected readings will introduce the student to both methodological and content issues in the field of disability.

Students will master basic research skills through selected assignments and exercises. Scholarly criticism will be encouraged. The influence of currently accepted paradigms of knowledge on disability and disability policy will be discussed. Ethical dilemmas and protocols for the protection of human subjects in disability research will also be considered.

REQUIRED TEXTS AND READINGS

DePoy, E. & Gitlin, L. (1998). *Introduction to research: Understanding and applying multiple strategies.* St. Louis, MO: Mosby.

Pyrczak, F. (1991). *Success at statistics.* Los Angeles, CA: Pyrczak Publishing.

Article 1. Yelin, E. & Trupin, L. (2000). Successful labor market transitions for persons with disabilities. In B. M. Altman & S. N. Barnett (Eds.), *Expanding the scope of social science research on disability* (pp. 105-129). Stamford, CT: JAI Press, Inc.

Article 2. Hains, A. A., Davies, W. H., Behrens, D., & Biller, J. A. (1997). Cognitive behavioral interventions for adolescents with cystic fibrosis. *Journal of Pediatric Psychology, 22*(5), 669-687.

Article 3. Haller, B. (2000). How the news frames disability. In B. M. Altman & S. N. Barnett (Eds.), *Expanding the scope of social science research on disability* (pp. 55-83). Stamford, CT: JAI Press, Inc.

John's Hopkins University. (1999). *Manual for the child health and illness profile: Adolescent edition.* 1-7. For permission to use contact *http://www.outcomes-trust.org.*

University of Maine, Human Subject Review Policy and Procedures.
Go to: http://orspdocs.umesp.maine.edu/Ethical/humansubjects1.htm

COURSE OBJECTIVES

Upon successful completion of this course the student will be able to

1. View knowledge generation as an epistemological phenomenon.

2. Determine the usefulness of varying methodological approaches for evaluating disability practice and disability knowledge.

3. Critically analyze current research and determine its use for disability practice.

4. Master skills in information retrieval.

5. Pose a researchable question or query.

6. Organize existing literature and information to answer research questions and queries, suggest new questions and queries, and provide a rationale for method.

7. Examine research biases against disabled populations, and other groups, in order to eliminate the use of research as an oppressive tool.

8. Develop inquiry strategies to answer disability questions and queries, including questions and queries regarding evaluation of disability interventions.

9. Identify the ethical dilemmas in disability research and articulate useful resolutions consonant with social work values and ethics.

ASSIGNMENTS AND GRADING PROCEDURES

The assignments in this course are designed to give each student the opportunity to participate in analysis of research and in developing research skills in disability research.

COURSE OUTLINE

Note: Each assignment or task is due on the due date given. Readings are particularly important to your understanding and comprehension of the concepts and ideas presented in this course, thus you are expected to complete the readings assigned to you each week. (See below for analysis questions.)

Session 1 (Jan 24-30) Research as a Way of Knowing

- Assignment: Read Depoy & Gitlin, Chapters 1, 2, & 3; Pyrczak, Introduction & Section 1.

- Welcome! Please introduce yourself and tell us about your reasons for taking this course and any past experience with research you may have. Complete Assignment 1. Post all to the Topic 1 folder.

  Assignment 1—Research as a way of knowing

  Please answer the following questions and post your responses to the topic 1 folder:

  1. List and define the primary ways of knowing.

  2. Give an example of each way of knowing.

  3. Discuss the strengths and limitations of each way of knowing for the purpose of professional disability practice.

Session 2 (Jan 31-Feb 6) Reviewing the Literature

- Assignment: Read Depoy & Gitlin, Chapter 5; Pyrczak, Sections 2 & 3.

- Please select your topic for Assignment 2 and post to the Topic 2 folder (just the topic, not the whole assignment).

  Assignment 2 (for sessions 2 & 7)—Literature Review

  - Please conduct a literature search on a topic related the social benefits and limitations of delivering long term health and self care services to disabled individuals who are homebound. Limit your search to 1998-2001 and only select articles from the scholarly research literature. Write and post a literature review that is no longer than 2 pages, double spaced. Please note: we strongly encourage you to post versions of your review for instructor comment prior to the due date.

Session 3 (Feb 7-Feb 13) Query and Question

- Assignment: Read Depoy & Gitlin, Chapters 4, 6, & 7; Pyrczak, Sections 4 & 5.

- Post Assignment 3 to the Topic 3 folder.

Assignment 3 (for session 3)—Question and Query

- Read Articles 1 and 2 and post answers to study questions 1-5. Please note that study questions appear at the end of this syllabus.

Session 4 (Feb 14-20) Design Classifications: Introduction to Experimental-type Design

- Assignment: Read Depoy & Gitlin, Chapters 8 & 9 (pp. 108-116); Pyrczak, Sections 6, 7, & 8.
- No posting required.

Session 5 (Feb. 21-Feb. 27) The Continuum of Experimental-type designs

- Assignment: Read Depoy & Gitlin, Chapter 9 (pp. 117-126); Pyrczak, Sections 9, 10, & 11.
- Post Assignment 5 to Topic 5 folder.

    Assignment 5 (for session 5)—Experimental-type Design

    - Read Article 1 and post answers to study questions 6, 7, & 8.

Session 6 (Feb 28-Mar 5) Naturalistic Inquiry

- Assignment: Read Depoy & Gitlin, Chapter 10; Pyrczak, Sections 12, 13, 14, & 15.
- Post Assignment 6 to the Topic 6 folder.

    Assignment 6 (for session 6)—Naturalistic Design

    - Read Article 2 and post answers to study questions 6, 7, & 8.

Session 7 (Mar 5-Mar 10) Integrating Design

- Assignment: Read Depoy & Gitlin, Chapter 11; Pyrczak, Sections 16, 17, & 18.
- Post Assignment 7 to the Topic 7 folder.
- Post your final version of Task 2 to the Task 2 folder.

    Assignment 7 (for session 7)—Integrated Design

    - Read Article 3 and post answers to study questions 6, 7, 8.

March 12-25 Spring Break. Your assignment is to have a great break!

Session 8 (Mar 27-Apr 2) Setting Boundaries: Sampling and Domain

- Assignment: Read Depoy & Gitlin, Chapter 12, 13, & 14; Pyrczak, Sections 19, 20, 21, & 22.
- Post Assignment 8 to the Topic 8 folder.

    Assignment 8 (for session 8)—Boundaries

    Read Articles 1 and 2 and post answers to study questions 9 & 10.

Session 9 (Apr 3-Apr 9) Collecting Information: Introduction and Concern With Measurement

- Assignment: Read Depoy & Gitlin, Chapter 15 & 16; Pyrczak, Sections 27, 28, 29, & 30.
- Post Assignment 9 to the Topic 9 folder.

    Assignment 9 (for session 9)—Collecting Information

    - Read Article 1 and post answers to study question 11-17.

Session 10 (Apr 10-Apr 16) Instrumentation Continued-Analyzing Quantitative Data

- Assignment: Read Depoy & Gitlin, Chapter 18 & 19 (pp. 246-260); Pyrczak, Sections 33, 34, & 35, re-read Sections 21, 22, & 23 on the Pearson r.
- Post Assignment 10 to the Topic 10 folder.

    Assignment 10 (for session 10)—Collecting Information

    - Analyze the validity and reliability of the CHIP and post analysis. Post answers to study questions 11-17 about Article 2.

Session 11 (Apr 17-Apr 23) **Analytic Strategies for Experimental-type Design I**

- Assignment: Read Depoy & Gitlin, Chapter 19 (pp. 260-271) & Chapter 21 (pp. 287-291); Pyrczak, Sections 36, 37, 38, 39, & 40.
- Post Assignment 11 to the Topic 11 folder.

    Assignment 11 (for Session 11)—Analysis

    - Conduct a statistical analysis using the data in your course pack and the appropriate online sites.

Session 12 (Apr 24-Apr 30) **Analytic Strategies for Naturalistic Data**

- Assignment: Read Depoy & Gitlin, Chapter 17, 18 (pp. 240-244), 20 (pp. 273-279), & 21 (pp. 291-295); Pyrczak, Sections 41, 42, 47, & 48.
- No posting required.

    Assignment 12 (for Session 13)—Analysis

    - Conduct a thematic analysis using the narrative supplied in your course pack, to be posted next week.

Session 13 (May 1-May 7) **Analytic Strategies for Naturalistic Data**

- Assignment: Read Depoy & Gitlin, Chapter 20 (pp. 279-286); Pyrczak, Sections 49, 50, & 51.

    Assignment 13

    - Post Assignment 12 to the Topic 13 folder.

Session 14 (May 8-May 14) **Wrap Up and Summary**

- Assignment: Read Depoy & Gitlin Chapter 21.
- Post Task 12 to the Task 12 folder.

    Assignment 14 (for Session 14)—Final Paper

    - Select a topic that you believe is necessary to investigate in your area of disability. Post an outline of what literature needs to be reviewed, and suggest an inquiry, including question or query, and design.

Completion of the online course evaluation is required (please). Names and ratings are sent to different databases, but we will know if you don't complete the survey!

ACCOMMODATIONS

Any student who may need special arrangements or accommodations to meet the requirements of this course because of a disability is encouraged to contact us at your earliest convenience.

Students with Disabilities

If the accommodation the student requests requires material resources or for some reason cannot be provided by the faculty member, please inform the school's disability liaison in writing of your request. In turn, you may be asked to file documentation with a central university office. It is possible that university experts will confer with the liaison to determine what kind of accommodations should be made to facilitate your participation in the class.

QUESTIONS FOR ARTICLE ANALYSIS (STUDY QUESTIONS)

1. What is the research question or query? Is the question or query sound? Is it researchable?
2. What is the purpose of the study (usually found in the introduction)? Stated purpose? Implied purpose?
3. Describe the theoretical underpinnings (important ideas presented in the literature review) of the question or query.
4. What are the important constructs discussed in the literature review? Critically evaluate the literature for clarity and its ability to create a conceptual foundation for the study.

5. What level of abstraction (concept, construct, relationship, principle, theory) is discussed in the literature review? Is it appropriate to the development of theory in the field of study? Why or why not?

6. What is the rationale for the design implied or stated in the literature review? Is it a sound rationale? Do you agree with the investigator's choice of design based on the rationale and level of theory development presented in the literature review?

7. Diagram or describe the design.

8. Does the design answer the research question or query? Why or why not? (This question requires an analysis of design validity, reliability, or trustworthiness and authenticity).

9. What is the domain or population?

10. How is the sample selected or the domain explicated? How does sampling impact external validity? How does domain explication affect how the knowledge derived from the study can be used by the reader?

11. How is information obtained? Critically evaluate the data collection plan and process.

12. What data analytic strategies are used? Critically evaluate these strategies.

13. What are the strengths of the study?

14. What are its weaknesses?

15. What knowledge is generated? Level, content, use?

16. What use does this knowledge have for disability? For evaluation?

17. Are there ethical dilemmas presented in this article? What are they? Did the author resolve the dilemmas?

LITERATURE REVIEW ASSIGNMENT

The type of literature review that is appropriate for a research proposal is done differently from how you might have done one before. This is not an exhaustive and lengthy summary of the literature. Rather, articles should be selected for the following reasons (see also chapter 5 in DePoy & Gitlin):

- They describe concepts and or provide operational definitions that you will use in your research proposal.

- They indicate a need for further research and your proposal addresses the identified need.

- They provide evidence that the type of methodology or the survey you plan to use has been used before.

- They provide evidence that the methodology and survey have been used for studies of related topics.

- They provide steps in the rationale that you build for your proposal.

As you put together your literature review, look at the assigned study articles. Note that studies are cited in order to build a logical argument, explaining the problems, the current state of knowledge, the concepts under consideration and what they mean, populations that have been studied, special ethical issues, and methods that have been used.

Literature Search: Please contact the instructors if you need help searching the literature. Limit your search to 1998-2001 and only select articles from the scholarly research literature. Write and post a literature review that is no longer than 2 pages, 12 pt. double-spaced, with one inch margins. Please note that we encourage you to post versions of your review for instructor comment prior to the Session 7 due date.

STATISTICAL DATA ANALYSIS ASSIGNMENT

Conduct data analysis on the CHIP data set (course pack) using the assigned online statistical calculators. Directions for using each of the calculators are included in the following pages. Alternatively, data will be available on the website as an Excel file. If you have Excel on your computer, you can conduct the analysis using Excel.

First, you will need to look at the codesheet to understand your data. Then enter numerical values into the online calculators.

- Run frequencies on B9 using WEBSTAT.
- Run mean and standard deviation on B1, B2, & B3 using CSBSJU calculator.
- Run Pearson r on B9 and B12 using CSBSJU calculator.
- Run (unpaired) Student's independent t-test comparing A14 and B12 using CSBSJU calculator.
- Run Chi square on A4 & A15 using CSBSJU calculator.
- Run one-way ANOVA on B1, B5, & B11 using CSBSJU calculator.

Report your findings as numerical values. Using one or two sentences for each test, interpret the findings. What do these tests tell you in relation to the questions that were used to elicit responses?

USING WEBSTAT

http://www.stat.sc.edu/webstat/

- Select WEBSTAT 2.0
- Enter values in table under "var 1", use down-arrow to move through table.
- Select "Graphics" and then "pie chart" on spreadsheet.
- Select variable.
- Results will be calculated when you create graph. You may not be able to print results.

USING CSBSJU

http://bardeen.physics.csbsju.edu/stats/

Coursepack contents include the menu page and sample screens for descriptive statistics. Use appropriate links to complete analysis.

- Mean and Standard deviation are completed under the link similarly named.
- Students t-test are completed under similarly named link, then select the unpaired version.
- Pearson r test is completed as part of the Ordinary Least Squares analysis.
- Chi square is completed under contingency tables link, then select 2x2.
- ANOVA is completed under the similarly named link.

Annotated Bibliography

ARTICLES, DISSERTATIONS, AND CHAPTERS | BOOKS | WEBSITES | VIDEOS AND FILMS

SOCIAL WORK ARTICLES, DISSERTATIONS, AND CHAPTERS ON DISABILITY

With this section of the bibliography we provide a comprehensive listing of recent social work articles on the topic of disability. To assist the work of practitioners, students, teachers, and administrators, the entries are arranged categorically. The decision regarding which category to place the article in was based on the editors' evaluation of the primary focus of the article. We have listed each item only once. In each category selected references are annotated; in categories with fewer entries, a higher percentage of annotations appear than for those categories with numerous entries. The selection of an article for annotation does not reflect the editors' determination of the worth or value of the article in comparison or contrast to those not annotated. Annotated articles should not be considered endorsed by the editors. Annotations were made directly from hard copies of the article.

The bibliography was developed primarily from four searches using the electronic version of *Social Work Abstracts*. Search terms included disable, disabled, handicap, handicapped, and cripple for the years 1997-2001. The decision to limit the search to articles published after 1997 was made to assure that listed sources are most current. The decision to conduct four searches was based on a determination of the best way to collect recent publications while the annotation process progressed.

The general parameters which delimited the search included: (1) the article was written by a social worker, (2) the source of the publication was a social work journal or identified social work book publisher, or (3) the content and focus discussed social work and disability.

The usefulness of publication databases for tracking faculty scholarship was reported in a 1999 study by Green, Kvarfordt, & Hayden. Subsequent to completing the search in *Social Work Abstracts* it was evident to the editors that numerous important articles on disability written by or for social workers were not listed. Consequently, the decision was made by the editors to include articles published in some journals not covered by *Social Work Abstracts* and also to include other known articles about disability that were not picked up by the search terms. Again, the inclusion of articles in this phase of the project in no way reflects judgments about the superiority of one article over another, but rather familiarity with the work of some authors and searches through selected journals not abstracted by *Social Work Abstracts*. Finally, several articles that had not been identified through the electronic search, and were unknown to the editors, were forwarded to the senior editor by an author or another interested source.

The listings are arranged in five categories: Disability in the Field of Social Work, Disability-Specific Articles, Cultural Perspectives and Issues in Disability, Gender and Disability, and Miscellaneous Disability Articles. While some articles may seem relevant to more than one category, each has been placed in only one category. Articles assigned to the category of Disability in the Field of Social Work encompass social work micro, mezzo, and macro practice issues, theoretical/ethical concerns, teaching considerations, and the like. Those articles which address issues that relate to specific disabilities appear in Disability-Specific Articles. Comparative studies of specific ethnic/cultural populations are in Cultural Perspectives and Issues in Disability and in Gender and Disability. The Miscellaneous category contains a range of other issues, including abuse and gay, lesbian, bisexual, or transgendered experience. The size of each category serves as a marker for the extent to which social workers have engaged in scholarly work in these areas.

Reference

Green, R.G., Kvarfordt, C.L., & Hayden, M.A. (1999). The middle years of the decade publication project. 1994-97. *Journal of Social Work Education, 35*(2), 195-202.

Social Work and Disability

Allison, C. E. (1999). Disability as diversity: A socio-linguistic construct for the new millennium. *Reflections, 5*(4), 47-51.

Aronsson, G., Astvik, W., & Thulin, A. B. (1998). Home-care workers: Work conditions and occupational exclusion: a comparison between carers on early-retirement and regular pensions. *Home Health Care Services Quarterly, 17*(2), 71-91.

Bader, J. E. (1999). Bridging personal and professional perspectives: A continuous process. *Reflections, 5*(4), 27-32.

Batavia, A. I., & Beaulaurier, R. L. (2001). The financial vulnerability of people with disabilities: Assessing poverty risks. *Journal of Sociology and Social Welfare, 28*(1), 139-162.

This paper presents an overview of reasons why persons with disabilities have disproportionately high rates of poverty, compared with persons without disabilities. Factors include: lower levels of education, lower levels of income, higher health care and other disability-related expenses, and lower employment rates. In general, persons with disabilities have less stable and more vulnerable financial levels. Conclusions call for more research into the factors that create financial vulnerability for disabled people.

Beinecke, R. H., Shepard, D. S., Goodman, M., & Rivera, M. (1997). Assessment of the Massachusetts Medicaid managed behavioral health program: Year three. *Administration and Policy in Mental Health, 24*(3), 205-220.

Beresford, P. (2000). Service users' knowledge and social work theory: Conflict or collaboration? *British Journal of Social Work, 39*(4), 489-503

Blair, R. G. (1999). Integrating my disability: My journey. *Reflections, 5*(4), 7-15.

Bricout, J. C., & Bentley, K. J. (2000). Disability status and perceptions of employability by employers. *Social Work Research, 24*(2), 87-95.

To explore the low employment rates of persons with disabilities, a survey was sent by mail to a randomly selected group of employers belonging to a national association of human resources managers. Participants rated the "hiring climate" and "negotiation latitude," read and answered questions on a job vignette, and answered questions about themselves. Results showed that nondisabled applicants were more likely to be hired that applicants with disabilities. Unexpectedly, results also showed that people with physical disabilities and people with psychiatric disabilities were rated as equally employable or nonemployable.

Brzuzy, S. (1997). Deconstructing disability: The impact of definition. *Journal of Poverty, 1*(1), 81-91.

Bucaro, T. (1999). The disability experience: New voices, new images [Editorial]. *Reflections, 5*(4), 4-6.

Bucaro, T., & Kopfstein, R. (1999). Coming out: Claiming disability in and out of the classroom. *Reflections, 5*(4), 71-81.

Burge, P., Druick, D., Caron, M.C., Oullette-Kuntz, H.,& Paquette, D. (1999). Coursework on developmental disabilities: A national survey of Canadian schools of Social Work. *Canadian Social Work Review, 16*(1), 49-64.

The survey of Canadian schools in this article contained questions about course-work and field-work in the area of developmental disabilities. Using 28 completed questionnaires (16 bachelor's programs and 12 master's programs), statistical analyses revealed that only two schools (master's programs) scored in the range of content coverage considered adequate; all others scored below that range. Lack of faculty expertise and lack of student interest were among the primary reason cited for a low rate of course coverage.

Caplan, G., & Caplan, R. (2000). Principles of community psychiatry. *Community Mental Health Journal, 36*(1), 7-24.

> This article presents a set of principles to be used in the delivery and practice of community psychiatry. These principles are predicated on the basic assumption that programs should be designed to fit the needs of a bounded (geographic) population. Based on an existing program, the authors differentiate between their individual approach and the more traditional population-focused approach.

Caro, F. G. (1998). Commentary on the closing of a social health maintenance organization. *Journal of Aging and Social Policy, 10*(2), 1-6.

Chisanga, B., Masiye, G., Billups, J., & Julia, M. (1999). Poverty experiences in Zambia: What next for civil society and socioeconomic development? *Social Development Issues, 21*(1), 37-46.

Deal, L. W., & Shiono, P. H. (1998). Medicaid managed care and children: An overview. *The Future of Children, 8*(2), 93-104.

Degenholtz, H. B., Kane, R. A., Kane, R. L., & Finch, M. D. (1999). Long-term care case managers' out-of-home placement decisions: An application of hierarchical logistic regression. *Research on Aging, 21*(2), 240-274.

> This study used hierarchical logistic progression analysis to analyze factorial survey data and test theories about case managers' decision making. Results indicated that client preferences are taken into account in the decision making process, except in instances of cognitive disability. Greater case manager specialization in intake tasks and higher workloads were associated with lower weight being placed on client preferences and a greater likelihood of nursing home placement.

Farmer, R. L., & Pandurangi, A. K. (1997). Diversity in schizophrenia: Towards a richer biopsychosocial understanding of Social Work practice. *Health and Social Work, 22*(2), 109-116.

> This article discusses a quasi-experimental study designed to determine whether persons with chronic schizophrenia who have larger ventricle-to-brain (VBR) ratios or cortical atrophy (CA) demonstrate different psychosocial adaptation than those who do not. Using a series of standardized measures, psychosocial adaptation was operationalized as quality of life, course of illness, self-esteem, and stress. Results were inconclusive in answering the research hypothesis. However, significant differences between genders were found. Women had higher self-esteem and better psychosocial adaptation than men. Of additional interest, for a follow-up study, African American participants seemed to have a more benign form of schizophrenia, compared with White participants.

Fleming, E., Ma, C. A., & McGuire, T. G. (2000). Behavioral health expenditures and state organizational structure. *Administration and Policy in Mental Health, 27*(3), 91-111.

Fortune, A. E. (2000). Work [Editorial]. *Social Work Research, 24*(2), 67-68.

Gething, L. (1997). Sources of double disadvantage for people with disabilities living in remote and rural areas of New South Wales, Australia. *Disability and Society, 12*(4), 513-531.

> This study illustrates how persons with disabilities living in rural and remote areas experienced double disadvantages with regard to receiving services. Data collection involved consultation with people with disabilities, disability groups, service providers, families, and caregivers/providers. Major difficulties with access included transportation, staff availability, and preparedness issues. The similarity between these findings and those done in other countries was discussed.

Gilson, S. F. (1997). Personal assistance services and case management. *Journal of Case Management, 6*(1), 13-17.

Gilson, S. F., & DePoy, E. (2000). Multiculturalism and disability: A critical perspective. *Disability and Society, 15*(2), 207-215.

Gilson, S. F., Bricout, J. C., & Baskind, F. R. (1998). Listening to the voices of individuals with disabilities. *Families in Society, 79*(2), 188-196.

The authors sought to illuminate how social work treats disability as non-normative. Using both a literature search and interviews with persons with disabilities, the authors reported that the dearth of professional literature that fosters growth and the realization of aspirations of persons with disabilities is paralleled by individual reports that social workers pay less attention to the aspirations of persons with disabilities.

Gilson, S. F., & Netting, F. E. (1997). When people with pre-existing disabilities age in place: Implications for social work practice. *Health and Social Work, 22*(4), 290-298.

This article distinguished between two groups of aging persons with disabilities: those who had been disabled for many years and are very familiar with acquiring accommodations, and those who were aging rapidly and were unfamiliar with acquiring accommodations. The authors used case studies to illuminate ways in which the differences between these groups affected relationships when persons with disabilities partner with social workers.

Gold, M., Nelson, L., Brown, R., Ciemnecki, A., Aizer, A., & Docteur, E. (1997). Disabled medicare beneficiaries in HMOs. *Health Affairs, 16*(5), 149-162.

Goulet, J. L., Rosenheck, R., & Leslie, D. (1999). Effectiveness of a targeted mailing outreach program on SSI applications and awards. *Social Service Review, 73*(4), 579-587.

Helton, L. R. (1998). Riding the giraffe: A social worker's nine year journey. *Reflections, 2*(4), 40-48.

Helton, L. R. (1999). From my view everything is clear: Building on family strengths. *Reflections, 5*(4), 53-63.

Himes, C. L., & Reidy, E. B. (2000). The role of friends in caregiving. *Research on Aging, 22*(4), 315-336.

This study used the National Survey of Family and Households to examine how women caring for female friends are different from women caring for family members. Results indicated that women provided care to a friend were older and less likely to be married than women caring for family. The importance of informal care in today's health care climate was discussed.

Jimenez, M. A. (1999). Letter from the editor. *Reflections, 5*(4), 2.

Johnson, K. (1997). Deinstitutionalization: The management of rights. *Disability and Society, 13*(3), 375-387.

This article was based on an ethnographic study of the closure of an institution for people with intellectual disabilities in Australia. Results indicated that two main stresses that existed during this process concerned the residents who were being moved out and management concerns about efficiency and cost. The authors discussed the two incompatible discourses, about which participants in similar processes should be aware and self-reflexive.

Kilty, K. M., Richardson, V. E., & Segal, E. A. (1997). Editors' introduction. *Journal of Poverty, 1*(1), 1-3.

Kim, R. Y. (2000). Factors associated with employment status of parents receiving Temporary Assistance for Needy Families. *Social Work Research, 24*(4), 211-222.

Li, L., & Moore, D. (1998). Acceptance of disability and its correlates. *Journal of Social Psychology, 138*(1), 13-25.

Lordan, N. (2000). Finding a voice: Empowerment of people with disabilities in Ireland. *Journal of Progressive Human Services, 11*(1), 49-69.

McCallum, J. (1999). Policy implications of Australian ageing: The graying of a young-society. *Journal of Sociology and Social Welfare, 26*(1), 87-106.

Meldrum, B. K. (1999). Bringing the darkness into light: A disability rights struggle. *Reflections, 5*(4), 33-41.

Meyers, M. K., Lukemeyers, A., & Smeeding, T. (1998). The cost of caring: Childhood disability and poor families. *Social Service Review. 72*(2), 209-223.

This study explored the dimensions of poverty in families of children with disabilities. A telephone survey was conducted of welfare recipients in California that addressed prevalence of disability, cost of care, and the impact of cost of care on family well-being. Results suggested that "the rate of disabilities and chronic illnesses in children receiving AFDC is about twice that of children in the general population." The costs of caring were significant, both in terms of out-of-pocket expenses and loss of wages.

Michailakis, D. (1997). When opportunity is the thing to be equalized. *Disability and Society, 12*(1), 17-30.

This article discusses the goal set out by the United Nations in its Standard Rules on the Equalization of Opportunities for Persons with Disabilities. Two conflicting approaches to handicap are inherent in the document: the individual-centered approach and the person-environment approach. The article suggests that the individual-centered approach functions as a formal relationship, no matter what the setting in which it occurs, while the person-environment approach is related with an active social policy informed by an understanding of equal treatment as a question of substantial right.

Middleton, L. (1998). Services for disabled children: Integrating the perspective of social workers. *Child and Family Social Work, 3*(4), 239-246.

Noonan, A. E., Tennstedt, S. L., & Rebelsky, F. G. (1999). Getting to the point: Offspring caregivers and the nursing home decision. *Journal of Gerontological Social Work, 31*(3/4), 5-27.

Ondersma, S. J., Lumley, M. A., Corlis, M. E., Tojek, T. M., & Tolia, V. (1997). Adolescents with inflammatory bowel disease: The roles of negative affectivity and hostility in subjective versus objective health. *Journal of Pediatric Psychology, 22*(5), 723-738.

Overman, W. H., & Morgan, R. C. (2000). Aging and elder law in the 21st century. *Journal of Mental Health and Aging, 6*(2), 115-117.

Pardeck, J. T. (1999). Disability discrimination in social work education: Current issues for social work programs and faculty. *Journal of Teaching in Social Work, 19*(1/2), 151-163.

Peek, M. K., & Coward, R. T. (2000). Antecedents of disability for older adults with multiple chronic health conditions. *Research on Aging, 22*(4), 422-444.

This article reports on the findings of a longitudinal panel survey of community-dwelling older adults with two or more chronic health conditions. The survey was designed to examine factors associated with the presence and development of activities of daily living (ADL) and instrumental activities of daily living (IADL) disabilities. Discussion points include the differences between predictors of disability and predictors of IADL disabilities, and the finding of certain types of co-morbidity (e.g., obesity, arthritis) that predict the development of ADL disabilities.

Piastro, D. B. (1999). Coping with the transitions in our lives: From "afflicted" identity to personal empowerment and pride. *Reflections, 5*(4), 42-46.

Rasmussen, D. W., Megbolugbe, I. F., & Morgan, B. A. (1997). The reverse mortgage as an asset management tool. *Housing Policy Debate, 8*(1), 173-194.

Rose, A. (1997). "Who causes the blind to see": Disability and the quality of religious life. *Disability and Society, 12*(3), 395-405.

This article discusses the less-than-welcoming attitudes of some religious organizations experienced by disabled people. The reasons for this are theorized as stemming from historical religious views about disabilities and their relationships to God's wishes. Four central Judeo-Christian views are analyzed.

Sellers, J. (1999). Bridging disabilities and work. *Policy and Practice, 57*(2), 18-25.

Sheehan, N. W., & Stelle, C. (1998). The mixed-population issue in state-subsidized elderly housing: Management problems posed by non-elderly and elderly tenants. *Journal of Aging and Social Policy, 10*(2), 29-48.

Sherman, C. (1999). Alice in social work wonderland: Reflections on disability policy and services during student placement. *Australian Social Work, 52*(3), 57-61.

Smith, D. (1997). Implementing disability management: A review of basic concepts and essential components. *Employee Assistance Quarterly, 12*(4), 37-50.

Sidell, N. L. (1997). Adult adjustment to chronic illness. *Health and Social Work, 22*(1), 5-11.

This article explores issues of importance to clinical social workers and case managers in working with people with chronic illness. The importance and complexity of grief and loss issues, coping, and developmental issues is presented, along with suggestions for conceptual social work that can be employed to address them.

Soifer, S., & Singer, J. (1999). The campaign to restore the Disability Assistance and Loan Program in the state of Maryland. *Journal of Community Practice, 6*(2), 1-10.

Soissons, S. A. (1997). Healer/healee, my journey. *Reflections, 3*(2), 21-24.

Steiner, S. J. (1997). AFDC recipients and family caregiving responsibilities. *Journal of Poverty, 1*(2), 63-79.

Temkin, G. H., Meiners, M. R., & Fatula, J. E. (1999). Continuing care network: Building a disability-based payment and delivery mode. *Policy and Practice, 57*(3), 38-44.

Tracy, P. D. (1997). The emergence of social services in rural Russia: The case of Togliatti and Samara. *Social Development Issues, 19*(1), 122-127.

Wardell, F., Lishman, J., & Whalley, L. J. (2000). Who volunteers? *British Journal of Social Work, 30*(2), 227-248.

Whitelaw, N. A., & Warden, G. L. (1999). Reexamining the delivery system as part of Medicare reform. *Health Affairs, 18*(1), 132-143.

Specific Disabilities

Abels, P. (1998). Retrospective: Riding with Batman, Superman and the Green Hornet. *Reflections, 4*(3), 69-73.

Appleton, P. L., Ellis, N. C., Minchom, P. E., Lawson, V., Boll, V., & Jones, P. (1997). Depressive symptoms and self-concept in young people with spina bifida. *Journal of Pediatric Psychology, 22*(5), 707-722.

Bradley, V. J. (2000). Challenges to services and supports for people with developmental disabilities: New challenges to established practice. *Health and Social Work*, *25*(3), 191-200.

Explored in this article was the impact of a terminology of ideals that have been associated with changes in the field of developmental disabilities. These included words such as "inclusion," "normalization," and "participation." The analysis included consideration of the power of each word across time to effect change and contexts in which the ideals represented become problematic and difficult to realize.

Brown, H., & Thompson, D. (1997). The ethics of research with men who have learning disabilities and abusive sexual behavior: A minefield in a vacuum. *Disability and Society*, *12*(5), 695-707.

Burge, P., Druick, D., Caron, M. C., & Kuntz, O. H. (1998). Fieldwork: Are students prepared to work with persons with developmental disabilities? *The Social Worker*, *66*(3), 15-27.

Cambridge, P. (1999). Building care management competence in services for people with learning disabilities. *British Journal of Social Work*, *29*(3), 393-415.

Carnaby, S. (1997). A comparative approach to evaluating individual planning for people with learning disabilities: Challenging the assumptions. *Disability and Society*, *12*(3), 381-394.

Considered in this manuscript are aspects of individualized service planning in London compared to a system of normalization with an individualized, family centered system operating in Milan, Italy. The role of professionals and the involvement of service users are among the key factors considered.

Collins, M. E., Mowbray, C. T., & Bybee, D. (1999). Measuring coping strategies in an educational intervention for individuals with psychiatric disabilities. *Health and Social Work*, *24*(4), 279-291.

Cook, J. A., Cohler, B. J., Pickett, S. A., & Beeler, J. A. (1997). Life-course and severe mental illness: Implications for caregiving within the family of later life. *Family Relations*, *46*(4), 427-436.

Cook, J. A., Pickett, S. A., & Cohler, B. J. (1997). Families of adults with severe mental illness the next generation of research: Introduction. *American Journal of Orthopsychiatry*, *67*(2), 172-176.

Cooper, B., & Picton, C. (2000). The long-term effects of relocation on people with an intellectual disability: Quality of life, behavior, and environment. *Research on Social Work Practice*, *10*(2), 195-208.

The longitudinal study reported here involved 58 people with mental retardation who were moved from institutional to community (group home) care. Outcome measures constructs included quality of life, community living skills, challenging behavior, and quality of care. Data gathering employed face-to-face structured interviews, using a number of standardized scales. Results indicated that relocation was associated with modest increases in quality of life and quality of care, and short-term decreases in disruptive behavior and no change in community living skills.

Cummins, R. A. (2001). Self-rated quality of life scales for people with an intellectual disability: A reply to Ager and Hatton. *Journal of Applied Research in Intellectual Disabilities*, *14*(1), 1-11.

Davis, A. (1999). Critical commentaries: Mental health and poverty. *British Journal of Social Work*, *29*(4), 631-638.

Deselle, D. D., & Pearlmutter, D. (1997). Navigating two cultures: Deaf children, self-esteem, and parents' communication patterns. *Social Work in Education*, *19*(1), 23-29.

Desselle, D. D., & Proctor, T. K. (2000). Advocating for the elderly hard-of-hearing population: The deaf people we ignore. *Social Work*, *45*(3), 277-281.

Dyer, S., & Quine, L. (1998). Predictors of job satisfaction and burnout among the direct care staff of a community learning disability service. *Journal of Applied Research in Intellectual Disabilities*, *11*(4), 320-332.

Frizzell, L. B. (1997). Fitness and exercise for older adults with developmental disabilities. *Activities, Adaptation & Aging, 21*(3), 37-51.

Fullagar, S., & Owler, K. (1998). Narratives of leisure: Recreating the self. *Disability and Society, 13*(3), 441-450.

This article explored the use of narrative in the leisure experiences of people with mild intellectual disability. These narratives related attributes of capability that run counter to the typical story of lack associated with disability. The implications for this approach for developing alternative leisure support services are discussed.

Gamliel, S., Singer, B., & Marconi, K. (1998). HIV healthcare delivery and managed care: Applications and implications from the special projects of national significance program. *Home Health Care Services Quarterly, 17*(1), 101-109.

Gillman, M., Swain, J., & Heyman, B. (1997). Life history or 'case history': The objectification of people with learning difficulties through the tyranny of professional discourse. *Disability and Society, 12*(5), 675-693.

This article argues that people with learning difficulties have been objectified by professional practices. This objectification is furthered by professional reliance on case histories that do not contain background material, or that fail to include statements and wishes of the person with a learning difficulty as well.

Greenberg, J. S., Seltzer, M. M., Krauss, M. W., & Kim, H. (1997). The differential effects of social support on the psychological well-being of aging mothers of adults with mental illness or mental retardation. *Family Relations, 46*(4), 383-394.

This article reports on a longitudinal study designed to explore possible differences between the supports experienced by aging mothers of adults with mental illness versus those of aging mothers of adults with mental retardation. The sample included 360 families and used structured and semi-structured interviews. A number of conceptual reasons for differences are advanced, including mother-blaming for the mental illness of offspring. Results indicated significant differences in caregiving and social support.

Hains, A. A., Davies, W. H., Behrens, D., & Biller, J. A. (1997). Cognitive behavioral interventions for adolescents with cystic fibrosis. *Journal of Pediatric Psychology, 22*(5), 669-687.

Hall, J. A., Schlesinger, D. J., & Dineen, J. P. (1997). Social skills training in groups with developmentally disabled adults. *Research on Social Work Practice, 7*(2), 187-201.

Hall, L. L., & Purdy, R. (2000). Recovery and serious brain disorders: The central role of families in nurturing roots and wings. *Community Mental Health Journal, 36*(4), 427-441.

This paper advanced the view that the involvement of family members in mental health consumer recovery efforts is crucial. The development of consumer- and family-accessible service networks is advised.

Hall, J. A., Dineen, J. P., Schlesinger, D. J., & Stanton, R. (2000). Advanced group treatment for developmentally disabled adults with social skill deficits. *Research on Social Work Practice, 10*(3), 301-326.

This article reported on the results of a trial use of a group social skills training program with adults with mental retardation. The participants were identified as having moderate to borderline mental retardation. Training in social skills occurred across nine sessions with six adults. Results indicated that the group skills training program was not effective.

Haveman, M., van, Berkum, G., Reijnders, R., & Heller, T. (1997). Differences in service needs, time demands, and caregiving burden among parents of persons with mental retardation across the life cycle. *Family Relations, 46*(4), 417-425.

Heller, T., Roccoforte, J. A., & Cook, J. A. (1997). Predictors of support group participation among families of persons with mental illness. *Family Relations*, *46*(4), 437-442.

Heller, T., Hsieh, K., & Rowitz, L. (1997). Maternal and paternal caregiving of persons with mental retardation across the lifespan. *Family Relations*, *46*(4), 407-415.

Heller, T., Roccoforte, J. A., Hsieh, K., Cook, J. A., & Pickett, S. A. (1997). Benefits of support groups for families of adults with severe mental illness. *American Journal of Orthopsychiatry*, *67*(2), 187-198.

Heller, T., Miller, A. B., & Hsieh, K. (1999). Impact of a consumer-directed family support program on adults with developmental disabilities and their family caregivers. *Family Relations*, *48*(4), 419-427.

This article is based on a mixed-methods study of participants in a family support program for adults with developmental disabilities and their families. Results were based on responses to questionnaires given to either post hoc experimental and control groups, or longitudinally evaluated (four years) experimental and control groups. Measures included service use and unmet service needs, service satisfaction, caregiving self-efficacy, caregiver burden, out-of-home placement plans, community integration, and monthly wage. Results indicated that consumer-directed programs provided positive outcomes for adults with developmental disabilities and their families.

Herman, K. C. (1997). Increasing counselor awareness of Scotopic Sensitivity/Irlen Syndrome. *Journal of College Student Psychotherapy*, *11*(3), 65-73.

Hicks-Coolick A., & Kurtz, P. D. (1997). Preparing students with learning disabilities for success in postsecondary education: Needs and services. *Social Work in Education*, *19*(1), 31-42.

This article reports on a qualitative study with school learning disability personnel, conducted to determine what key issues should concern school social workers assisting youth with learning disabilities. Numerous important support activities were identified in four intervention areas: individual counseling, group counseling, parent support, and working with colleagues.

Hunt, A. (1998). A comparison of the abilities, health and behavior of 23 people with tuberous sclerosis at age 5 and as adults. *Journal of Applied Research in Intellectual Disabilities*, *11*(3), 227-238.

Janicki, M., McCallion, P., Force, L. T., Bishop, K., & LePore, P. (1998). Area agency on aging outreach and assistance for households with older carers of an adult with a developmental disability. *Journal of Aging and Social Policy*, *10*(1), 13-36.

Due to the longer life expectancies of persons with developmental disabilities, Area Agencies on Aging (AAAs) are increasingly becoming involved in providing outreach care to this population. In this article the feasibility of AAAs providing day-to-day support and outreach to disabled elder was examined. Based on data sheets, qualitative interviews, and *post facto* follow-up interviews, the authors concluded that AAAs are in a position to provide this care in close collaboration with developmental disabilities service systems.

Jones, L., & Menchetti, B. M. (2001). Identification of variables contributing to definitions of mild and moderate mental retardation in Florida. *Journal of Black Studies*, *31*(5), 619-634.

Kropf, N. P. (1997). Older parents of adults with developmental disabilities: Practice issues and service needs. *Journal of Family Psychotherapy*, *8*(2), 37-54.

This article explored a variety of issues and needs of older parents of adults with disabilities. While there are stresses, such as health, cost, and relocation planning for sons or daughters, there are also rewards for caring for adult children with disabilities, such as expressive support or help with housework. Intervention suggestions included psychoeducational issues, resources management, casework, and policy reform.

Levitas, A. S., & Gilson, S. F. (2001). Predictable crises in the lives of people with mental retardation. *Mental Health Aspects of Developmental Disabilities*, *4* (3), 1-12.

Lindsay, W. R., Olley, S., Jack, C., Morrison, F., & Smith, A. H. W. (1998). The treatment of two stalkers with intellectual disabilities using a cognitive approach. *Journal of Applied Research in Intellectual Disabilities*, *11*(4), 333-344.

Malone, D. M., McKinsey, P. D., Thyer, B. A., & Straka, E. (2000). Social work early intervention for young children with developmental disabilities. *Health and Social Work*, *25*(3), 169-181.

In the context of support for social workers as coordinators of early intervention teams, this article encourages appropriate preparation for social workers in consideration of the formal recognition of the importance of the profession in the Individuals with Disabilities Education Act (IDEA). The article provided a review of developmental disabilities and the roles of social work in early intervention, skills, and competencies required.

Nochi, M. (1997). Dealing with the "void": Traumatic brain injury as a story. *Disability and Society*, *12*(4), 533-555.

This naturalistic study employed unstructured taped interviews and thematic analysis to explore the experience of four people with traumatic brain injury (TBI). Themes related to the persons' sense of self were described as: (a) dealing with the "void" in the memory; (b) recovering from the void, and (c) living with the void. The importance of the void in the context of rehabilitation is stressed, as is the importance of counseling relationships that are nonpathologizing.

Palley, H. A., & Van, H. V. (2000). Long-term care for people with developmental disabilities: A critical analysis. *Health and Social Work*, *25*(3), 181-189.

This article explores today's deinstitutionalization trend in long-term care, tracing the historical manners of care in consideration of increasing population rates, public sentiment, and such. The authors included parallel consideration of long term care for elderly persons as well. Concluding remarks call for more flexibility in program design to allow for tailoring services to individual needs.

Phillips, R. S. C. (1999). Intervention with siblings of children with developmental disabilities from economically disadvantaged families. *Families in Society*, *80*(6), 569-577.

Pickett, S. A., Cook, J. A., Cohler, B. J., & Solomon, M. L. (1997). Positive parent/adult child relationships: Impact of severe mental illness and caregiving burden. *American Journal of Orthopsychiatry*, *67*(2), 220-230.

Raiz, L. (1997). The transplant trap: The impact of health policy on employment status following renal transplantation. *Journal of Health and Social Policy*, *8*(4), 67-87.

Rosen, A. L., & Persky, T. (1997). Meeting mental health needs of older people: Policy and practice issues for social work. *Journal of Gerontological Social Work*, *27*(3), 45-54.

This article reviews problems with the current delivery system for mental health for the elderly. The article identifies barriers to service use and calls for a separate and specific analysis of service delivery needs for elderly mental health.

Sanders, J. L., & Morgan, S. B. (1997). Family stress and adjustment as perceived by parents of children with Autism or Down Syndrome: Implications for intervention. *Child and Family Behavior Therapy*, *19*(4), 15-32.

Scott, B. S., Atkinson, L., Minton, H. L., & Bowman, T. (1997). Psychological distress of parents of infants with Down syndrome. *American Journal on Mental Retardation*, *102*(2), 161-171.

Slivinske, L. R., Fitch, V. L., & Wingerson, N. W. (1998). The effect of functional disability on service utilization: Implications for long-term care. *Health and Social Work*, *23*(3), 175-185.

Tedrick, T. (1997). Issues resolved and unresolved: A look to the future. *Activities. Adaptation & Aging*, *21*(3), 91-103.

Thapar, N., & Bhardwaj, S. M. (1999). Overcoming the tyranny of space: Experiences of multiple sclerosis patients. *Reflections*, *5*(4), 64-70.

Turner, H. A., Pearlin, L. I., & Mullan, J. T. (1998). Sources and determinants of social support for caregivers of persons with AIDS. *Journal of Health and Social Behavior*, *39*(2), 137-151.

White, B. (1997). Permanency planning for deaf children: Consideration of culture and language. *Arete*, *21*(2), 13-24.

Williams, V., & Robinson, C. (2001). More than one wavelength: Identifying, understanding and resolving conflicts of interest between people with intellectual disabilities and their family carers. *Journal of Applied Research in Intellectual Disabilities*, *14*(1), 30-46.

Young, J. M., & McNicoll, P. (1998). Against all odds: Positive life experience of people with advanced amyotrophic lateral sclerosis. *Health and Social Work*, *23*(1), 35-43.

Young, S., Young, B., & Ford, D. (1997). Parents with a learning disability: Research issues and informed practice. *Disability and Society*, *12*(1), 57-68.

> This paper begins with an examination of the concept of parenting and then applies its findings to parents who have a learning disability. The article suggests that no matter what skills, beliefs, or knowledge a parent with a disability may have about parenting, what is most important is how these are applied.

Disability and Ethnicity

Belgrave, F. Z.,& Bowe, F. (2000). Psychosocial aspects of chronic illness and disability among African Americans. *Contemporary Psychology*, *45*(2), 164.

Blacher, J., Lopez, S., Shapiro, J., & Fusco, J. (1997). Contributions to depression in Latina mothers with and without children with retardation: Implications for caregiving. *Family Relations*, *46*(4), 325-334.

> A multimethod study designed to evaluate the extent to which Californian Latina mothers with children with mental retardation were depressed, compared with peers whose children do not have mental retardation, was presented in this study. Based on a total sample size of 249, the study identified that mothers whose children have mental retardation are not only depressed at a higher rate than the controls, but are also more depressed.

Calderon, V., & Tennstedt, S. L. (1998). Ethnic differences in the expression of caregiver burden: Results of a qualitative study. *Journal of Gerontological Social Work*, *30*(1/2), 159-179.

> This article reports on a study that explored the accuracy of research reports that African Americans experience less caregiver burden than other groups. Eighteen caregivers representing three ethnic groups (African American, White, and Latino) were interviewed about their caregiving experiences. While all three groups reported feelings of anger and caregiver burden, the Latino group identified social isolation as a source of burden. Likewise, African Americans reported the time consuming nature of caregiving as a burden.

Cook, P., Cook, M., Tran, L., & Tu, W. (1997). Children enabling change: A multicultural, participatory, community-based rehabilitation research project involving Chinese children with disabilities and their families. *Child and Youth Care Forum*, *26*(3), 205-219.

Delgado, M., & Tennstedt, S. (1997). Making the case for culturally appropriate community services: Puerto Rican elders and their caregivers. *Health and Social Work, 22*(4), 246-255.

This study was designed to illuminate the caregiving characteristics of Puerto Rican women, in response to possible changing utilization needs by an ethnic group that historically has been committed to family provision of long-term care for its disabled members. Telephone, in-home and proxy interviews were conducted using a two-stage field design. Interview questions addressed demographics, functional abilities, caregiver characteristics, and extent of care. Results indicated that the participants were primarily cared for by family members, but that in many cases the caregiver was "virtually absent. "The need for social service development to reach Puerto Rican elders is discussed.

Fowler, L., Seekins, T., Dwyer, K., Duffy, S., Brod, R. L., & Locust, C. (2000). American Indian disability legislation and programs. *Journal of Disability Policy Studies, 10*(2), 166-185.

This article presented the results of participatory action research study with indigenous American tribal leaders designed to determine the extent to which tribes have disability programs available and accessible. Six percent of the respondents indicated their tribe was aware of federal legislation on disability, while 58% indicated they would be interested in establishing such legislation in their tribe. The authors suggests the need for coordinated federal support to develop programs to serve indigenous peoples who are disabled.

Hazuda, H. P., Wood, R. C., Lichtenstein, M. J., & Espino, D. V. (1998). Sociocultural status, psychosocial factors, and cognitive functional limitation in elderly Mexican Americans: Findings from the San Antonio longitudinal study of aging. *Journal of Gerontological Social Work, 30*(1/2), 99-121.

Reported in this article are the findings of a longitudinal study of Mexican American and European American elders. Multivariate analysis on socioeconomic status, education psychosocial supports, psychosocial burdens, and functional integration showed correlations between low educational levels and low levels of assimilation, as well as lower levels of psychosocial support to help prevent the deterioration of cognitive functioning.

Keigher, S. M. (1997). America's most cruel xenophobia. *Health and Social Work, 22*(3), 232-237.

The author of this article discusses the difficulties that immigrants to the United States experience as a result of the restrictive changes to Medicaid when Temporary Aid to Needy Families (TANF) was implemented.

Lau, J. T., & Cheung, C. (1999). Discriminatory attitudes to people with intellectual disability or mental health difficulty. *International Social Work, 42*(4), 431-444.

Reported in this study were the findings of a telephone survey designed to evaluate the attitudes of residents of Hong Kong toward people with psychiatric disabilities and people with intellectual difficulties. Respondents were significantly more negative in perception and attitude toward people with psychiatric disabilities, compared with people with intellectual disabilities. Further, respondents indicated that people with psychiatric disabilities should remain in their group homes, and that group homes should be located on the perimeter or outside of a town.

Loveland, C. (1999). The experiences of African Americans and Euro-Americans with multiple sclerosis. *Sexuality and Disability, 17*(1), 19-37.

McCallion, P., Janicki, M., & Grant, G. L. (1997). Exploring the impact of culture and acculturation on older families caregiving for persons with developmental disabilities. *Family Relations, 46*(4), 347-357.

Reviewed in this article are the themes discussed in focus group meetings with African American, Chinese American, Haitian American, Hispanic/Latino American, Korean American, and indigenous American groups. The groups were asked to respond to questions about family caregiving for members with developmental disabilities, perceptions of disability, and community and provider support.

Niu, X. (1999). Chinese-American students with learning difficulties: A pilot study. *International Journal of Disability, Development, and Education, 46*(1), 117-131.

Pixa, K. U. (1998). Parents with intellectual disability in Germany: Results of a nation-wide study. *Journal of Applied Research in Intellectual Disabilities, 11*(4), 355-364.

Potocky, M. (1997). Predictors of refugee economic status: A replication. *Journal of Social Service Research, 23*(1), 41-70.

Pruchno, R., Patrick, J. H., & Burant, C. J. (1997). African American and White mothers of adults with chronic disabilities: Caregiving burden and satisfaction. *Family Relations, 46*(4) 335-346.

> The authors describe a large study intended to illuminate differences in reported caregiver burden between African American and White mothers of adults with chronic disabilities. It has regularly been reported that African American mothers, in contrast to White mothers, consistently identify lower caregiver burden, despite lower socioeconomic, educational, and health status. The analysis of data from 841 structured interviews while demonstrating results that were consistent with other studies, indicating statistically significant differences in the level of caregiving satisfaction and caregiving burden between the two groups, provided analysis suggesting that these differences are attributable to demographic characteristics, and not to race per se.

Singh, N. N., McKay, J. D., & Singh, A. N. (1998). Culture and mental health: Nonverbal communication. *Journal of Child and Family Studies, 7*(4), 403-409.

Tennstedt, S. L., Chang, B., & Delgado, M. (1998). Patterns of long-term care: A comparison of Puerto Rican, African American, and non-Latino White elders. *Journal of Gerontological Social Work, 30*(1/2). 179-199.

Torres, G. F. M., & Kuo, T. (1998). Social policy and the politics of Hispanic aging. *Journal of Gerontological Social Work, 30*(1/2), 143-158.

Wallace, S. P., Levy, S. L., Andersen, R. M., & Kington, R. S. (1997). The impact by race of changing long-term care policy. *Journal of Aging and Social Policy, 9*(3), 1-20.

Weiss, M. (1997). Territorial isolation and physical deformity: Israeli parents' reaction to disabled children. *Disability and Society, 12*(2), 259-271.

> Three case study responses of Israeli parents to their disabled children are reported in this article. Using participant observation and interviews, the researcher found that parents isolated the child from the common family living space, and defined the child as a nonperson.

Disability and Gender

Barron, K. (1997). The bumpy road to womanhood. *Disability and Society, 12*(2) 223-239.

> A qualitative study dealing with societal constraints on the womanhood of physically disabled young women in Sweden is presented. While both women and people with disabilities are constrained by social expectations, results suggest that women with disabilities are constrained from being women, and relegated to a social role of disabled. The importance of providers and role models is discussed.

Jimenez, A. L., Alegria, M., Pena, M., & Vera, M. (1997). Mental health utilization in women with symptoms of depression. *Women and Health, 25*(2), 1-21.

Kallianes, V., & Rubenfeld, P. (1997). Disabled women and reproductive rights. *Disability and Society*, *12*(2), 203-221.

> The article reviews issues and concerns of women with disabilities with respect to reproductive rights, social barriers to reproductive health care, supportive information, and risks for undesirable outcomes, including those that stem from coercive social interventions.

Van, D. J. (1997). Body image of non-clinical and clinical populations of men: A literature review. *Occupational Therapy in Mental Health*, *13*(1), 37-57

MISCELLANEOUS DISABILITY

Adler, A. K., & Wahl, O. F. (1998). Children's beliefs about people labeled mentally ill. *American Journal of Orthopsychiatry*, *68*(2), 321-326.

Albrecht, G. L., & Devlieger, P. J. (1998). The disability paradox: High quality of life against all odds. *Social Science and Medicine*, *48*(8), 977.

Ammerman, R. T. (1997). Physical abuse and childhood disability: Risk and treatment factors. *Journal of Aggression, Maltreatment and Trauma*, *1*(1), 207-224.

Atkins, B. S., & Allen, M. P. (2000). Infants and toddlers with disabilities: Relationship-based approaches. *Social Work*, *45*, 371-379.

Bigby, C. (1997). Parental substitutes? The role of siblings in the lives of older people with intellectual disability. *Journal of Gerontological Social Work*, *29*(1), 3-21.

> The study reported was designed to identify the characteristics of people who take over the care of an older sibling with an intellectual disability, primarily in cases where the parents are no longer able to do so. Results indicated that while care of a sibling with an intellectual disability is taken over by most siblings after the loss of care-giving parents, this is not a situation that lasts.

Bosch, L. (1998). Early intervention in the new millennium: The critical role of school social workers. *Social Work in Education*, *20*(2), 139-143.

Bould, S., Smith, M. H., & Longino, C. F., Jr. (1997). Ability, disability, and the oldest old. *Journal of Aging and Social Policy*, *9*(1), 13-31.

Brzuzy, S. (1997). Deconstructing disability: The impact of definition. *Journal of Poverty*, *1*(1), 81-91.

Chiou, A. F., & Buschmann, M. T. (1999). The factors associated with excess disability in arthritic elderly patients. *Journal of Mental Health and Aging*, *5*(2), 151-164.

Corrigan, D., & Bishop, K. (1997). Creating family-centered integrated service systems and interprofessional educational programs to implement them. *Social Work in Education*, *19*, 149-161.

Cramer, E. P., & Gilson, S. F. (1999). Queers and crips: Parallel identity development processes for persons with nonvisible disabilities and lesbian, gay, and bisexual persons. *Journal of Gay, Lesbian, and Bisexual Identity*, *4*(1), 23-37.

> This article explored similarities in identity development for lesbian, gay, and bisexual persons (LGB) and persons with nonvisible disabilities, none of whom are likely to be raised and socialized by someone who shares in their experiences of marginalization. The authors applied and analyzed identity development of LGB persons and persons with non-visible disability through four models, and propose an interactional model that incorporates the influence of multiple identities, the fluidity of identity and other factors.

Damiani, V. B. (1999). Responsibility and adjustment in siblings of children with disabilities: Update and review. *Families in Society*, *80*(1), 34-40.

DePoy, E., Gilmer, D., Haslette, D. (2000). Adolescents with disabilities and chronic illness in transition: A community action needs assessment. *Disability Studies Quarterly, 20*, 17-25.

DePoy, E., & Miller, M. (1997). Attitudes towards inclusion: As Political-economic ideology? *Disability Studies Quarterly*, Spring, 1997.

Farmer, M. M., & Ferraro, K. F. (1997). Distress and perceived health: Mechanisms of health decline. *Journal of Health and Social Behavior, 38*(3), 298-311.

Findler, L. S. (2000). The role of grandparents in the social support system of mothers of children with a physical disability. *Families in Society, 81*(4), 370-381.

Finn, J. (1999). An exploration of helping processes in an online self-help group focusing on issues of disability. *Health and Social Work, 24*(3), 220-231.

> The use of online support groups by persons with disabilities is reviewed in this article. Posted messages were downloaded and coded for the extent to which therapeutic processes were involved. The study found that online groups were used for support in much the same way as face-to-face help, such as mutual sharing, catharsis, and empathy.

Floyd, F. J., & Gallagher, E. M. (1997). Parental stress, care demands, and use of support services for school-age children with disabilities and behavior problems. *Family Relations, 46*(4), 359-371.

Gilson, S. F. (1998). Case management and supported employment: A good fit. *Journal of Case Management, 7*(1), 10-17.

Gilson, S. F., Baskind, F., & Bricout, J. (1998). Social work's perspective on disability and our reality. *Families in Society, 79,*188-196.

Gilson, S. F., & Casebolt, G. M. (1997). Personal assistance services and case management. *Journal of Case Management 6*(1), 13-17.

Gilson, S. F., Cramer, E. P., & DePoy, E. (2001). Linking the assessment of self reported functional capacity with abuse experiences of women with disabilities. *Violence against Women, 7*, 418-431.

Gilson, S. F., Cramer, E., & DePoy, E. (2001). Redefining abuse of women with disabilities: A paradox of limitation and expansion. *Affilia, 16*(2), 220-235.

> This naturalistic study employed focus group interviews and thematic and taxonomic data analysis to explore the abuse experiences of women with disabilities. Within the theme of abuse, subthemes included assault, neglect, and control/restraint. Within the theme of response, subthemes included bad self, stuck, and movement. Overall, types of abuse unique to women with disabilities were related to the limitations that their disabilities present.

Gilson, S. F., Tusler, A. T., & Gill, C. (1997). Identity formation and the politics of community. *Journal of Vocational Rehabilitation, 9,* 7-17.

Hartman, A., DePoy, E., Francis, C., & Gilmer, D. (2000). Adolescents with special health care needs in transition: Three life histories. *Social Work in Health Care, 31*(4), 43-58.

Hendy, N., & Pascall, G. (1998). Independent living: Gender, violence and the threat of violence. *Disability and Society, 13*(3), 415-427.

> A qualitative study of young adults with severe physical disabilities and their choices about independent living, based on fears of, and experiences with, violence. Violence and abuse were found to be matters of major concern to this group of young adults.

Itzhaky, H., & Schwartz, C. (2000). Empowerment of parents of children with disabilities: The effect of community and personal variables. *Journal of Family Social Work, 5*(1), 21-36.

Jimenez, M. A. (1999). Letter from the editor. *Reflections, 5*(4), 2.

Johnson, H. C., Renaud, E. F., Schmidt, D. T., & Stanek, E. J. (1998). Social workers' views of parents of children with mental and emotional disabilities. *Families in Society, 79*(2), 173-187.

This article explores concerns expressed about possible negative perceptions among social workers of parents of children with disabilities, concerns expressed by the parents themselves. The authors conducted a survey by mail to evaluate worker attitudes and beliefs. While the majority of responses were parent-friendly, some were parent-blaming. Worker belief in the usefulness of medication was positively correlated with parent-friendly attitudes. In general, dynamic approaches were more likely to be parent-blaming than other approaches.

Kvam, M. H. (2000). Is sexual abuse of children with disabilities disclosed? A retrospective analysis of child disability and the likelihood of sexual abuse among those attending Norwegian hospitals. *Child Abuse and Neglect, 24*(8), 1073-1084.

Lau, J. T., & Cheung, C. (1999). Discriminatory attitudes to people with intellectual disability or mental health difficulty. *International Social Work, 42*(4), 431-444.

Leclerc, C., Lesage, A. D., Ricard, N., Lecomte, T., & Cyr, M. (2000). Assessment of a new rehabilitative coping skills module for persons with schizophrenia. *American Journal of Orthopsychiatry, 70*(3), 380-388.

Liese, H., Clevenger, R., & Hanley, B. (1999). Joining University Affiliated Programs and schools of social work: A collaborative model for disabilities curriculum development and training. *Journal of Social Work Education, 35*, 63-69.

Beginning with a report on previous survey findings that few social work schools offer developmental disabilities content in their curricula despite their professed interest in doing so, this study surveyed 58 University Affiliated Programs (UAPs) to determine to what extent they were involved with practitioner training activities in the field of mental retardation and developmental disabilities. Results showed that UAP/School of Social Work involvement occurred in 51%-76% of the UAPs surveyed, depending on the activity being evaluated. Conclusions were that ongoing and increasing cross-involvement between UAPs and schools of social work has potential to ultimately improve the practice of social work practitioners with people with disabilities.

McCreadie, C., & Hancock, R. (1997). Elder abuse: Can the British OPCS disability surveys throw any light? *Journal of Elder Abuse and Neglect, 8*(4), 31-42.

McCroskey, J., & Meezan, W. (1998). Family-centered services: Approaches and effectiveness. *The Future of Children: Protecting Children from Abuse and Neglect, 8*(4), 54-71.

McNamara, J., & Brooker, D. J. (2000). The Abuse Disability Questionnaire: A new scale for assessing the consequences of partner abuse. *Journal of Interpersonal Violence, 15*(2), 170-183.

The Abuse Disability Questionnaire, which is designed to evaluate the degree to which a victim of interpersonal violence has been disabled by the experience is presented in this article. The evaluation is predicated on the view that violence is psychologically disabling, to the extent that a negative psychological perspective is acquired. The evaluation rests on self-appraisals of how impaired people judge themselves to be in a number of areas. Positive psychometric results are discussed.

Mitchell, L. M., & Buchele-Ash, A. (2000). Abuse and neglect of individuals with disabilities: Building protective supports through public policy. *Journal of Disability Policy Studies, 10*(2), 225-243.

The authors of this article discuss the disproportionately high incidence of abuse and neglect experienced by disabled individuals. They then suggest how service providers can influence policy making to decrease risk.

Monahan, K., & O'Leary, K. D. (1999). Head injury and battered women: An initial inquiry. *Health and Social Work, 24*(4), 269-278.

This descriptive study examined the case records of residents in a domestic violence center, determining that 35% of the residents had experienced a head injury during a battering incident. The study discusses numerous challenges to working with this group of women, related to the head injury.

Neath, J. (1997). Social causes of impairment, disability and abuse: A feminist perspective. *Journal of Disability Policy Studies, 8,* 195-230.

Orelove, F. P., Hollahan, D. J., & Myles, K. T. (2000). Maltreatment of children with disabilities: training needs for a collaborative response. *Child Abuse and Neglect, 24*(2), 185-194.

Oravec, J. (2000). Online counseling and the Internet: Perspectives for mental health care supervision and education. *Journal of Mental Health, 9*(2), 121-136.

Quinn, P. (1997). Computer resources for people with disabilities. *Computers in Social Service, 14,* 83-84.

Quinn, P. (1999). Supporting and encouraging father involvement in families of children who have a disability. *Child and Adolescent Social Work Journal, 16*(6), 439-454.

The importance of father involvement in the lives of their children is reviewed. Barriers to father involvement include a lack of external support and guidance. Guided by a developmental model, this article proposes that the involvement of fathers in the lives of their disabled children would be furthered by the development of support groups and networks specifically for fathers.

Savemen, B. I., Astrom, S., Bucht, G., & Norberg, A. (1999). Elder abuse in residential settings in Sweden. *Journal of Elder Abuse and Neglect, 10*(1/2), 43-60.

Schilmoeller, G. L., & Baranowski, M. D. (1998). Intergenerational support in families with disabilities: Grandparents' perspectives. *Families in Society, 79,* 465-476.

Seltzer, M. M., Greenberg, J. S., Krauss, M. W., Gordon, R. M., & Judge, K. (1997). Siblings of adults with mental retardation or mental illness: Effects on lifestyle and psychological well-being. *Family Relations, 46*(4), 395-405.

Seltzer, M. M., & Heller, T. (1997). Families and caregiving across the life course: Research advances on the influence of context. *Family Relations, 46*(4), 321-323.

Four aspects of caregiving are identified: cultural, type of disability, socioeconomic characteristics, and formal services.

Trent, J. W. (1998). Defectives at the World's Fair. *Remedial and Special Education, 19*(4), 201-211.

Tymchuk, A. J., Lang, C. M., Dolyniuk, C. A., Berney, F. K., & Spitz, R. (1999). The Home Inventory of Dangers and Safety Precautions-2: Addressing critical needs for prescriptive assessment devices in child maltreatment and in healthcare. *Child Abuse and Neglect, 23*(1), 1-14.

Witkin, S. L. (1998). Chronicity and invisibility [Editorial]. *Social Work, 43,* 293-295.

The author discusses discrimination faced by people with invisible disabilities, even within the profession of social work. In an effort to spark debate, the semiotic importance of the term 'chronic' is discussed, as an indicator of what is untreatable. However, the author urges that the relative truth of this belief may be illuminated by cross cultural examination of other beliefs, believed by the insider but unnoticeable by the outsider.

Zeanah, P. D., & Hamilton, M. L. (1998). Staff perceptions of sexuality-related problems and behaviors of psychiatrically hospitalized children and adolescents. *Child Psychiatry and Human Development, 29*(1), 49-64.

Dissertations

DeHart, P. H. (1999). The relationship among social background, family support and life satisfaction of adults with spina bifida. Unpublished doctoral dissertation, New York University.

Horsley, C. L. (1999). Equal access and equal opportunity in higher education: The implementation of the Americans with Disabilities Act of 1990 in Region II colleges and universities. Unpublished doctoral dissertation, Bryn Mawr College.

Kropf, N. P. (1990). Stress and social support of parents with an adult mentally retarded child. Unpublished doctoral dissertation, Virginia Commonwealth University.

Nannini, A. (1998). Understanding sexual assault of women with disabilities: A feminist perspective. Unpublished doctoral dissertation, Brandeis University.

Book Chapters

Beaulaurier, R. L., & Taylor, S. H. (1999). Self-determination and consumer control: Guiding principles in the empowerment model as utilized by the disability rights movement. In W. Shera & L. Wells (Eds.), *Empowerment practice: Developing richer conceptual foundations* (pp. 159-177). Toronto: Canadian Scholars Press.

DePoy, E., & Gilson, S. F., (2000). Disability within a multicultural context. In C. D. Bryant (Ed.), *The encyclopedia of criminology and deviant behavior* (vol. 4 , pp. 202-205). London: Taylor & Francis.

DePoy, E. & Gitlow, L. (2000) Evidence-based practice. In L. Pedretti & M.B. Early, (Eds.), *Physical Disabilities in Occupational Therapy* (5th ed., pp.58-68). St. Louis, MO: Mosby

Gilson, B. B., & Gilson, S. F. (1998). Making friends and building relationships. In P. Wehman, & J. Kregel (Eds.), *More than a Job: Securing Satisfying Careers for People with Disabilities* (pp. 301-318). Baltimore, MD: Paul H. Brookes.

Gilson, S. F. (2000). Disability and the sick role. In C. D. Bryant (Ed.), *The encyclopedia of criminology and deviant behavior* (vol. 4, pp. 184-187). London: Taylor & Francis.

Gilson, S. F. (2000). Aging and disability. In R. L. Schneider, N.P. Kropf, & A. Kisor (Eds.), *Gerontological social work: Knowledge, service settings, and special Populations* (2nd ed.). Pacific Grove, CA: Wadsworth.

Gilson, S. F. (1998). Choice and self-advocacy: A consumer's perspective. In P. Wehman & J. Kregel (Eds.), *More Than a Job: Securing Satisfying Careers for People with Disabilities* (pp. 3-23). Baltimore, MD: Paul H. Brookes.

Gilson, S. F., Chilcoat, H. D., & Stapleton, J. M. Drug use by persons with disabilities. (1998). In B. A. Rouse (Ed.), *Substance Abuse and Mental Health Statistics Source Book, 1998*. Rockville, MD: Substance Abuse and Mental Health Administration, Government Publications Office.

Gilson, S. F., & Gilson, B. B. (2000). Underground advocacy: Emergence of the consumer voice. In D. Fauri, E. F. Netting, & S. P. Wernet (Eds.), *Cases in Macro Social Work Practice* (pp. 187-202). Boston: Allyn and Bacon.

Levitas, A. S., & Gilson, S. F. (2000). Transference/counter transference, reaction/counter-reaction: Resolution of dependency in individual psychotherapy for persons with mild and moderate mental retardation. In R. J. Fletcher & W. Gardner (Eds.), *Effective Therapy Approaches with Persons Who Have Mental Retardation*. Kingston, NY: NADD.

Sheriden, M. A. (1999). Personal narrative: Martha Sheridan. In R. Mackelprang R & Salsgiver (Ed.), *Disability: A diversity model approach in human service practice* (pp. 118-121). Pacific Grove, CA: Brooks/Cole.

Sheriden, M. A. (2000). Images of self and others: Stories from the children. In P. S. Spencer, C. Erting, & M. Marshark (Eds.), *The deaf child in the family and at school* (pp. 5-19). Mahwah, NJ: Lawrence Erlbaum.

Sheriden, M. A. (2001). Deaf women now. In L. Bragg (Ed.), *Deaf world: A historical reader and primary sourcebook* (pp. 380-389). New York: New York University Press.

Trent, J. W. (2000). Disability, subculture (culture) of. In C. D. Bryant (Ed.), *The encyclopedia of criminology and deviant behavior* (vol. 4, pp. 213-216). London: Taylor and Francis.

White, B. (2001). This child is mine: Deaf parents and their adopted deaf children. In L. Bragg (Ed.), *Deaf world* (pp. 68-80). New York: New York University Press.

BOOKS ON DISABILITY

This section is comprised of books on disability, primarily compiled from searches using the Library of Congress online catalog and relevant books referred to the senior editor. Additionally, recent landmark works in the field of disability studies were included to the extent that they were judged likely by the editors to advance social work disability knowledge, teaching, research, and practice. For the electronic search, the terms used were disabled, disability, handicapped, and handicap.

The listing is by no means exhaustive. Particularly in the area of disability-specific texts, the works presented here are a fraction of what is currently available. Additional works are readily identifiable, through electronic searches, in a wide variety of academic disciplines by using specific diagnostic labels and desired qualifiers as search terms. Examining texts outside of disciplines commonly considered—such as political science, economics, modern language studies, occupational therapy, allied health, and linguistics—can be helpful to social workers as well.

In general, the works cited were first published within the past 10 years. However, if in the judgment of the editors, a work continues to have significant influence on current conceptualizations and research, those works have been included.

References have been organized categorically.

Disability Studies

Albrecht, G. L., Seelman, K. D., & Bury, M. (Eds.). (2001). *Handbook of disability studies*. Thousand Oaks, CA: Sage.

> This is an extensive edited work with three broad topical areas: the shaping of disability studies as a field; experiencing disability; and disability in context. The book seeks to illuminate the private and public experience of disability as well as emergent academic approaches to studying disability. Extensive consideration is given to disability and social welfare and cross-cultural and policy issues.

Barnes, C. (1990). *The cabbage syndrome: The social construction of dependence*. New York: Falmer.

Barnes, C., & Mercer, G. (Eds.). (1996). *Exploring the divide: Illness and disability*. Leeds, UK: Disability Press.

Barnes, C., Mercer, G. & Shakespeare, T. (1999). *Exploring disability: A sociological introduction.* Malden, MA: Polity.

> The authors seek to distinguish between the American version of the "social model" of disability and the British version of the social model. The American version treats disability as an issue of minority populations and restricted civil rights, while the British issue focuses on the distinction between impairment and disability that is socially imposed as a result of impairment.

Barton, L. (1989). *Disability and dependency.* New York: Falmer.

Barton, L. (Ed.). (1996). *Disability and society: Emerging issues and insights.* New York: Longman.

Batshaw, M. L., & Perret, Y. M. (1992). *Children with disabilities: A medical primer (3rd ed.).* Baltimore, MD: Paul H. Brookes.

> This text is intended to be used as a college textbook for students and professionals who plan to work or already work with children having developmental disabilities. The authors begin by discussing what happens before, during, or after birth to cause a child to have a developmental disability. In the chapters that follow, the authors focus on individual developmental disabilities highlighting new medical, rehabilitative, and educational material. Separate chapters on ethical dilemmas and family caring and coping are included.

Bogdan, R., & Taylor, S. (1994). *The social meaning of mental retardation: Two life studies.* New York: Teachers College Press.

Bruggemann, B. J. (1999). *Lend me your ear: Rhetorical constructions of deafness.* Washington, DC: Gallaudet University Press.

Campbell, J., & Oliver, M. (1996). *Disability politics: Understanding our past, changing our future.* New York: Routledge.

Charlton, J. I. (1998). *Nothing about us without us: Disability oppression and empowerment.* Berkeley: University of California Press.

> Entitled with the words that have become the rallying cry of the disability rights movement, this book challenges the notion that dependency on the part of persons with disabilities dictates a loss of power. The analysis explores oppressive features of social and economic systems worldwide, and suggests ways to empowerment for disability activists.

Corbett, J. (1996). *Bad-mouthing: The language of special needs.* Washington, DC: Falmer Press.

Corker, M. (1998). *Deaf and disabled, or deafness disabled? Towards a human rights perspective.* Philadelphia: Open University Press.

Corker, M., & French, S. (Eds.). (1999). *Disability discourse.* Philadelphia: Open University Press.

> This text explores power in discursive reciprocal relationships from the theoretical standpoint that the "linguistic turn" in intellectual discourse of this century is an active part of disabling people with sensory impairments.

Crutchfield, S., & Epstein, M. (Eds.). (2000). *Points of contact: Disability, art, and culture.* Ann Arbor: University of Michigan Press.

Davis, L. (1995). *Enforcing normalcy: Disability, deafness, and the body.* New York: Verso.

Davis, L. (1997). *The disability studies reader.* New York: Routledge.

Donley, C., & Buckley, S. (1996). *The tyranny of the normal: An anthology.* Kent, OH: Kent State University Press.

> An anthology of fiction and nonfiction about people whose "physical abnormalities make them disturbingly deviant from cultural norms." Includes essays that explore the problems faced by these "others" as they try to find a place in society.

Fawcett, B. (2000). *Feminist perspectives on disability.* New York: Pearson Education.

Fiedler, L. (1993). *Freaks: Myths and images of the secret self.* New York: Anchor Books.

Fleischer, D. Z., & Zames, F. (2001). *The Disability Rights Movement: From charity to confrontation.* Philadelphia: Temple University Press.

> A history of the disability rights movement, from the time of charity and institutionalization through the present day. Discussion of important legislation is included as it relates to specific topics (e.g., physician assisted suicide, access to jobs).

Hevey, D. (1992). *The creatures that time forgot: Photography and disability imagery.* New York: Routledge.

Johnstone, D. (2001). *An introduction to disability studies* (2nd ed.). London: David Fulton Publishers.

Linton, S. (1998). *Claiming disability: Knowledge and identity.* New York: New York University Press.

Longmore, P. K. U., L. (Ed.). (2001). *The new disability history: American perspectives.* New York: New York University Press.

Mitchell, D., & Snyder, S. (Eds.). (1997). *The body and physical difference: Discourses of disability.* Ann Arbor: University of Michigan Press.

Pointon, A., Davies, C., & Pointon, A. (Eds.). (1998). *Framed: Interrogating disability in the media.* London: British Film Institute, Arts Council of England.

> An introduction to the critical analysis of film and media images of disabled people. The second segment of the book is devoted to access to employment and training and the development of a disability arts movement.

Polsky, A. J. (1991). *The rise of the therapeutic state.* Princeton, NJ: Princeton University Press.

Read, J. (2000). *Disability, the family and society: Listening to mothers.* Philadelphia: Open University Press.

> Presented in this book are the results of a qualitative study about the experiences of mothers with children who have disabilities. The author reports that acting as intermediaries between their children and a stigmatizing society is important to these mothers.

Reinders, H. S. (2000). *The future of the disabled in liberal society: An ethical analysis.* Notre Dame, IN: University of Notre Dame Press.

> Explores the ethical paradox around accepting people with disability by looking at the paradigm shift from medical to normalization paradigms. Conflicting approaches suggest that for existing people with disabilities the prevailing sentiment is, "Since you're here we're going to everything we can for you, but it'd be better for all of us if you weren't here at all." The author seeks to widen the current view, and discusses policy challenges that arise.

Rioux, M. H. & Bach, M. (Eds.). (1994). *Disability is not measles: New research paradigms in disability.* North York, Canada: Roeher Institute.

Rogers, L. J., & Swadener, B. B. (Eds.). (2001). *Semiotics and dis/ability : Interrogating categories of difference.* Albany: State University of New York Press.

Scotch, R. K. (2001). *From good will to civil rights: Transforming federal disability policy (2ⁿᵈ ed.).* Philadelphia, PA: Temple University Press.

Shakespeare, T. (Ed.). (1998). *The disability reader: Social science perspectives.* New York: Cassell.

Smart, J. (2001). *Disability, society and the individual.* Gaithersburg, MD: Aspen.

Stiker, H.-J. (1999). *A history of disability.* Ann Arbor: University of Michigan Press.

Thomas, C. (1999). *Female forms: Experiencing and understanding disability.* Philadelphia: Open University Press.

Thomson, R. G. (Ed.). (1996). *Freakery: Cultural spectacles of the extraordinary body.* New York: New York University Press.

This collection explores the movement of freakery from "the embodiment of wonder to the embodiment of error." The analysis includes interdisciplinary conversations such as those from art, social, and medical discourse to demonstrate and evaluate the change in freak status over time.

Wilson, J. C., & Lewiecki-Wilson, C. (Eds.). (2001). *Embodied rhetorics: Disability in language and culture.* Carbondale: Southern Illinois University Press.

Wolfensberger, W. (1998). A brief Introduction to Social Role Valorization: A high-order concept for addressing the plight of societally devalued people, and for structuring human services. Syracuse, NY: Training Institute for Human Service Planning, Leadership and Change Agentry, Syracuse University.

Disability and Practice

Altman, B. M., & Barnartt, S. N. (Eds.). (2000). *Expanding the scope of social science research on disability.* Stamford, CT: JAI Press.

This book presents an introduction to research on disability issues in a manner designed to educate social science researchers to the extensive social issues that affect the lives of people with disabilities ("An invitation to social scientists to 'get it'"). Included articles highlight the broad array of issues facing this population.

Anchor, K. N., & Felicetti, T. C. (Eds.). (1999). *Disability analysis in practice: framework for interdisciplinary science.* Dubuque, IA: Kendall/Hunt.

Belgrave, F. Z. (1998). *Psychosocial aspects of chronic illness and disability among African Americans.* Westport, CT: Auburn.

Barnartt, S. & Scotch, R. (2001). *Disability protests: Contentious politics, 1977-1999.* Washington, DC: Gallaudet University Press.

Barret, R. P. (Ed.). (1986). *Severe behavior disorders in the mentally retarded: Nondrug approaches to treatment.* New York: Plenum.

Brantlinger, E. A. (1994). *Fighting for Darla: Challenges for family care and professional responsibility.* New York: Teacher's College Press.

The case study of a pregnant adolescent with autism.

Briggs, M. H. (1997). *Building early intervention teams: Working together for children and families.* Gaithersburg, MD: Aspen.

Corker, M. (1995). *Counseling the deaf challenge.* Bristol, PA: J. Kingsley.

This book is written for counselors and counselors in training who wish to prepare themselves to best serve clients who are deaf. Valuable background into the politics of deafness provides information about some of the social challenges that people who are deaf may face in an all-Deaf community.

Crossley, R. (1997). *Speechless: Facilitating communication for people without voices.* New York: Dutton.

Dale, N. O. (1996). *Working with families of children with special needs: Partnership and practice.* New York: Routledge.

Darling, R.B., D., & Baxter, C. (1996). *Families in focus: Sociological methods in early intervention.* Austin, TX: Pro-Ed.

Dunst, C., Trivette, C. M., & Deal, A. G. (Eds.). (1994). *Supporting and strengthening families.* Cambridge, MA: Brookline Books.

Fletcher, R. J. (2000). Therapy approaches for persons with mental retardation. Kingston, NY: NADD Press.

Gardner, J. F. & Chapman, M. S. (1993). *Developing staff competencies for supporting people with developmental disabilities: An orientation handbook.* Baltimore, MD: Paul H. Brookes.

Gething, L. (1997). *Person to person : A guide for professionals working with people with disabilities.* Baltimore, MD: Paul H. Brookes.

Gray, B. R. G. (1999). *Lifemaps of people with learning difficulties.* Philadelphia: J. Kingsley.

GreyHouse Publishing Company. (1998). *The complete directory for people with disabilities: A one-stop source-book for individuals and professionals.* Lakeview, CT: Author.

Harry, B., Kalyanpur, M. & Day, M. (1999). *Building cultural reciprocity with families: Case studies in special education.* Baltimore, MD: Paul H. Brookes.

Kroll, K., & Klein, E. L. (1992). *Enabling romance: A guide to love, sex and relationships for the disabled.* New York: Harmony Books.

This is an illustrated guide to romantic and sexual relationships for persons with physical disabilities, their friends, families, and helping professionals. Includes safe sex strategies, family planning, and how to establish intimacy for those who need caregivers or personal attendants for physical assistance.

LaPlante, M. P. (1991). *Disability in basic life activities across the life span.* Washington, DC: National Institute on Disability and Rehabilitation Research, U.S. Department of Education, Office of Special Education and Rehabilitative Services.

LaPlante, M. P. (1991). *Disability risks of chronic illnesses and impairments.* Washington, DC: National Institute on Disability and Rehabilitation Research, U.S. Department of Education, Office of Special Education and Rehabilitative Services.

Levison, L. & St. Onge, I. (1999). *Disability awareness in the classroom: A resource tool for teachers and students.* Springfield, IL: Charles C. Thomas.

Lovett, H. (1997). *Learning to listen: Positive approaches and people with difficult behavior.* Baltimore, MD: Paul H. Brookes.

A clinical psychologist talks about his approach to working with people with difficult behavior. He discusses the shortcomings of behavior modification and the damaging effects of negative staff and organizational attitudes. The author describes his own strategies and approaches to including people with problem behaviors in everyday life.

Mackelprang, R., & Salsgiver, R. O. (1999). *Disability: A diversity model approach in human service practice.* Pacific Grove, CA: Brooks/Cole.

The authors review the development of the current models of disability theory and culture. The authors discuss categories of disability from a life stage development approach and offer practice guidelines for human service workers.

McGee, J. J. (1991). *Beyond gentle teaching: A non-aversive approach to helping those in need.*

Miller, N. B., & Sammons, C. C. (1999). *Everybody's different : Understanding and changing our reactions to disabilities.* Baltimore, MD: Paul H. Brookes.

Written by two social workers, this book is about understanding one's own reaction to the difference of disability. The content includes additional resources, awareness activities and skill building exercises.

Moore, M., Beazley, S., & Maelzer, J. (1998). *Researching disability issues.* Philadelphia: Open University Press.

Neufeldt, A. H., & Albright, A. (Eds.). (1998). *Disability and self-directed employment: Business development models.* Ottawa, Canada: International Development Research Centre.

Oliver, M. (Ed.). (1991). *Social work: Disabled people and disabling environments with disabled people.* London: J. Kingsley.

Oliver, M. (1996). *Understanding disability: From theory to practice.* New York: St. Martin's Press.

Oliver presents his view of disability as a social construction and traces the enduring nature of the social construction through an analysis and critique of existing policies. The oppression of disabled people as restriction of civil rights is discussed.

Olkin, R. (1999). *What psychotherapists should know about disability.* New York: Guilford.

This volume provides a comprehensive view of disability and issues of treatment that are important when working clinically with persons with disabilities. The theoretical perspective is that of the social model of disability. Considerable discussion is devoted to the influence of attitudes and stereotypes towards disability, of which therapists must be aware to practice effectively.

Orenstein, M. (2000). *Smart but stuck: What every therapist needs to know about learning disabilities and imprisoned intelligence.* Binghamton, NY: Haworth.

Pardeck, J. T. (1998). *Social work after the Americans with Disabilities Act: New challenges and opportunities for social service professionals.* Westport, CT: Auburn House.

Working from the standpoint that the Americans with Disabilities Act (ADA) is aligned with the antidiscrimination philosophies and traditions of social work, Pardeck provides an overview and analysis of the ADA that will help professional social workers and students realize the significance of the new rights and protections extended under the ADA legislation.

Pilling, D. (1992). *Approaches to case management for people with disabilities.*

Priestly, M. (2001). *Disability and the life course: Global perspectives.* New York: Cambridge University Press.

Rothman, J. (1994). Practice with highly vulnerable clients: A case management and community-based service. Englewood Cliffs, NJ: Prentice Hall.

Sharlin, S. S., M. (2000). *Therapeutic intervention with poor, unorganized families: From distress to hope.* Binghamton, NY: Haworth Clinical Practice Press.

Ward, L. (1997). *Don't leave us out: Involving young people in research and development projects.* York, United Kingdom: Joseph Rowantree Foundation.

Weisgerber, R. A. (1991). *Quality of life for persons with disabilities: Skill development and transitions across life stages.* Gaithersberg, MD: Aspen.

Disability and Social Justice

Armstrong, F., & Barton, L. (Eds.). (1999). *Disability, human rights and education: Cross cultural perspectives*. Philadelphia: Open University Press.

This volume looks at multinational versions of educational programming for persons with disabilities. Each section provides an analysis of the sociopolitical context that underpins educational policy. The final chapter comments on those preceding and questions whether education has historically been the primary concern in developing policy for placing children.

Baquer, A., & Sharma, A. (1997). *Disability: Challenges vs. responses*. New Delhi, India: Concerned Action Now.

Barnartt. S. N., & Scotch, R. (2001). *Disability protests: Contentious politics 1970-1999*. Washington, DC: Gallaudet University Press.

Bound, J., Schoenbaum, M., & Waidmann, T. (1996). *Race differences in labor force attachment and disability*. Cambridge, MA: National Bureau of Economic Research.

Bryan, W. V. (2001). *Sociopolitical aspects of disabilities: The social perspectives and political history of disabilities and rehabilitation in the United States*. Springfield, IL: Charles C. Thomas.

Christensen, C. R., F. (Ed.). (1996). *Disability and the dilemmas of education and justice*. Philadelphia: Open University Press.

Crichton, A., & Jongbloed, L. (1998). *Disability and social policy in Canada*. North York, Canada: Captus.

This book has both specific and general use as an analysis of how disability policy was and is developed in the context of existing social policy. Specific policy development areas covered are habilation/rehabilitation, employment, shelter, income support, access and disability-related supports.

Doyle, B. J. (1995). *Disability, discrimination and equal opportunities: A comparative study of the employment rights of disabled persons*. New York: Mansell.

Duster, T. (1990). *Backdoor to eugenics*. New York: Routledge.

The author critiques the growing acceptance for preventing "defective" babies, which "screens a new type of eugenics based on a new social order, in which the working agreement about what makes babies unwanted is never overtly discussed." The subsequent analysis is designed to spur public debate about these issues.

Ellis, A., & Llewellyn, M. (1997). *Dealing with differences: Taking action on class, race, gender, and disability*. Thousand Oaks, CA: Corwin.

Fries, K. (1997). *Body, remember: A memoir*. New York: Dutton.

Goffman, E. (1961). *Asylums: Essays on the social situation of mental patients and other inmates*. New York: Anchor.

Goffman, E. (1963). *Stigma: Notes on the management of a spoiled identity*. New York: Simon and Schuster.

A critical work in the development of disability studies theory, Goffman analyzes the development and maintenance of stigma in society. The author explores the roles of stigmatized individuals as well as questions about identity.

Goldman, C. D. (1991). *Disability rights guide: Practical solutions to problems affecting people with disabilities*. Lincoln, NE: Media.

Hales, G. (1996). *Beyond disability toward an enabling society*. Thousand Oaks, CA: Sage.

Indiana Governor's Planning Council for People with Disabilities. (1999). *Overcoming double discrimination: Defeating prejudices of ethnicity and disability*. Indianapolis, IN: Author.

Kent, D. (1996). *The disability rights movement*. New York: Children's Press.

This is a brief and easy-to-read account of the disability rights movement, from the major players to the highlights of activism and the legislation enacted.

Leicester, M. (1999). *Disability voice: Towards an enabling education*. Philadelphia: J Kingsley.

Marks, D. (1999). *Disability: controversial debates and psychosocial perspectives*. New York: Routledge.

Minuchin, P., Colapinto, J., & Minuchin, S. (1998). *Working with families of the poor*. New York: Guilford.

A discussion of a systems approach to working with the families of poor children, including children who have been institutionalized. The book includes a discussion about the context of origin for the children and what it means for their behavior within the therapeutic milieu.

Potok, A. (2002). *A matter of dignity: Changing the lives of the disabled*. New York: Bantam.

Racino, J. (1999). *Policy, program evaluation, and research in disability*. Binghamton, NY: Haworth.

Russell, M. (1998). *Beyond ramps: Disability at the end of the social contract*. Monroe, ME: Common Courage.

Russell challenges political rhetorical dodges and details how social policies underlying oppression of persons with disabilities violate the social contract. Her analysis of the ADA reveals what it was intended, and has yet failed, to do.

Shapiro, J. (1993). *No pity: People with disabilities forging a new civil rights movement*. New York: Times Books.

Shaw, B. (Ed.). (1994). *The ragged edge: the disability experience from the pages of the first fifteen years of The Disability Rag*. Louisville, KY: Avocado.

Silvers, A., Wasserman, D., & Mahowald, M. B. (1998). *Disability, difference, discrimination*. Lanham, MD: Rowman and Littlefield.

In this volume three authors contribute their views on justice and the place of persons with disabilities in society. Issues under consideration include genetic engineering, access to resources, and the ability to contribute.

Sobsey, D. (1991). *Disability, sexuality and abuse: Annotated bibliography*. Baltimore, MD: Paul H. Brookes.

Weaver, C. (Ed.). (1991). *Disability and work: Incentives, rights and opportunities*. Washington, DC: AEI Press.

Wilson, J. C., & Lewiecki-Wilson, C. (200). *Embodied Rhetorics: Disability in language and culture*. Carbondale: Southern Illinois University Press.

This volume critically examines the past and present rhetoric that has labeled and formed social stereotypes of persons with disabilities. Special consideration is given to deafness and literacy as well as "cultural and spatial rhetorics of disability."

Disability and Ethnic Culture

Abrams, J. (1998). *Judaism and disability: Portrayals in ancient texts from the Tanach through the Bavli*. Washington, DC: Gallaudet University Press.

Ahmad, W. I. U. (2000). *Ethnicity, disability and chronic illness*. Buckingham, United Kingdom: Open University Press.

Bedirhan, T. (2000). *Disability and culture: Universalism and diversity*. Kirkland, WA: Hogrefe and Huber.

Belgrave, F. Z. (1998). *Psychosocial aspects of chronic illness and disability among African Americans*. Westport, CT: Auburn.

This book presents chronic illness and disability disparities between African American and other groups, and examines cultural considerations that influence health care, medical and rehabilitation utilization in this population. Disability outcomes and adaptive functioning are discussed, again from the perspective of cultural difference/congruence. Alternative policies and practices are suggested.

Bruhns, B. I. (1995). *Disability and rehabilitation in Namibia: A national survey*. Windhoek, Namibia: Namibian Economic Policy Research Unit.

Bryan, W. V. (1999). *Multicultural aspects of disabilities: A guide to understanding and assisting minorities in the rehabilitation process*. Springfield, IL: Charles C. Thomas.

Written primarily for a rehabilitation counselors, this book explores the intersection of disability and specific cultural groups. Disability incidence statistics, healthcare, employment, social, family and cultural issues are reviewed for Black, Asian, Hispanic/Latino and Native American populations. Rehabilitation strategies are provided.

Cohen, C. (1999). *The boundaries of blackness: AIDS and the breakdown of black politics*. Chicago: University of Chicago Press.

Fadiman, A. (1997). *The spirit catches you and you fall down: A Hmong child, her American doctors, and the collision of two cultures*. New York: Farrar Straus and Giroux.

An account of the clash between a Hmong family and their child's American doctors. Treatment events are interspersed with musing about the Hmong culture, both of the culture native to Southeast Asia and the immigrant (refugee) population in the United States.

Fowler, L. (1996). *American Indian approaches to disability policy establishing legal protections for tribal members with disabilities: Five case studies*. Missoula, MO: Montana University Affiliated Rural Institute on Disabilities.

Goodluck, C. T. (1991). *Utilization of genograms and eco-maps to assess American Indian families who have a member with a disability (making visible the invisible)*. Flagstaff, AZ: American Indian Rehabilitation Research and Training Center, Institute for Human Development, Northern Arizona University.

Ingstad, B., & Whyte, S. R. (1995). *Disability and culture*. Berkeley: University of California Press.

This landmark text explores the notion of a universal definition of disability, and the differences between culture that are apparent. As anthropologists, these authors ask questions designed to illuminate the process by which cultures identify disability.

Joe, J. R., & Miller, D. (1987). *American Indian cultural perspectives on disability*. Tucson, AZ: University of Arizona, Native American Research and Training Center.

Leavitt, R. L. (1992). *Disability and rehabilitation in rural Jamaica: An ethnographic study*. Rutherford, NJ: Fairleigh Dickinson University Press.

Makas, E. (1995). *The development of the MIDS-AI/AN: The American Indian/Alaska Native version of the Modified Issues in Disability Scale*. Flagstaff, AZ: American Indian Rehabilitation Research and Training Center, Northern Arizona University, Institute for Human Development.

Martin, L. G., & Soldo, B. J. (1997). *Racial and ethnic differences in the health of older Americans*. Washington, DC: National Academy Press.

This volume provides a series of studies that compare specific aspects of health differences among older adults. The studies are intended to illuminate health disparities between cultural groups in the US.

Retish, P., & Reiter, S. (Eds.). (1999). *Adults with disabilities: International perspectives in the community*. Mahwah, NJ: Lawrence Erlbaum.

Santiago, A. M. (1996). *The economic consequences of disability status: A comparison between Anglo, black and Latino men*. East Lansing, MI: Julian Sammora Research Institute, Michigan State University.

Thomson, N., & Snow, C. (1994). Disability and handicap among Aborigines of the Taree area of New South Wales. Canberra: Australian Government Publications Service.

Biographies/Autobiographies

Anserine, C. (1994). *The me in the mirror*. Seattle: Seal.

Connie Planarian's candid account of growing up with a severe disability. Topics include daily life, relationships, personal attendants, social barriers and her work as a civil servant.

Casuist, S. (1998). *Planet of the blind*. New York: Dial.

Casuist discusses the experiences and challenges of growing up legally blind. In addition to discussing his admission or self-identification as a blind and disabled person, Casuist describes the reception that society has held for him because of his disability status.

Edgerton, R. B., & Gaston, M. A. (Eds.). (1991). *"I've seen it all!*. Baltimore, MD: Paul H. Brookes.

Older people with mental retardation living in the community talk about their experiences and their lives.

Finger, A. (1990). *Past due: A story of disability, pregnancy and birth*. Seattle, WA: Seal.

Fries, K. (1998). *Staring back: The disability experience from the inside out*. New York: Plume.

Gallagher, H. (1998). *Blackbird fly away: Disabled in an ablebodied world*. Arlington, VA: Vandemere.

Hugh Gallagher writes about his life after contracting polio during his teen years. Gallagher describes his personal feelings at different times, aging, and social, and physical barriers to career, travel, and environments. He also describes his involvement in the creation of federal policies such as the Architectural Barriers Act and the ADA.

Gallagher, H. G. (1998). *FDR's splendid deception, FDR memorial edition*. New York: Dodd, Mead.

Gitter, E. (2001). *The imprisoned guest: Samuel Howe and Laura Bridgman, the original deaf-blind girl*. New York: Farrar, Straus and Giroux.

Grandin, T. (1995). *Thinking in pictures: And other reports on my life with autism*. New York: Doubleday.

Griffin, S. (1999). *What her body thought: A journey into the shadows*. San Francisco: Harper.

The personal account of a woman with chronic fatigue syndrome.

Hathaway, K. B. (2000). *The little locksmith*. New York: Feminist Press at the City University of New York. (Originally published 1943.)

The story of a woman with scoliosis.

Huckleberry, J. (1995). *Moving violations: War zones, wheelchairs and declarations of independence*. New York: Hyperion.

Radio correspondent Huckleberry writes about his life and travels as an individual with paraplegia.

Jacobson, D. S. (1999). *The question of David: A disabled mother's journey through adoption, family and life*. Berkley, CA: Creative Arts.

Kingsley, J., & Levitz, M. (1994). *Count us in: Growing up with Down syndrome*. New York: Harcourt Brace.

Lynden, J. (1997). *Daughter of the Queen of Sheba*. Boston: Houghton Mifflin.

Mars, N. (1997). *Waist-high in the world: A life among the non-disabled*. Thorndike, ME: G.K. Hall.

Murphy, R. F. (1987). *The body silent*. New York: Holt.

An anthropologist writes of his experience with progressive paralysis.

Russo, H., O'Malley, S. G., & Severance, M. (1988). *Disabled, female and proud! Stories of ten women with disabilities*. Boston, MA: Exceptional Parent Press.

Williams, D. (1992). *Nobody, nowhere: The extraordinary autobiography of an autistic*. New York: Times Books.

Williams, D. (1994). *Somebody somewhere: Breaking free from the world of autism*. New York: Times Books.

Wright, M. H. ((1999). *Sounds like home: Growing up black and deaf in the South*. New York: Gallaudet University Press.

The story of an African American deaf child writing from the perspective of a student and a student teacher in a black deaf and blind school. Includes discussion of important black figures as well as major events in American history such as the Depression and World War II.

Disability, Policy, and Service Provision

Burke, P. C., K. (1996). *Support for families: Helping children with learning disabilities*. Brookfield, VT: Ashgate.

Cameron, G., & J., V. (1997). *Protecting children and supporting families: Promising programs and organizational realities*. New York: Aldine de Gruyter.

Crepe, J. J. W., & Graffito, J. (1995). *A family's guide to the individualized family service plan*. Baltimore, MD: Paul H. Brookes.

Gardner, A., Lipsky, D. K., & Turnbull, P. (1991). *Supporting families with a child with a disability: An international outlook*. Baltimore, MD: Paul H. Brookes.

Miry, R. (1996). *Disability and the city: International perspectives*. New York: St. Martin's Press.

In this volume the development of the modern city is explored in contrast to the access needs of persons with disabilities. Policies governing accessibility are analyzed, with suggestions for changes. Targeted policies are primarily those in Britain.

Martin, E. D. (2001). Significant disability: Issues affecting people with significant disabilities from a historical, policy, leadership and systems perspective. Springfield, IL: Charles C. Thomas.

Percy, S. (1989). *Disability, civil rights and public policy: The politics of implementation.* Tuscaloosa: University of Alabama Press.

Priestly, M. (1999). *Disability politics and community care.* Philadelphia: J. Kingsley.

> The conflicts between the values of community care and independent living and those of the social welfare state are discussed in depth. Although the system being reviewed is British, the value conflicts between true independent life and choice versus subsistence level poverty are consistent with those experienced by persons with disabilities in the United States.

Racino, J.A. (2001). Personnel preparation in disability and community life: Toward universal approaches to support. Springfield, IL: Charles C. Thomas.

Reno, V. P., & Macaw, J. L. (Eds.). (1997). Disability: Challenges for social insurance, health care financing, and labor market policy. Washington, DC: National Academy of Social Insurance.

Retish, P. & Reiter, S. (Eds.). (1999). *Adults with disabilities: International perspectives in the community.* Mahwah, NJ: Lawrence Erlbaum.

> In this book an international look at programs to assist youth with disabilities in transitioning to adulthood is presented. The authors Highlight the importance of considering cultural diversity in planning and implementing transition programs. Roberts, R. N., Rule, S. & Innocent, M. (1998). *Strengthening the family-professional partnership in services for young children.* Baltimore, MD: Paul H. Brookes.

Routledge Institute. (1996). *Disability, community and society: Exploring the links.* North York, Canada: Author

Seligman, M., & Darling, R. B. (1997). *Ordinary families, special children: A systems approach to childhood disability* (2nd ed.). New York: Guildford.

Szymanski, E. M., & Parker, R. M. (Eds.). (1996). *Work and disability: Issues and strategies in career development and job placement.* Austin, TX: Pro-Ed.

Turnbull, H. R., Turnbull, A. P., Bronchi, G. J., Summers, J. A., & Roeder-Gordon, C. (1989). *Disability and the family: A guide to decisions for adulthood.* Baltimore, MD: Paul H. Brookes.

Disability-Specific Texts

Batshaw, M. L. (Ed.). (1997). *Children with disabilities* (4th ed.) Baltimore, MD: Paul H. Brookes Publishing Co.

Bragg, L. (Ed.). (2001). *Deaf world: A historical reader and primary sourcebook.* New York: New York University Press.

> This volume is a sourcebook on Deaf history, politics, and culture. Articles on the proper treatment and training of deaf people by industry are placed in contrast with current challenges to social stereotypes.

Corker, M. (1996). *Deaf transitions: Images and origins of deaf families, deaf communities and deaf identities.* Bristol, PA: J. Kingsley.

Godley, D. (2000). *Self-advocacy in the lives of people with learning difficulties: the politics of resilience.* Philadelphia: Open University Press.

> This guide for teachers and practitioners examines self-advocacy in the lives of persons with learning difficulties. The analysis is grounded in the experience of the people themselves, and redresses the predominant focus on learning difficulties as pathology. Suggestions for supporters are provided.

Hallowell, E. M., & Rate, J. J. (1994). *Driven to distraction: Recognizing and coping with ADD from childhood to adulthood*. New York: Touchstone.

Lane, H. (1989). *When the mind hears: A history of the deaf*. New York: Vintage.

Latke, J. R. (1994). *Ecobehavioral family interventions in developmental disabilities*. Pacific Grove, CA: Brooks/Cole.

> Provided in this text is a model of ecobehavioral family intervention, and a history of the ecobehavioral approach. Social issues such as in-home service delivery, as well as ethics and skills training for staff and research personnel are also covered.

Limas, N. G., & Patria, R. (Eds.). (1997). *Disability and chronic fatigue syndrome: Clinical, legal, and patient perspectives*. Binghamton, NY: Haworth Medical Press.

McLaughlin, P., & Wehman, P. (Eds.). (1996). *Mental retardation and developmental disabilities*. Austin, TX: Pro-ed.

Meyer, L. H., Peck, C., & Brown, L. (Eds.). (1991). *Critical issues in the lives of people with severe disabilities*. Baltimore, MD: Paul H. Brookes.

Munson, P. (Ed.). (2000). *Stricken: Voices from the hidden epidemic of chronic fatigue syndrome*. Binghamton, NY: Haworth.

> According to the editor's Introduction, *Stricken* is not only a collection of literary writings about the CFIDS epidemic, "but a critique of the mythology and language surrounding an illness population and a collection of untold stories."

Orenstein, M.O. (2001). *Smart but stuck: Emotional aspects of learning disabilities and imprisoned intelligence*. Binghamton, NY: Haworth.

> Examined in this text is how growing up with imprisoned Intelligence creates difficulties and continues to cause problems for many individuals.

Sutton, E., Factor, A. R., Hawkins, B. A., Heller, T., & Seltzer, G. (1993). *Older adults with developmental disabilities: Optimizing choice and challenge*. Baltimore, MD: Paul H. Brookes.

Taylor, S. (1999). *Living well with a hidden disability: Transcending doubt and shame and reclaiming your life*. Oakland, CA: New Harbinger.

Disability and Spirituality

Black, K. (1996). *A healing homiletic: Preaching and disability*. Nashville, TN: Abingdon.

Campbell, A. (1995). *Health as liberation: Medicine, theology and the quest for justice*. Cleveland, OH: Pilgrim.

Dale, M. (1995). *The Corinthian body*. New Haven: Yale University Press.

Davie, A. R., & Thornburgh, G. I. (2000). *That all may worship: An interfaith welcome to people with disabilities*. Washington, DC: National Organization on Disability.

Deyer Bouldoc, K. (1999). *His name is Joel: Searching for God in a son's disability*. Louisville, KY: Bridge Resources.

Eisland, N. (1994). *The disabled God: Towards a liberatory theology of disability*. Nashville, TN: Abingdon.

Eisland, N. L., & Saliers, D. (Eds.). (1998). *Human disability and the service of God: Reassessing religious practice*. Nashville, TN: Abingdon.

Hauerwas, S. (1990). *Naming the silences: God, medicine and the problem of suffering*. Grand Rapids, MI: Eerdmans.

> Hauerwas explores the question of suffering and death, not in a search for answers but rather to address the question of why we seek such explanations. The reality of medicine as both a source of hope and an imperfect answer is discussed.

Isherwood, L., & Stuart, E. (1998). *Introducing body theology*. Sheffield, UK: Sheffield Academic Press.

> The theology of "the body of God" as experienced by diverse populations, including persons with disabilities is explored in this volume. "People with disabilities bespeak the essential contingency of embodiment which can be both a source of grief and source of creativity," the authors say.

Kutz-Mellem, S. (1998). *Different members, one body: Welcoming the diversity of abilities in God's family*. Louisville, KY: Witherspoon.

Mellor, P., & Shilling, C. (1997). *Re-forming the body: Religion, community and modernity*. London: Sage.

> This analysis builds on Durkheim's view of religion as the keystone of society in the sense that somatic experiences symbolize the sacred and also reflect the feelings, passions, and beliefs that characterize particular forms of social life. The formation and re-formation of this embodiment is viewed through Christianity.

Vash, C. L., & McCarthy, H. (1995). *Spirituality, disability and rehabilitation*. Athens, GA: Elliot and Fitzpatrick.

Webb-Mitchell, B. (1994). *Unexpected guests at God's banquet: Welcoming people with disabilities into the Church*. New York: Crossroad.

Disability and Health Care

Abel, E. K. (2000). *Hearts of wisdom: American women caring for kin, 1850-1940*. Cambridge, MA: Harvard University Press.

Albrecht, G. L. (1992). *The disability business: Rehabilitation in America*. Newbury Park, CA: Sage.

Birenbaum, A. (1999). *Disability and managed care: Problems and opportunities at the end of the century*. Westport, CT: Praeger.

> Presented in this book presents is an analysis of managed care from the perspective of frequent users: persons with disabilities. The approach includes consideration of safety-net services, gains and losses, access to specialists, quality of care, and a consumer bill of rights.

Bloch, F. S. (1992). *Disability determination: The administrative process and the role of medical personnel*. Westport, CT: Greenwood.

Quinn, J. (1993). *Successful case management in long-term care*. New York: Springer.

> This volume on case management long-term care covers intake, assessment, careplanning, specific issues related to disability, and management issues.

Rupp, K., & Stapleton, D. C. (1998). *Growth in disability benefits: Explanations and policy implications*. Kalamazoo, MI: W.E. Upjohn Institute for Employment Research.

Stalker, K. (1996). *Development in short-term care: Breaks and opportunities*. Bristol, PA: J. Kingsley.

Young, T. K. (1994). *The health of Native Americans: Toward a biocultural epidemiology*. New York: Oxford University Press.

Disability and Law

Cooper, J., & Vernon, S. (1996). *Disability and the law*. Bristol, PA: J. Kingsley.

Francis, L. P., & Silvers, A. (Eds.). (2000). *Americans with disabilities: Exploring the implications of the law for individuals and institutions*. New York: Routledge.

Explored in this book is the state of the ADA following its enactment over 10 years ago. Court challenges, failures in implementation, and the extent to which this legislation can remediate the social oppression experienced by persons with disabilities are discussed.

Jones, M., & Basser Marks, L. (Eds.). (1998). *Disability, divers-ability and legal change*. The Hague, the Netherlands: M. Nijhoff.

Tucker, B. (1998). *Federal Disability Law in a Nutshell*. St. Paul, MN: West.

Summarized in this volume are the text of major disability legislation, as well as that rulings on significant challenges to that legislation.

Miscellaneous

Brown, D. S. (2000). *Learning a living: A guide to planning your career and finding a job for people with learning disabilities, attention deficit disorder, and dyslexia*. Bethesda, MD: Woodbine House.

Brownworth, V., & Raffo, S. (Eds.). (1999). *Restricted access: Lesbians on disability*. Seattle: Seal.

Lesbians talk about the experience of being "dually disabled" and reveal how they live, who they look to for support, and legal issues specific to being unmarried and disabled.

Casebolt, G. M., & Gilson, S. F. (Eds.). (2000). *Managing personal assistants: A consumer guide*. Washington, DC: Paralyzed Veterans of America.

Ginsberg, L. (1992). *Social work almanac*. Washington, DC: NASW Press.

Johnson, K. (1998). *Deinstitutionalising women: An ethnographic study of institutional closure*. Cambridge: Cambridge University Press.

Explored here are the lives of 21 women living in a large institution for people with intellectual disabilities. The author examines their lives and the impact of deinstitutionalization on them, raising a number of broad questions about our understanding of the nature of disability, and the ways in which individuals with disabilities are objectified.

Kaye, H. S. (2000). *Computer and Internet use among people with disabilities*. Washington D.C: National Institute on Disability and Rehabilitation Research, U.S. Department of Education.

Klauber, J. (1994). *Disability information at your fingertips*. Centrereach, NY: Disability Resources.

Knight, A. (1998). *Valued or forgotten?: Independent visitors and disabled young people*. London: National Children's Bureau.

Luczak, R. (Ed.). (1993). *Eyes of desire: A Deaf gay and lesbian reader*. Boston: Allson.

Michalko, R. (2002). *The difference that disability makes*. Philadelphia: Temple University Press.

Okumu, D. (1993). *A gender analysis of disability*. Nairobi, Kenya: Women's Bureau, Ministry of Culture and Social Services.

Paciorek, M. J. & Jones, J. A. (2001). *Disability sport and recreation resources*. Traverse City, MI: Cooper Publishing.

Preiser, W. F. E., & Ostroff, E. (Eds.). (2001). *The universal design handbook*: McGraw-Hill.

> A very extensive volume that contains the principles of universal design, and United Nations standards and rules for indoor and outdoor access. Examples of universal design are provided from numerous cultures as well as the challenges that specific disabilities present to universally designed access.

Quinn, P. (1998). Understanding disability: A lifespan approach. Thousand Oaks, CA: Sage.

Roulstone, A. (1998). *Enabling technology: Disabled people, work, and new technology*. Philadelphia: Open University Press.

Rousso, H. W., M. (2001). *Addressing gender equity in special education*. Albany: State University of New York Press.

Sobsey, D., Wells, D., Lucardie, R. & Mansell, S. (1995). *Violence and disability: An annotated bibliography*. Baltimore, MD: Paul H. Brookes.

Stone, D. (1984). *The disabled state*. Philadelphia: Temple University Press.

> Stone takes a unique perspective in exploring disability as an administrative category in the welfare state that entitles its members to particular privileges in the form of social aid and exemptions from certain obligations of citizenship. She demonstrates that disability is a moveable social boundary whose limits depend on cultural consensus.

Tremain, S. (Ed.). (1996). *Pushing the limits: Disabled dykes produce culture*. Toronto: Women's Press.

DISABILITY RESOURCES WEBSITES

Center for Research on Women with Disabilities

http://www.bcm.tmc.edu/crowd/index.htm

> The Center for Research on Women with Disabilities is a research center that focuses on issues related to health, aging, civil rights, abuse, and independent living. CROWD's purpose is to promote, develop, and disseminate information to expand the life choices of women with disabilities so that they may fully participate in community life. More specifically, researchers develop and evaluate models for interventions to address specific problems effecting women with disabilities.

Consortium for Citizens with Disabilities

http://www.c-c-d.org

> The Consortium for Citizens with Disabilities is a Coalition of national consumer, advocacy, provider and professional organizations headquartered in Washington, DC. CCD has worked to achieve federal legislation and regulations that assure that the 54 million children and adults with disabilities are fully integrated into the mainstream of society. CCD does this by:
>
> - Identifying and researching public policy issues, developing testimony and policy recommendations, and encouraging innovative solutions to public policy concerns.
>
> - Educating members of Congress to improve public policies and programs that foster independence, productivity, integration, and inclusion of people with disabilities.
>
> - Encouraging people with disabilities and their families to advocate for themselves and coordinating grassroots efforts to support these advocacy efforts.

Disability Radio Worldwide

http://www.independentliving.org/radio/

This links to the site of the radio show that features the experiences of people with disabilities around the world. Issues, events, and political analysis affecting people with disabilities are the subject matter of the weekly half-hour program. Recent programs have included: reproductive health care and women with disabilities in the U.S. and Africa; disability in history and literature; the values of disability culture; people with disabilities in the Holocaust; community-building and community organizing in South Africa and the Middle East; the experiences of women with disabilities at the NGO Forum on Women in Beijing; the progress of children with disabilities in Nicaragua; and the effects of Agent Orange on the children of Vietnam veterans.

Disability Related Issues: A Web Pathfinder for Student Research

http://www.disrights.org/guide/research.html#db

This guide focuses on researching disability-related issues on the World Wide Web

The Empowerment Zone

http://www.empowermentzone.com

The motto of Empowerment Zone is "helping individuals and communities achieve self actualization and full citizenship." Its resources may be viewed online or downloaded with any web browser, text or graphical. The Empowerment Zone has extensive public, plain-text, organized collections on the following subjects: accessible education; accessible housing; accessible travel; civil rights; employment; financial advice; funding assisstive technology; gender, relationships, and sexuality; health care; HTML, CGI, and Perl; independent living; Java; legal help; political action; popular applications, including Eudora, Internet Explorer, Lynx, Netscape, Notes, Pine, Microsoft Word, and WordPerfect; rehabilitation; self-development; Social Security; telecommunications; and Microsoft Windows

Half the Planet

www.halftheplanet.com

HalfthePlanet Foundation is a nonprofit organization that supports the application of technology to promote the values of the Americans with Disabilities Act—independent living, social inclusion, equality of opportunity, economic self-sufficiency, and empowerment. This site provides links to extensive resources for daily living.

National Empowerment Center

http://www.power2u.org/

The mission of the National Empowerment Center Inc. is to carry a message of recovery, empowerment, hope and healing to people who have been diagnosed with mental illness. A consumer, survivor, ex-patient-run organization, NEC is committed to the belief that "recovery and empowerment are not the privilege of a few exceptional leaders, but rather are possible for each person who has been diagnosed with mental illness."

On a Roll (Disability Radio online)

http://www.onarollradio.com/

On a Roll is a weekly talk radio show about life and disability sponsored by DIMENET. This site provides a link to the current radio show and to searchable archived shows.

Society for Disability Studies

http://www.uic.edu/orgs/sds/links.html

> The Society for Disability Studies is a nonprofit scientific and educational organization established to promote interdisciplinary research on humanistic and social scientific aspects of disability and chronic illness. Its membership includes social scientists, scholars in the humanities, and disability rights advocates concerned with the problems of disabled people in society. The purpose of the society is to bring together people from diverse backgrounds and substantive concerns.

Yahoo Disability Search Page

http://dir.yahoo.com/society_and_culture/disabilities

> Yahoo's search page on disabilities, with extensive links categorically arranged.

VIDEOS AND FILMS ON DISABILITY

The videos and films listed do not include all that are available, nor do they reflect works necessarily produced or directed by social workers. However, the editors believe they add an essential teaching and learning resource. The videos listed are those that the editors have "discovered" during the course of their general research on disability, through attending conference screenings, from producer pamphlets, and by suggestion of colleagues. Inclusion in this list does not reflect endorsement of their quality or usefulness. They are considered by the editors to be educational films, art films, disability studies films, or films in similar categories. We have not included in the annotated list reference to popular culture films (see section below).

Unless otherwise noted all the videos were screened by the editors. In some cases video annotations were provided by Carrie Sandahl, whom we thank, or they were provided by the video producers. The status of the video or film's accessibility by deaf and hard-of-hearing viewers is identified where known. Where videos are identified as "Uncaptioned," a later version with either open or closed captioning may be available. If an uncaptioned video is listed and might be useful if made accessible, individuals are encouraged to contact the producers. Names of production companies or distributors have been included after the publication date.

Resources for Disability-Related Video Materials

- Fanlight Productions: http://www.fanlight.com
- Program Development Associates: http://www.pdassoc.com
- Library Media Foundation: http://www.librarymedia.org/health/disability.html
- Advocating Change Together (ACT): http://www.selfadvocacy.com. 1-(800)-641-0059.
- Axis Consultation and Training, Ltd.: http://www.normemma.com 1-(250)-754-9939

60 Minutes: Necessity is the mother of invention. (1998). CBS.

> Lesli Stahl reports on unique assistive technology for people with disabilities. Problem identification includes restrictive health care policies. (Uncaptioned) (7 min.)

Able to laugh. (1993). Fanlight Productions.

> Six disabled comics are featured interpreting the disability experience. (Captioned) (27 min.)

Access theatre. (1996). Storm Reading Video Productions.

> Humorous skits/song/dance depicting prejudicial stereotypes and attitudes encountered in daily living activities by people with disabilities. (Signed) (50 min.)

An untold story: People with disabilities speak out on health care. (1993). Colorado Cross-Disability Coalition.

> The video includes highlights of the 1993 Colorado Cross Disability Coalition Public Hearings. The hearings were designed to give consumers the chance to tell personal stories about experiences with health care and the impact of health-related issues on our lives. (Uncaptioned) (25 min.)

And then came John. (1988). Telesis Productions International.

> The triumphant story of John McGough, a man of many accomplishments with Down syndrome, living in a warm and accepting community in northern California. (Uncaptioned) (36 min.)

Asylum. (1988). Stone Lantern Films Inc.

> Traces the history of treatment policy for people with mental illness through the story of St. Elizabeth's Hospital in Washington, DC. Addresses the debate about institutionalization of people with mentally illness. Discussion section follows. (Uncaptioned) (90 min.)

Body beautiful. (1991). Women Make Movies. (http//:www.wmm.com)

> White mother and Black daughter in England deal with issues of disability, illness (breast cancer and rheumatoid arthritis), body image, sexuality, and the mother-daughter bond. (Uncaptioned) (23 min.)

Breaking ground: Opportunity for students with disabilities. (1998). Orono, ME: Center for Community Inclusion, University of Maine.

> Several college students with disabilities talk about their experiences in attending college. Addresses the difficulty of asking for accommodations and describes the accommodations that facilitate their attendance. (Open captioned) (10 min.)

Breaking silence: The rape of people with physical disabilities. (1988). Ann Arbor: Citizen's Advisory Committee on Rape Prevention, University of Michigan.

> People with physical disabilities talk about their experiences with rape and abusive practices directed at their disabilities. Discussion focuses on the impact of being marginalized, the vulnerability of dependence, risk factors, blaming the victim. Includes footage for self-defense training (Uncaptioned) (23 min.)

Breathing lessons. (1996). Fanlight Productions.

> A documentary about Mark O'Brien, a published poet-journalist who spends much of his time in an iron lung. "Both through the medium of his poetry through poignant and wry interviews, Mark reflects on sex, God, work and death, and what makes a life worth living," say the producers. (Open captioned) (35 min.)

Closing the doors, opening the windows: The closing of the Laconia State School. (1991). Image-In-That! Videographic Productions.

> A documentary about the closing of the Laconia State School and Training Center for people with developmental and other disabilities. Features interviews with former residents, administrators, and staff of the school and the parents and activists involved in its closure. Footage and testimony depict the dismal conditions in the institution, and raise issues that have been important in the national deinstitutionalization of disabled people. (Uncaptioned) (20 min.)

Coming to terms. (1990). H. Gallagher, director.

> This remarkable documentary combines history and biography in telling the story of Hugh Gregory Gallagher who became disabled by paralytic polio at the age of 19 and whose personal odyssey led him to confront stereotypes of the disabled and the public image of his childhood hero, adult role model, and fellow polio sufferer, President Franklin D. Roosevelt. Gallagher reflects honestly on the life-long physical and psychological adjustments that had to be made before he could come to terms with his disability. The author of *FDR's Splendid Deception*, Gallagher also compares his coping mechanisms with those of his childhood idol. (Closed caption) (57 min.)

Creating equity. (1993). Orono, ME: University of Maine.

> Features several disabled university students who describe how their disabilities interfere with their studies. Students describe the accommodations that have been helpful to them. Instructors talk about their approach to accommodations as well. (Uncaptioned) (26 min.)

Disability culture rap: Advocating change together. (2000). Tools for Change.

> A montage of stills and live images depicting the lives and culture of disabled people. Identified activists declare their wish to live in freedom through performance pieces. Tracks major events in the disability rights movement. Topically arranged segments narrated by artist Cheryl Marie Wade. Comes with a facilitators manual. (Open captioned) (22 min.)

Disabled women: Visions and voices. (1996). Program Development Associates.

> From the Fourth World Conference on Women in Beijing, disabled women from around the world share their concerns and successes demonstrating the diversity and commonality of women's issues. (Captioned) (12 min.)

The disabling bullet. (1999). Chicago: University of Illinois at Chicago, Department of Disability and Human Development.

> A documentary that traces the life stories of four African-American men on Chicago's West Side who have become disabled because of gang violence. (Reviewed by Carrie Sandahl) (Open captioned) (55 min.)

Enable: People with disabilities and computers. (1999). Microsoft Corporation.

> People with disabilities talk about the importance of computers in their lives. Narrated by the Flying Brothers Karamazov, people with a wide range of disabilities describe how computers make competitive functioning and independence possible. (Captioned) (45 min.)

Fred's story. (1996). Brookline, MA: Pennycorner Press, produced in association with Storyline Motion Pictures.

> A first-person narrative by an individual with developmental disabilities who tells of his horror story of institutional life in Mansfield Training Center compared with independent living. (Uncaptioned) (27 min.)

Full circle: African Americans with disabilities. (1992). Reno, NV: KNPB/Channel 5.

> Presents the human drama which led from the Civil Rights movement to the passage of the Americans with Disabilities Act in the 1990s. The program follows the stories of several young people and adults as they describe the initial trauma of their injuries and the paths they took to adapt to their disabilities. (Description by Kristine Tower) (Uncaptioned) (26 min.)

Here. (1991). CMW Out-of-Pocket-Productions.

> Cheryl Marie Wade performs a series of her own wry and saucy poetry. Uppity, unflinching, and direct pieces target stereotypes about people with disabilities and life experiences. (Captioned) (13 min.)

If I can't do it. (1998). Fanlight Productions.

> "This is the story of a man born with cerebral palsy, living in an isolated home and restricted by a lack of opportunities until he breaks out of his sheltered life and enters the world of politics." (Description by producers) (Captioned) (57 min.)

I'm a person too. (1987). Bayside, NY: Dick Young Productions.

> Features the stories of several individuals who have Tourette's syndrome. Describes social supports and barriers that affect the lives of these individuals. (Uncaptioned) (21 min.)

King Gimp. (2000). HBO.

> An exploration of the commitment and struggles of a disabled artist. Winner of an Academy Award. (Captioned) (39 min.)

Lasting leadership: Popular education and self advocacy. (1999). Advocating Change Together (ACT).

> A guide for teachers of self-advocates, advocating the use of a popular education approach. All participants in the classroom contribute to knowledge through formal learning and through experience. Narrated by Chris Burke. (Closed captioned) (17 min.)

A little history worth knowing. (1998). Program Development Associates.

> A brief history of the disabled in society highlighting key philosophical issues, including the Americans with Disabilities Act, the Independent Living Movement, and how disability is portrayed in the media. (Uncaptioned) (22 min.)

Making community a reality. (1996). Bloomington: Indiana Employment Initiative, Center for School and Community Integration, Indiana University.

> Introduces specific organizational and community change necessary to support inclusive community living for people with disabilities. (Closed captioned) (18 min.)

Making contact: Communicating with adults with mental retardation. (1990). Ames: University of Iowa Video Center.

> Provides specific guidance for professionals who communicate with people with mental retardation/developmental disabilities. (Uncaptioned) (19 min.)

Mending spirits: Native Americans with disabilities. (1992). Reno, NV: KNPB/Channel 5.

> Young indigenous Americans are three times more likely than nonindigenous Americans to incur life-changing disabilities. Indigenous Americans who live in rural settings where resources for rehabilitation are scarce face the greatest challenges. Several young indigenous people in various stages of adaptation to traumatic injury or congenital disability are featured in this documentary. Featured speakers talk about resources and access to opportunity. (Description by Kristine Tower) (Uncaptioned) (58 min.)

Movin on. (1993). The Riley Development Center.

> Several professionals with disabilities talk about accommodations that support their employment. (Closed captioned) (24 min.)

My country: The civil rights movement that created the Americans with Disabilities Act. (1997). Program Development Associates.

> This 60-minute video explains the history of the ADA and highlights the powerful stories of three handicapped persons who share insight about their life and the impact of the ADA on them and on society. (Uncaptioned) (60 min.)

Not just surviving: Women living a full life with a spinal cord injury. (1998). Fanlight Productions.

Four women talking about living with spinal cord injury. Topics covered include working with healthcare professionals, rehabilitation, sexuality, menstruation, pregnancy, parenting, menopause, careers. (Uncaptioned) (40 min.)

Pathways: Latinos with disabilities. (1992). Reno, NV: KNPB/Channel 5.

Explores the impact of disability on Americans of Hispanic heritage. The program examines physical and mental problems of both children and adults, as well as relevant issues in their education and employment and the effect on family and community. Practical information about obtaining support resources appeals to both parents and health care professionals. (Description by Kristne Tower) (Uncaptioned) (27 min.)

People in motion: Ready to live. (1995). Distributed through Films for the Humanities and Sciences.

People with disabilities talk about the role of technologies in providing them with independence, and the role of negative attitudes in restricting their access. Featured guests include disability activist Ed Roberts, users of prosthetic racing legs, innovative wheelchair users/designers, and a user of prosthetic hands. (Captioned) (60 min.)

People in motion: Without barriers or borders. (1996). Thirteen WNET.

Explores the burgeoning global movement for independent living and how people with disabilities are reshaping the world. Features disabled high school students from Russia, Japanese activists, and a Cambodian clinic and wheelchair factory. (Captioned) (56 min.)

Small differences. (1995). Program Development Associates.

"Small Differences is a disability awareness film produced by, for and about children. This video received a National Educational Media Award for its excellent content and appropriateness for the education setting. Children with and without disabilities explore the realities and perceptions about individuals with disabilities. The children learn two facts: that everyone is unique, and that most of us want the same things in life. Comes with an age appropriate study guide". (Description by producers) (Uncaptioned) (20 min.)

Sound and fury. (2000). Next Wave Films.

Portrays a family struggle about the cochlear transplant surgery, and the struggle for identity among deaf people today. (Closed captioned) (55 min.)

Special kids, special dads: Fathers of children with disabilities. (1989). Maternal and Child Health/ SEFAM Vision Productions.

Three fathers talk about their experiences related to having children with disabilities. Fathers discuss role challenges, emotional responses, and spousal communication issues. Contains discussion questions. (Uncaptioned) (24 min.)

Still/Here with Bill Moyers. (1997). Distributed through Films for the Humanities and Sciences.

A Bill Moyers documentary about dancer/choreographer Bill T. Jones's development of a dance piece, Still/Here, which incorporates the stories and movement vocabulary of people with terminal illnesses. (Review by Carrie Sandahl) (Closed captioned) (60min.)

The story of the stranger. (1993). Axis Consultation and Training.

In a humorous talk to an audience of high school students, Norman Kunc describes what it was like to have cerebral palsy and go to a regular high school. He shares with the students his discovery that he didn't need to hide his disability in order to be liked. He generalizes this message and points out that most people believe that they're not good enough as they are, and continuously strive to find a place where they feel they belong. (Uncaptioned) (60 min.)

Tell them I'm a mermaid: Women with mixed disabilities. (1983). San Francisco State University

Commentary and humorous skits depicting daily experiences of women with disability encountering social attitudes, stigma, living, and dating. (Uncaptioned) (23 min.)

Ticket to work. (2000). Gainesville, FL: Institute for Child Health Policy.

An informational video on the benefits of the Ticket to Work, the services that the ticket accesses and how to apply. Young people talk about their wish to work and be independent. (Captioned) (10 min.)

Twitch and shout, a New Day Production. Fanlight Productions.

A somewhat humorous documentary on people living with Tourette's syndrome. (Uncaptioned)

Understanding the disabled: Dances with the Minotaur. (1998). Charleston, WV: Cambridge Educational.

"A story about two disabled high school students at an integrated school. The phrase 'separate but equal' is challenged by their struggles to be included in social life. The students worry about their future prospects, with dating and careers, and experiment with adult responsibilities." (Description by producers) (Captioned) (20 min.)

Vital signs: Crip culture talks back. (1996). Brace Yourself Productions.

"A documentary about a national disability arts community that explores disability as a shared experience among a politically disenfranchised constituency. Features interviews with artists, activists and academics and includes performances from a number of artistic traditions, including fiction, poetry, stand-up comedy, street theater and performance arts. Vital Signs pursues a definition of disability culture through questions of architectural inaccessibility, political activism, mainstream representations of disability in literature, film, art and television, and in a narrative of shared struggle to gain access to influential cultural institutions." (Description by producers) (Captioned) (48 min.)

Weirded out and blown away. (1986). MacArthur Foundation Library Video Project.

Film address public's negative attitudes toward physical disability. The film focuses on personal and social relationships of disabled men and women, personal perceptions of their professional image versus their physical image, the hierarchical ranking of physical disabilities, sexuality and disability, and dealing with particular difficulties encountered in job interviews. (Review by Carrie Sandahl.) (Captioned) (43 min.)

What about Lindsay? (1998). Maine Public Broadcasting System.

A family talks about the transition of their developmentally disabled daughter to a group home. They discuss their struggle to create transition opportunities for their daughter, including a state petition drive, that culminated in systems changes that provided transition opportunities for many developmentally disabled people. Features interviews with developmentally disabled adults who are living independently. (Captioned) (52 min.)

When Billy broke his head and other tales of wonder. (1996). Fanlight Productions.

Billy Golfus was brain damaged as a result of a motor scooter accident. In this documentary, he goes on the road to meet people with disabilities around the country, blending humor with politics and individual voices to explore what it is like to live with a disability in America-where bureaucratic 'helping' systems too often keep people with disabilities trapped in a labyrinth of government rules and legislated poverty. (Captioned) (57min.)

Disability in Feature Films

Following is a list of feature films that represent disabilities. Unlike other areas of the annotated bibliography, this section relies exclusively on a list of resources from a third party. Despite having viewed several of these films, the senior editor decided not to proceed with the process of developing annotations. Because feature films commonly represent historic and contemporary social climates, the editors believe that their use can provide an important educational resource and tool for social work education.

For more on the subject, visit http://www.disabilityfilms.co.uk.

And Now Tomorrow (hard of hearing)

Antonia's Line (learning disability)

As Good As It Gets (asthma, obsessive compulsive disorder)

At First Sight (blind)

At the End of the Day. The Sue Rodriguez Story (amiotrophic lateral sclerosis)

Autumn Sonata (general)

Awakenings (persistent vegetative state)

Beautiful Dreamers (mental illness)

Benny and Joon (illness)

Best Boy (mental retardation)

The Best Years of Our Lives (loss of limb)

Birdy (facial disfigurement)

Born on the Fourth of July (paraplegia)

The Boy Who Could Fly (autism)

Breathing Lessons (polio)

A Brief History of Time (amiotrophic lateral sclerosis)

Butterflies are Free (blind)

Cactus (blind)

Children of a Lesser God (hard of hearing)

City Lights (blind)

Clean and Sober (drug and alcohol addiction)

Clean Shaven (schizophrenia)

Coming Home (paraplegia)

The Connection (drug addiction)

Cries and Whispers (cancer)

Cripples Go Christmas (paraplegia)

Cutter's Way (loss of limb, blindness)

Cyrano de Bergerac (Facial Disfigurement)

Dance Me to My Song (Cerebral Palsy)

Days of Wine and Roses (alcohol addiction)

The Deer Hunter (loss of limb)

The Doctor (cancer)

Dr. Jekyll and Mr. Hyde (mental illness)

Dr. Strangelove (mental illness, loss of limb)

Echoes of a Summer (heart disease)

Edward Scissorhands (limb disfigurement)

Elephant Man (proteus syndrome)

The English Patient (disfigurement)

For the Love of My Child: The Anissa Ayala Story (leukemia)

Frankie Starlight (short stature)

Freaks (disfigurement)

Gaby, A True Story (cerebral palsy)

Gattaca (genetic engineering)

Go Now (multiple sclerosis)

The Heart Is a Lonely Hunter (hard of hearing, learning disabled, mobility impairment, alcohol addiction)

The Horse Whisperer (loss of limb)

The Hunchback of Notre Dame (disfigurement)

I Don't Want to Talk about It (short stature)

Jacknife (mental illness, loss of limb)

Johnny Belinda (hard of hearing)

Johnny Got His Gun (loss of limb)

Johnny Handsome (facial disfigurement)

Knocking on Heaven's Door (alcohol addiction)

Leaving Las Vegas (alcohol addiction)

The Lost Weekend (alcohol addiction)

Mandy (hard of hearing)

Mask (facial disfigurement)

The Men (paraplegia)

The Miracle Worker (hard of hearing/blindness)

Mr. Holland's Opus (hard of hearing)

My Girl (Alzheimer's)

My Left Foot (cerebral palsy)

Niagara, Niagara (Tourette's syndrome)

One Flew Over the Cuckoo's Nest (mental illness)

Ordinary People (Mental Dysfunction)

Paradise Lost (Learning Difficulty)

Passion Fish (paraplegia)

People vs. Larry Flynt (autoimmune deficiency syndrome, paraplegia)

Philadelphia (autoimmune deficiency syndrome)

The Piano (hard of hearing)

Rain Man (autism)

Roxanne (facial disfigurement)

Running Against (cerebral palsy)

Savage Nights (autoimmune deficiency syndrome)

The Secret Garden (chronic illness)

Shadowlands (cancer)

Shine (mental illness)

Simon Birch (Corquio Syndrome)

The Sixth Happiness (brittle bone disease)

Sling Blade (Learning disability)

Steel Magnolias (diabetes)

Tell Me That You Love Me, Junie Moon (disfigurement, epilepsy)

Terms of Endearment (cancer)

Vertigo (compulsion)

The Waterdance (paraplegia)

What's Eating Gilbert Grape (autism)

Whose Life Is It Anyway? (quadriplegia)

A Woman under the Influence (mental illness)

Contributors

STEPHEN FRENCH GILSON

Stephen French Gilson, associate professor in the School of Social Work at the University of Maine, serves as a Commissioner on the Council on Social Work Education's Commission on Disability and Persons with Disabilities. His primary areas of research and writing focus on sexual assault and intimate partner violence toward women with disabilities; the socio-political and economic context of disability identity, culture, and community; the interrelationship of multiculturalism and disability; local, state, and federal disability policies and legislation; the interrelationships of the experiences of health/illness and disability; and disability advocacy and self-advocacy. Stephen identifies as a disabled man who is active in seeking to promote social justice and fight discrimination against and oppression of marginalized populations.

ELIZABETH DEPOY

Elizabeth DePoy, PhD is professor in the School of Social Work and Coordinator of Research and Evaluation at the Center for Community Inclusion, Maine's University Center of Excellence, both at the University of Maine. Her areas of inquiry, teaching, and practice include research and evaluation design, with particular emphasis on participatory and mixed method strategies, and disability. Dr. DePoy is a disabled woman whose work is aimed at promoting social justice for all populations, including those who have been and continue to be oppressed.

HEATHER MACDUFFIE

Heather MacDuffie, licensed clinical social worker, completed her MSW at the University of Maine. She is currently completing an individualized doctoral program in Disability and Cultural Studies at the University of Maine, where she works as Project Specialist on a federal grant to develop disability and long term care education for allied health professionals.

KATHERINE MEYERSHON

Katherine Meyershon, MSW is a graduate of the School of Social Work at Virginia Commonwealth University.

MICHELLE S. BALLAN

Michelle S. Ballan, MSW is a doctoral student at the University of Texas at Austin, School of Social Work, where she specializes in clinical practice and research with children and families with developmental disabilities. Ms. Ballan developed the course Introduction to Developmental Disabilities in 1997 and teaches the course yearly as an elective. Ms. Ballan has received numerous awards for her research and curriculum development including the Hogg Foundation Evaluation Research Fellowship, Houston Endowment President's Excellence Scholarship, and the American Association on Mental Retardation 2000 Student Award. She has authored several publications including the book *Persons with Disabilities: Cultural Diversity Curriculum for Social Workers and Health Practitioners*. Ms. Ballan is a board member of the Texas Association on Mental Retardation and the faculty advisor for Best Buddies at the

University of Texas at Austin. She serves as an adjunct faculty member of the Psychology Department at Our Lady of the Lake University, where she teaches doctoral courses in qualitative research. Ms. Ballan will begin her tenure as an assistant professor at Columbia University's School of Social Work in July 2002. Ms. Ballan's current areas of interest include developmental disabilities, sexuality and atypical development, clinical practice research, research methodology and data analysis, and assessment and measurement.

JEFFREY J. BASSIN

Jeffrey J. Bassin, MSW, LCSW is the Director of Program Services at the Office for Productive Living Services, the administrative office of The Productive Living Board for St. Louis County Citizens with Developmental Disabilities (PLB). The PLB administers a special property tax that provides residential and vocational services for more than 4,800 St. Louis County residents with developmental disabilities. He has served as the Missouri Chapter President of TASH, an international advocacy and educational organization for persons with disabilities. He is also an adjunct professor at the George Warren Brown School of Social Work, Washington University, St. Louis, Missouri. It is in this capacity that his interest in family support and strength-based social work practice led to the development of a course designed to develop practice skills focused around families who have children with developmental disabilities. He currently serves as President of the Alumni Board at the George Warren Brown School of Social Work.

JEANETTE R. DREWS

Jeanette R. Drews is Associate Professor at the University of Utah's Graduate School of Social Work. She received a master's in counseling at Idaho State University and an MSW and a PhD at the University of Utah. Her teaching has been augmented with extensive community service work in the area of developmental disabilities. She has served on the Governor's Council for People with Disabilities, served as President of the Arc of Utah and has been on the Board of Directors of The Arc of the United States. Currently she is President-elect of the Avatar Board of Directors, a community service provider agency. She has conducted a number of research grants related to developmental disabilities in the state of Utah.

TERESA M. S. FAVUZZI

Teresa M. S. Favuzzi earned her MSW from San Francisco State University. She is currently the Program Manager at the Independent Living Resource Center San Francisco. Her research interests include the intersections of disability and queer identity, multicultural outreach strategies in disability communities, and the inclusion of disability rights education in the social work curriculum.

REIKO HAYASHI

Reiko Hayashi, PhD, is an assistant professor at the University of Utah, Graduate School of Social Work. Her research interests include disability, health care, welfare reform, poverty, and international social work.

ROMEL MACKELPRANG

Romel Mackelprang is a professor of social work with the Eastern Washington University School of Social Work and Human Services. He has been involved in the independent living movement for twenty years, including serving on CIL boards. He was a founder of the CSWE Task Force on Disabilities and is a member of the CSWE Commission on Disability and Persons with Disabilities (CDPD). With Richard Salsgiver, he authored *Disability: A Diversity Model Approach in Human Service Practice* published by Brooks/Cole. He is a liaison for the CDPD and the American Association of Spinal Cord Injury Psychologists and Social Workers to NASW, working on disability issues.

NANCY L. MARY

Dr. Nancy L. Mary has been an associate professor in the Department of Social Work at California State University, San Bernardino since 1989. Her main teaching areas include policy and macro practice (e.g., program development, community practice, and planning). From 1986 to 1989, Dr. Mary was a lecturer at California State University, Long Beach, where she taught policy, community practice, and field seminars. Dr. Mary's practice experience is primarily in the field of developmental disabilities and includes program evaluation, organizational development, planning, and community and group work. She worked at the Harbor Regional Center for Developmental Disabilities (South Bay) and is currently a Board Member of the Region II American Association on Mental Retardation (AAMR). Dr. Mary earned her MSW and DSW at the University of California, Los Angeles, her undergraduate degrees at Pitzer College, Claremont, California, and completed her field training at the Neuropsychiatric Institute, UCLA, Mental Retardation Program.

GARY E. MAY

Gary E. May is an associate professor of social work at the University of Southern Indiana. His teaching responsibilities are primarily in the social policy curriculum in the MSW program. Professor May created the course described here. He is a member of the Indiana Governor's Planning Council for People with Disabilities, the Indiana Protection and Advocacy Services Commission, the Society for Disability Studies, and other learned and professional organizations.

ROSALIE (ROSE) J. RUSSO

Rosalie (Rose) J. Russo received her DSW degree from the department of Social Welfare at the Graduate School and University Center (GSUC) of the City University of New York (CUNY) at the Hunter College School of Social Work. Her dissertation focused on social workers who work in the field of developmental disabilities. An earlier version of this course syllabus was submitted as a final class assignment for the doctoral elective course, Education in Social Welfare. From 1998 to the present, she is employed at a state government agency in New York city that provides employment services to individuals with disabilities. From 1995-1998, she worked at a large, voluntary, nonprofit organization serving adults with developmental disabilities and their families. She received the MSW degree from Wurzweiler School of Social Work at Yeshiva University, and a BA degree in Sociology from Brooklyn College (CUNY). The author is also a Certified Social Worker (CSW) in New York state. Correspondence can be addressed to the author at: Rose Russo, 201 West 70th Street, Apt. # 2-C, New York, NY 10023 or by email: RoseRusso@aol.com.

DIANE STROCK-LYNSKEY

Diane Strock-Lynskey is a professor of social work for the Baccalaureate Program at Siena College where she has also previously served as Department Chair/Program Director and Coordinator of Field Education. She received her MSW in Social Work from Syracuse University and a Bachelors in Sociology with a concentration in Social Work from Siena College. In addition to developing and conducting numerous workshops and presentations on disability-related issues and topics, Diane is one of the original members of the CSWE Task Force on Disability and has served as a Commissioner for the CSWE Commission on Disability and Persons with Disabilities since 1998. Currently the Chair of this Commission, she was also the founder and is the Chair of the Committee on Disability and Persons with Disabilities for the Association of Baccalaureate Program Directors (BPD).

EVELYN TOMASZEWSKI

Evelyn Tomaszewski is Project Director with the HIV/AIDS Spectrum: Mental Health Training and Education of Social Workers Project at the National Association of Social Workers and is responsible for the research and design of project materials; implementing a train the trainer education model; and oversight of continuing education and technology transfer content. Evelyn also works on gender and diversity issues as staff to the National Committee on Women's Issues and the National Committee on Lesbian, Gay, and Bisexual Issues.

Evelyn maintains a consultation practice as Director of Pearl Associates, a program providing consultation and training on gender equity issues to businesses, schools, membership organizations, and state and local government. Evelyn has authored numerous articles, book chapters, and training curricula, including the Disabilities Awareness Curriculum for Graduate Schools of Social Work (1993). Evelyn has a BSW and MSW from West Virginia University.

KRISTINE TOWER

Kristine Tower, LCSW, EdD, is an assistant professor at the University of Nevada, Reno. She earned her Master's degree in social work in 1987 and her doctorate in special education in 1996. Her primary practice experiences have been in medical (rehabilitation) and clinical social work. Since coming to the university, she has produced five television documentaries, including a series on culture and disability for PBS. She has authored several published articles and is currently working on a book about disability across the life span. Dr. Tower and her husband, Randy, are disability rights activists who have been involved in the independent living movement since the early 1980s. She was recently appointed by the Governor of Nevada to serve a three-year term on the state's Independent Living Council.

DEBORAH P. VALENTINE

Deborah P. Valentine is professor and director of the Division of Social Work at the University of Wyoming in Laramie. She received her MSSW and PhD in social work from the University of Texas at Austin. In addition to teaching, conducting research, and publishing in the field of disabilities, Deborah is an advisor to the Laramie Chapter of People First and state advisor to Wyoming People First. People First is a self-advocacy group for adult men and women with developmental disabilities.

NANCY VERDERBER

As Administrative Liaison for Disability Related Issues for The Special School District, Nancy Verderber works closely with 23 St. Louis County school districts. Formerly with Paraquad, Inc., the local Center for Independent Living, Ms. Verderber was Director of Independent Living Specialists. She holds a bachelor's degree in social welfare, a master's degree in rehabilitation administration, serves as an adjunct faculty member at Saint Louis University in the department of Social Work, and is a Missouri licensed professional counselor. Ms. Verderber served as a White House Commissioner on Presidential Scholars for eight years, is a former St. Louis City Civil Rights Enforcement Commissioner, and is a member of the National Institute for Urban School Improvement Leadership Team. As a person with a physical disability and an active member of the disability rights movement, Ms. Verderber brings firsthand knowledge and awareness of the social, personal, and environment issues involved in living with a disability.

Disability Resource Publication

Course Syllabus Evaluation Form

Reviewer/Evaluator: _____

Date: _____

Syllabus Course Number: _____

Instructor: _____

Title of Course: _____

On the form below, please indicate your full, honest, and complete evaluation of each syllabus and sample assignments from BSW- and MSW-level courses. The selected syllabi will comprise an exemplary compendium of courses that integrate disability into social work core curricula and that serve as model electives on social work and disability.

The form provides guidelines and criteria for review. Following the review process, all selected contributors will be asked to submit: a brief narrative about the course content and structure, sample assignments, reading lists, and course goals.

From the initial group, ten-to-fifteen course outlines with narratives that reflect the experience of disability will be selected for publication in the compendium of model syllabi.

Our intent is to cover a range of disability topics and issues in the compendium that reflect contemporary approaches to disability and that seek to analyze the past and current social issues and influences on disabled individuals through a systemic rather than a pathological perspective. Therefore, should you review two or more syllabi on the same topic, such as Social Work and Children with Developmental Disabilities, please rate the two syllabi to indicate which you would prefer to have included in the compendium. Use additional sheets of paper if necessary. Thank you in advance for your participation in this important project.

CRITERIA AND GUIDELINES

1. Stated focus of course: _____

2. Targeted degree level (BSW, MSW, PhD)?

3. Does the design of the course fit with the targeted degree level?

4. Degree to which the reading assignments support the stated focus:

5. Degree to which the assignments (presentations, essays, tests, and such) support the stated focus:

6. Required Readings: Author's Name, Title of Text or Journal Articles, Publication Date(s):

Do you consider these readings to reflect current disability scholarship ____Yes ____ No

Do you consider these readings to reflect a "social work" perspective ____ Yes ____ No

Discuss your reaction to/assessment of these readings

7. Supplemental or Suggested Readings: Author's Name, Title of Text or Journal Articles, Publication Date(s):

Do you consider these readings to reflect current disability scholarship ____Yes ____ No

Do you consider these readings to reflect a "social work" perspective ____ Yes ____ No

Discuss your reaction to/assessment of these readings

8. Does the instructor use videos as instruction tools? ___Yes ___ No

    If yes:

        Do you consider these readings to reflect current disability scholarship ____Yes ____ No

        Do you consider these to reflect a "social work" perspective __ Yes __ No

        Discuss your reaction to/assessment to the use of these videos

9. Is the weekly subject focus consistent with the stated focus of the course? ____ Yes ____ No

10. General format of the course (i.e., guest speakers, film, discussion, lecture, mix, other)

11. Are there adequate provisions for accommodations stated in the syllabus? Yes___ No___

12. What are your overall thoughts on the degree to which this syllabus aims to integrate disability from a contemporary diversity perspective into social work curricula?

13. Do you think that the syllabus should be included in the CDPD compendium?

___Accept

___Accept with revisions; Please specify_____

___Reject